P9-CEE-204

Teach Yourself
Microsoft®
Access 2000
VISUALLY™

IDG's **3-D Visual**™ Series

IDG BOOKS *From* **maranGraphics**™

IDG Books Worldwide, Inc.
An International Data Group Company
Foster City, CA • Indianapolis • Chicago • New York

Teach Yourself Microsoft® Access 2000 VISUALLY™

Published by
IDG Books Worldwide, Inc.
An International Data Group Company
919 E. Hillsdale Blvd., Suite 400
Foster City, CA 94404

Copyright©   1999 by maranGraphics Inc.
5755 Coopers Avenue
Mississauga, Ontario, Canada
L4Z 1R9

Library of Congress Catalog Card No.: 99-63954

ISBN: 0-7645-6059-X

Printed in the United States of America
10 9 8 7 6 5 4 3 2

Distributed in the United States by IDG Books Worldwide, Inc.

Distributed by CDG Books Canada Inc. for Canada; by Transworld Publishers Limited in the United Kingdom; by IDG Norge Books for Norway; by IDG Sweden Books for Sweden; by Woodslane Pty. Ltd. for Australia; by Woodslane (NZ) Ltd. for New Zealand; by TransQuest Publishers Pte Ltd. for Singapore, Malaysia, Thailand, Indonesia, and Hong Kong; by ICG Muse, Inc. for Japan; by Norma Comunicaciones S.A. for Colombia; by Intersoft for South Africa; by Le Monde en Tique for France; by International Thomson Publishing for Germany, Austria and Switzerland; by Distribuidora Cuspide for Argentina; by Livraria Cultura for Brazil; by Ediciones ZETA S.C.R. Ltda. for Peru; by WS Computer Publishing Corporation, Inc., for the Philippines; by Contemporanea de Ediciones for Venezuela; by Express Computer Distributors for the Caribbean and West Indies; by Micronesia Media Distributor, Inc. for Micronesia; by Grupo Editorial Norma S.A. for Guatemala; by Chips Computadoras S.A. de C.V. for Mexico; by Editorial Norma de Panama S.A. for Panama; by American Bookshops for Finland. Authorized Sales Agent: Anthony Rudkin Associates for the Middle East and North Africa.

For corporate orders, please call maranGraphics at 800-469-6616.
For general information on IDG Books Worldwide's books in the U.S., please call our Consumer Customer Service department at 800-762-2974.
For reseller information, including discounts and premium sales, please call our Reseller Customer Service department at 800-434-3422.
For information on where to purchase IDG Books Worldwide's books outside the U.S., please contact our International Sales department at 317-596-5530 or fax 317-596-5692.
For consumer information on foreign language translations, please contact our Customer Service department at 1-800-434-3422, fax 317-596-5692, or e-mail rights@idgbooks.com.
For information on licensing foreign or domestic rights, please phone 1-650-655-3109.
For sales inquiries and special prices for bulk quantities, please contact our Sales department at 650-655-3200.
For information on using IDG Books Worldwide's books in the classroom or for ordering examination copies, please contact our Educational Sales department at 800-434-2086 or fax 317-596-5499.
For press review copies, author interviews, or other publicity information, please contact our Public Relations department at 650-655-3000 or fax 650-655-3299.
For authorization to photocopy items for corporate, personal, or educational use, please contact maranGraphics at 800-469-6616.
Screen shots displayed in this book are based on pre-release software and are subject to change.

Trademark Acknowledgments

Permissions

©1999 maranGraphics, Inc.

The 3-D illustrations are the
copyright of maranGraphics, Inc.

U.S. Corporate Sales	U.S. Trade Sales
Contact maranGraphics at (800) 469-6616 or Fax (905) 890-9434.	Contact IDG Books at (800) 434-3422 or (650) 655-3000.

ABOUT IDG BOOKS WORLDWIDE

Welcome to the world of IDG Books Worldwide.

IDG Books Worldwide, Inc., is a subsidiary of International Data Group, the world's largest publisher of computer-related information and the leading global provider of information services on information technology. IDG was founded more than 30 years ago by Patrick J. McGovern and now employs more than 9,000 people worldwide. IDG publishes more than 290 computer publications in over 75 countries. More than 90 million people read one or more IDG publications each month.

Launched in 1990, IDG Books Worldwide is today the #1 publisher of best-selling computer books in the United States. We are proud to have received eight awards from the Computer Press Association in recognition of editorial excellence and three from Computer Currents' First Annual Readers' Choice Awards. Our best-selling ...For Dummies® series has more than 50 million copies in print with translations in 31 languages. IDG Books Worldwide, through a joint venture with IDG's Hi-Tech Beijing, became the first U.S. publisher to publish a computer book in the People's Republic of China. In record time, IDG Books Worldwide has become the first choice for millions of readers around the world who want to learn how to better manage their businesses.

Our mission is simple: Every one of our books is designed to bring extra value and skill-building instructions to the reader. Our books are written by experts who understand and care about our readers. The knowledge base of our editorial staff comes from years of experience in publishing, education, and journalism — experience we use to produce books to carry us into the new millennium. In short, we care about books, so we attract the best people. We devote special attention to details such as audience, interior design, use of icons, and illustrations. And because we use an efficient process of authoring, editing, and desktop publishing our books electronically, we can spend more time ensuring superior content and less time on the technicalities of making books.

You can count on our commitment to deliver high-quality books at competitive prices on topics you want to read about. At IDG Books Worldwide, we continue in the IDG tradition of delivering quality for more than 30 years. You'll find no better book on a subject than one from IDG Books Worldwide.

John Kilcullen
Chairman and CEO
IDG Books Worldwide, Inc.

Steven Berkowitz
President and Publisher
IDG Books Worldwide, Inc.

Eighth Annual Computer Press Awards ≥ 1992

WINNER
Ninth Annual Computer Press Awards ≥ 1993

WINNER
Tenth Annual Computer Press Awards ≥ 1994

WINNER
Eleventh Annual Computer Press Awards ≥ 1995

IDG is the world's leading IT media, research and exposition company. Founded in 1964, IDG had 1997 revenues of $2.05 billion and has more than 9,000 employees worldwide. IDG offers the widest range of media options that reach IT buyers in 75 countries representing 95% of worldwide IT spending. IDG's diverse product and services portfolio spans six key areas including print publishing, online publishing, expositions and conferences, market research, education and training, and global marketing services. More than 90 million people read one or more of IDG's 290 magazines and newspapers, including IDG's leading global brands — Computerworld, PC World, Network World, Macworld and the Channel World family of publications. IDG Books Worldwide is one of the fastest-growing computer book publishers in the world, with more than 700 titles in 36 languages. The "...For Dummies®" series alone has more than 50 million copies in print. IDG offers online users the largest network of technology-specific Web sites around the world through IDG.net (http://www.idg.net), which comprises more than 225 targeted Web sites in 55 countries worldwide. International Data Corporation (IDC) is the world's largest provider of information technology data, analysis and consulting, with research centers in over 41 countries and more than 400 research analysts worldwide. IDG World Expo is a leading producer of more than 168 globally branded conferences and expositions in 35 countries including E3 (Electronic Entertainment Expo), Macworld Expo, ComNet, Windows World Expo, ICE (Internet Commerce Expo), Agenda, DEMO, and Spotlight. IDG's training subsidiary, ExecuTrain, is the world's largest computer training company, with more than 230 locations worldwide and 785 training courses. IDG Marketing Services helps industry-leading IT companies build international brand recognition by developing global integrated marketing programs via IDG's print, online and exposition products worldwide. Further information about the company can be found at www.idg.com.   1/24/99

maranGraphics is a family-run business
located near Toronto, Canada.

At **maranGraphics**, we believe in producing great computer books–one book at a time.

Each maranGraphics book uses the award-winning communication process that we have been developing over the last 25 years. Using this process, we organize screen shots, text and illustrations in a way that makes it easy for you to learn new concepts and tasks.

We spend hours deciding the best way to perform each task, so you don't have to! Our clear, easy-to-follow screen shots and instructions walk you through each task from beginning to end.

Our detailed illustrations go hand-in-hand with the text to help reinforce the information. Each illustration is a labor of love–some take up to a week to draw!

We want to thank you for purchasing what we feel are the best computer books money can buy. We hope you enjoy using this book as much as we enjoyed creating it!

Sincerely,

The Maran Family

Please visit us on the web at:
www.maran.com

CREDITS

Author:
Ruth Maran

Copy Editors:
Cathy Benn
Jill Maran

Project Manager:
Judy Maran

**Editing &
Screen Captures:**
Roxanne Van Damme
Raquel Scott
Janice Boyer
Michelle Kirchner
James Menzies
Frances Lea
Stacey Morrison

**Layout Design &
Illustrations:**
Jamie Bell
Treena Lees

Illustrators:
Russ Marini
Peter Grecco
Sean Johannesen
Steven Schaerer

**Screens &
Illustrations:**
Jimmy Tam
Roben Ponce

Indexer:
Raquel Scott

Post Production:
Robert Maran

Editorial Support:
Michael Roney

ACKNOWLEDGMENTS

Thanks to the dedicated staff of maranGraphics, including
Jamie Bell, Cathy Benn, Janice Boyer, Francisco Ferreira,
Peter Grecco, Jenn Hillman, Sean Johannesen, Michelle Kirchner,
Wanda Lawrie, Frances Lea, Treena Lees, Jill Maran, Judy Maran,
Robert Maran, Sherry Maran, Russ Marini, James Menzies,
Stacey Morrison, Roben Ponce, Steven Schaerer, Raquel Scott,
Jimmy Tam, Roxanne Van Damme, Paul Whitehead
and Kelleigh Wing.

Finally, to Richard Maran who originated the easy-to-use
graphic format of this guide. Thank you for your
inspiration and guidance.

TABLE OF CONTENTS

Chapter 1

Getting Started

Chapter 2

Create Tables

Chapter 3

Edit Tables

Chapter 4

Design Tables

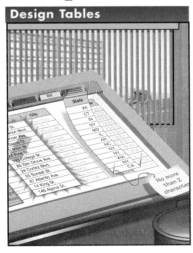

TABLE OF CONTENTS

Chapter 5

Establish Relationships

Chapter 6

Create Forms

Chapter 7

Design Forms

Chapter 8

Find Data

TABLE OF CONTENTS

Chapter 9

Create Queries

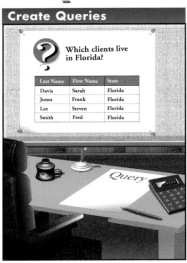

Chapter 10

Create Advanced Queries

Chapter 11

Create Reports

Chapter 12

Print Information

Chapter 13

Access and the Internet

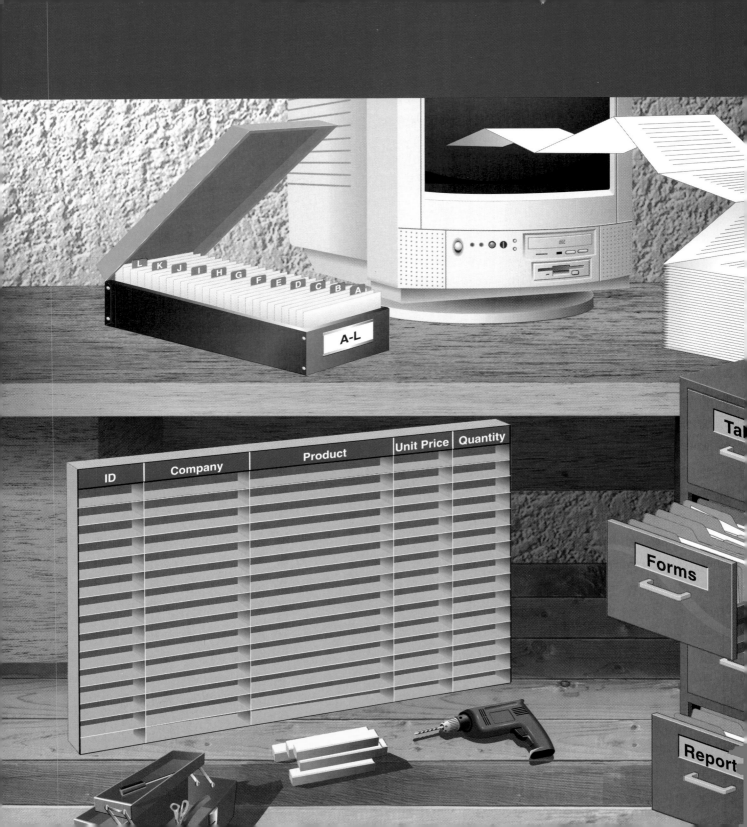

CHAPTER 1

Getting Started

Wondering where to start with Microsoft Access 2000? This chapter will show you the way.

INTRODUCTION TO ACCESS

Microsoft® Access is a database program that allows you to store and manage large collections of information.

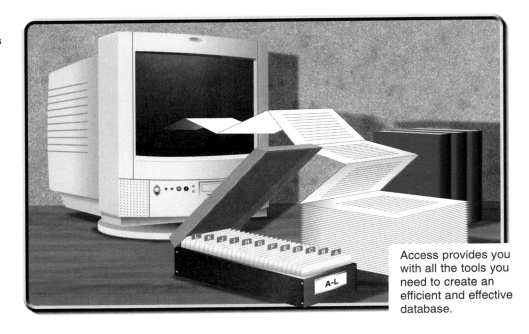

Access provides you with all the tools you need to create an efficient and effective database.

WHY WOULD I USE A DATABASE?

Personal Uses

Many people use databases to store personal information such as addresses, recipes, music collections and wine lists. Using a database to store and organize information is much more efficient than using sheets of paper or index cards.

Business Uses

Companies use databases to store information such as mailing lists, customer orders, expenses, inventory and payroll. A database can help a company effectively review, update and analyze information that constantly changes.

DATABASE APPLICATIONS

Store Information

A database stores and manages a collection of information related to a particular subject or purpose.

You can efficiently add, update, view and organize the information stored in a database.

Find Information

You can instantly locate information of interest in a database. For example, you can find all customers with the last name "Smith".

You can also perform more advanced searches, such as finding all customers living in California who purchased more than $100 of your product last year.

Analyze and Print Information

You can perform calculations on the information in a database to help you make quick, accurate and informed decisions.

You can neatly present the information in professionally designed reports.

PARTS OF A DATABASE

A database consists
of tables, forms,
queries and reports.

Tables

A table stores information
about a specific topic, such
as a mailing list. You can
have one or more tables
in a database. A table
consists of fields and
records.

Address ID	First Name	Last Name	Address	City	State/Province	Postal Code
1	Jim	Schmith	258 Linton Ave.	New York	NY	10010
2	Brenda	Petterson	50 Tree Lane	Boston	MA	02117
3	Todd	Talbot	68 Cracker Ave.	San Francisco	CA	94110
4	Chuck	Dean	47 Crosby Ave.	Las Vegas	NV	89116
5	Melanie	Robinson	26 Arnold Cres.	Jacksonville	FL	32256
6	Susan	Hughes	401 Idon Dr.	Nashville	TN	37243
7	Allen	Toppins	10 Heldon St.	Atlanta	GA	30375
8	Greg	Kilkenny	36 Buzzard St.	Boston	MA	02118
9	Jason	Marcuson	15 Bizzo Pl.	New York	NY	10020
10	Jim	Martin	890 Apple St.	San Diego	CA	92121

Field

A field is a specific
category of information,
such as the first names
of all your customers.

Record

A record is a collection
of information about one
person, place or thing,
such as the name and
address of one customer.

Forms

Forms provide a quick way to view, enter and change information in a database by presenting information in an attractive, easy-to-use format. Forms usually display one record at a time and display boxes that clearly show you where to enter information.

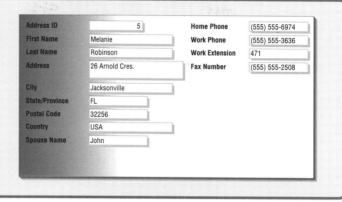

Queries

Queries allow you to find information of interest in a database. You can enter criteria in a query to specify what information you want to find. For example, you can create a query to find all customers who live in California.

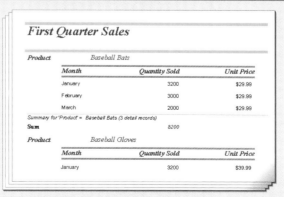

Reports

Reports are professional-looking documents that summarize data in a database. You can perform calculations in a report to help you analyze your data. For example, you can create a report that displays the total sales for each product.

PLAN A DATABASE

You should take the time to plan your database. A well-planned database ensures that you will be able to perform tasks efficiently and accurately.

Determine the Purpose of the Database

Decide what information you want your database to store and how you plan to use the information. If other people will use the database, you should consult with them to determine their needs.

Determine the Tables You Need

Gather all the information you want to store in your database and then divide the information into separate tables. A table should contain information for only one subject.

The same information should not appear in more than one table in your database. You can work more efficiently and reduce errors if you only need to update information in one location.

Determine the Fields You Need

➤ Each field should relate directly to the subject of the table.

➤ Make sure you break down information into its smallest parts. For example, break down names into two fields called First Name and Last Name.

➤ Try to keep the number of fields in a table to a minimum. Tables with many fields increase the time it takes Access to process information.

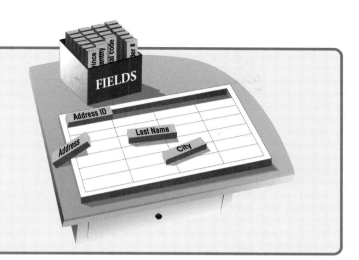

Determine the Primary Key

A primary key is one or more fields that uniquely identifies each record in a table. Each table in a database should have a primary key. For example, the primary key in a table containing employee information can be the social security number for each employee.

Social Security ID	First Name	Last Name	Address	City	State/Province	Postal Code
111-11-1111	Jim	Schmith	258 Linton Ave.	New York	NY	10010
222-22-2222	Brenda	Petterson	50 Tree Lane	Boston	MA	02117
333-33-3333	Todd	Talbot	68 Cracker Ave.	San Francisco	CA	94110
444-44-4444	Chuck	Dean	47 Crosby Ave.	Las Vegas	NV	89116
600-60-6000	Melanie	Robinson	26 Arnold Cres.	Jacksonville	FL	32256
777-77-7777	Susan	Hughes	401 Idon Dr.	Nashville	TN	37243
888-88-8888	Allen	Toppins	10 Heldon St.	Atlanta	GA	30375
999-99-9999	Greg	Kilkenny	36 Buzzard St.	Boston	MA	02118
000-00-0000	Jason	Marcuson	15 Bizzo Pl.	New York	NY	10020
000-11-2222	Jim	Martin	890 Apple St.	San Diego	CA	92121

Determine the Relationships Between Tables

Relationships between tables allow you to bring together related information in your database. You will usually relate the primary key in one table to a matching field in another table to form a relationship.

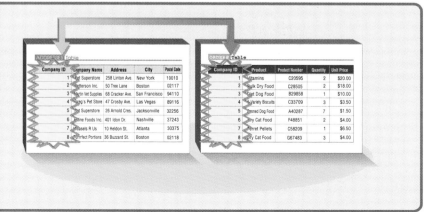

USING THE MOUSE

A mouse is a handheld device that lets you select and move items on your screen.

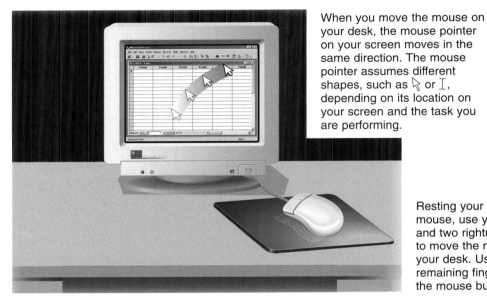

When you move the mouse on your desk, the mouse pointer on your screen moves in the same direction. The mouse pointer assumes different shapes, such as ▷ or I, depending on its location on your screen and the task you are performing.

Resting your hand on the mouse, use your thumb and two rightmost fingers to move the mouse on your desk. Use your two remaining fingers to press the mouse buttons.

MOUSE ACTIONS

Click

Press and release the left mouse button.

Double-click

Quickly press and release the left mouse button twice.

Right-click

Press and release the right mouse button.

Drag

Position the mouse pointer over an object on your screen and then press and hold down the left mouse button. Still holding down the button, move the mouse to where you want to place the object and then release the button.

You can start Access to create a new database or work with a database you previously created.

START ACCESS

1 Click **Start**.

2 Click **Programs**.

3 Click **Microsoft Access**.

■ The Microsoft Access window appears.

■ The Microsoft Access dialog box appears each time you start Access, allowing you to create or open a database.

Note: To create a database, see page 12 or 18. To open a database, see page 24.

■ The Office Assistant welcome appears the first time you start Access.

Note: For information on the Office Assistant, see page 30.

CREATE A DATABASE USING THE DATABASE WIZARD

You can use the Database Wizard to help you create a database. The wizard saves you time by providing ready-to-use objects, such as tables, forms, queries and reports.

You can use the Database Wizard to create many types of databases, such as databases for contact management, expenses, inventory control and order entry.

CREATE A DATABASE USING THE DATABASE WIZARD

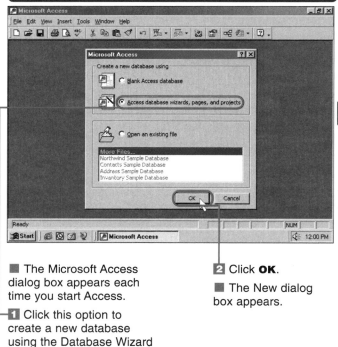

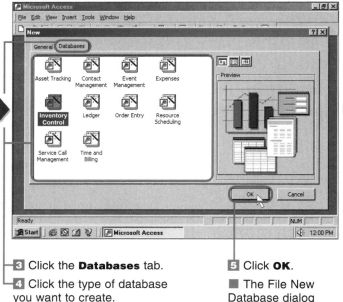

■ The Microsoft Access dialog box appears each time you start Access.

1 Click this option to create a new database using the Database Wizard (○ changes to ⊙).

2 Click **OK**.

■ The New dialog box appears.

3 Click the **Databases** tab.

4 Click the type of database you want to create.

5 Click **OK**.

■ The File New Database dialog box appears.

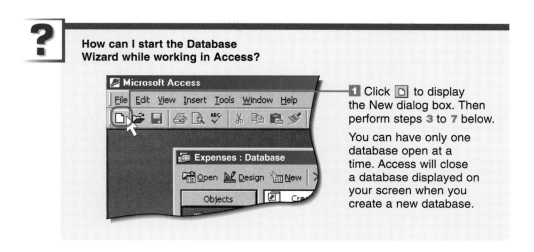

How can I start the Database Wizard while working in Access?

1 Click ▯ to display the New dialog box. Then perform steps **3** to **7** below.

You can have only one database open at a time. Access will close a database displayed on your screen when you create a new database.

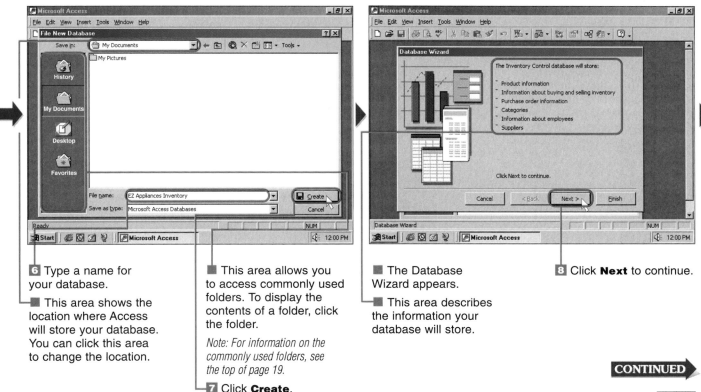

6 Type a name for your database.

■ This area shows the location where Access will store your database. You can click this area to change the location.

■ This area allows you to access commonly used folders. To display the contents of a folder, click the folder.

Note: For information on the commonly used folders, see the top of page 19.

7 Click **Create**.

■ The Database Wizard appears.

■ This area describes the information your database will store.

8 Click **Next** to continue.

CONTINUED ▶

CREATE A DATABASE USING THE DATABASE WIZARD

When creating a database, the Database Wizard displays the fields that each table will include. You can choose to include other optional fields.

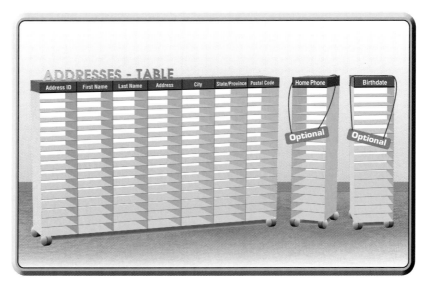

A field is a specific category of information in a table, such as the last names of your customers.

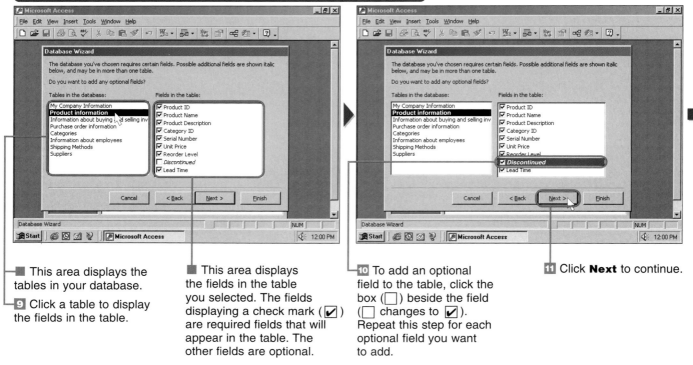

■ This area displays the tables in your database.

9 Click a table to display the fields in the table.

■ This area displays the fields in the table you selected. The fields displaying a check mark (✔) are required fields that will appear in the table. The other fields are optional.

10 To add an optional field to the table, click the box (☐) beside the field (☐ changes to ✔). Repeat this step for each optional field you want to add.

11 Click **Next** to continue.

14

Can I remove a required field from a table?

You can only remove a required field after you finish creating the database. To remove a field from a table, see page 47.

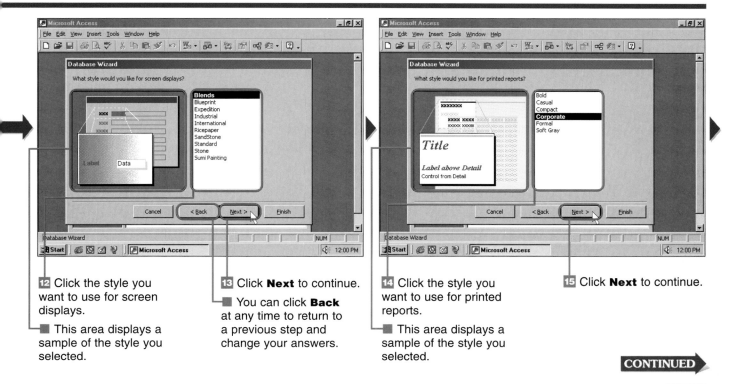

12 Click the style you want to use for screen displays.

■ This area displays a sample of the style you selected.

13 Click **Next** to continue.

■ You can click **Back** at any time to return to a previous step and change your answers.

14 Click the style you want to use for printed reports.

■ This area displays a sample of the style you selected.

15 Click **Next** to continue.

CONTINUED

CREATE A DATABASE USING THE DATABASE WIZARD

When you finish creating a database, Access displays a switchboard that can help you perform common tasks in the database.

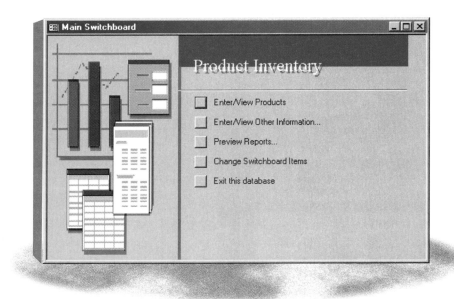

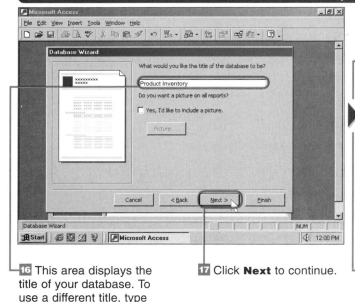

16 This area displays the title of your database. To use a different title, type the title.

17 Click **Next** to continue.

■ The wizard indicates that you have provided all the information needed to create your database.

18 Click **Finish** to create your database.

? **Why does this dialog box appear when I finish using the Database Wizard?**

Access needs you to enter information, such as your company name and address, to finish setting up the database.

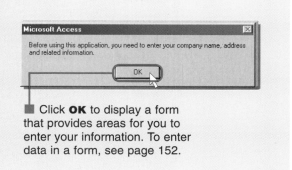

■ Click **OK** to display a form that provides areas for you to enter your information. To enter data in a form, see page 152.

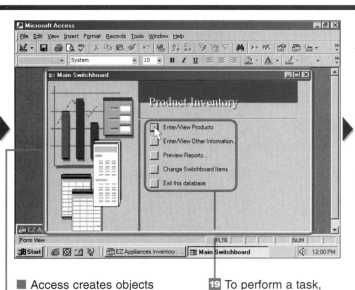

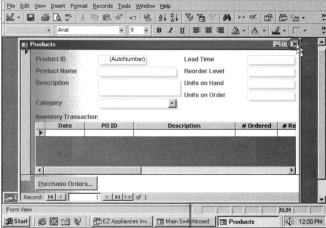

■ Access creates objects for your database, such as tables, forms, queries and reports.

■ The Main Switchboard window appears, which helps you perform common tasks in the database.

19 To perform a task, click the task you want to perform.

■ The object in the database that allows you to perform the task appears.

20 To close the object and return to the Main Switchboard window, click ✕.

CREATE A BLANK DATABASE

If you want to design
your own database,
you can create a blank
database. Creating a
blank database gives
you the most flexibility
and control.

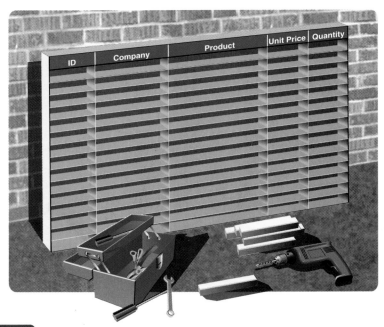

You can have only one
database open at a
time. Access will close
a database displayed
on your screen when
you create or open
another database.

CREATE A BLANK DATABASE

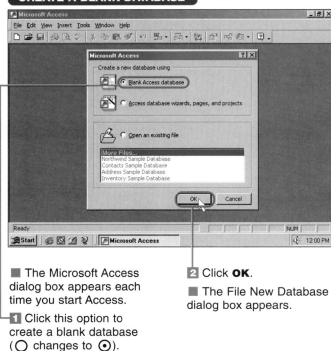

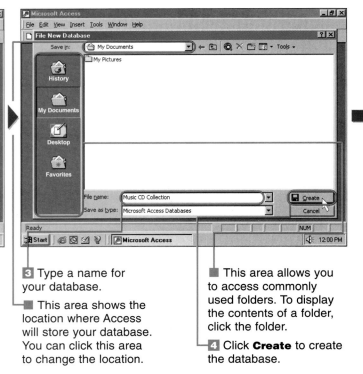

■ The Microsoft Access
dialog box appears each
time you start Access.

1 Click this option to
create a blank database
(○ changes to ⊙).

2 Click **OK**.

■ The File New Database
dialog box appears.

3 Type a name for
your database.

■ This area shows the
location where Access
will store your database.
You can click this area
to change the location.

■ This area allows you
to access commonly
used folders. To display
the contents of a folder,
click the folder.

4 Click **Create** to create
the database.

18

What are the commonly used folders I can access?

History

Provides access to folders and databases you recently used.

My Documents

Provides a convenient place to store a database.

Desktop

Lets you store a database on the Windows desktop.

Favorites

Provides a place to store a database you will frequently access.

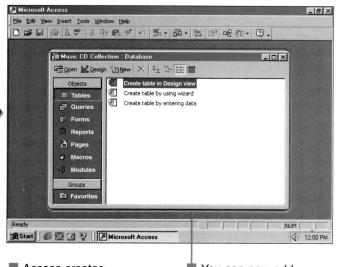

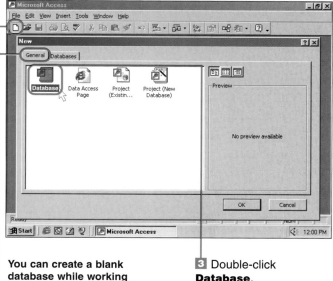

■ Access creates a blank database.

■ You can now add objects, such as tables and reports, to your database. The objects you add will appear in the Database window.

You can create a blank database while working in Access.

■1 Click ◻ to display the New dialog box.

■2 Click the **General** tab.

■3 Double-click **Database**.

■4 Perform steps 3 and 4 on page 18.

SELECT COMMANDS USING MENUS

You can select a command
from a menu to perform
a task. Each command
performs a different task.

SELECT COMMANDS USING MENUS

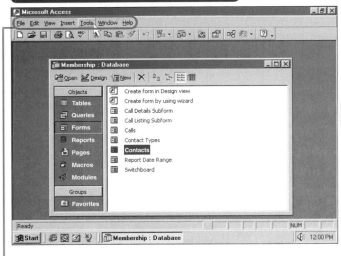

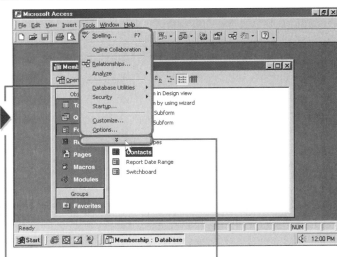

1 Click the name of
the menu you want
to display.

■ A short version of
the menu appears,
displaying the most
commonly used
commands.

2 To expand the menu
and display all the
commands, position
the mouse ⋟ over ⋟.

*Note: If you do not perform
step 2, the expanded menu
will automatically appear
after a few seconds.*

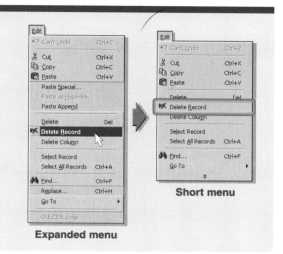

How can I make a command appear on the short version of a menu?

When you select a command from an expanded menu, Access automatically adds the command to the short version of the menu. The next time you display the short version of the menu, the command you selected will appear.

Short menu

Expanded menu

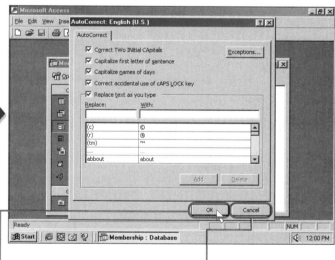

■ The expanded menu appears, displaying all the commands.

3 Click the command you want to use.

Note: A dimmed command is currently not available.

■ To close a menu without selecting a command, click outside the menu.

■ A dialog box appears if the command you selected displays three dots (...).

4 When you finish selecting options in the dialog box, click **OK** to confirm your changes.

■ To close the dialog box without making any changes, click **Cancel**.

SELECT COMMANDS USING TOOLBARS

A toolbar contains
buttons that you
can use to select
commands. Each
button allows you
to perform a
different task.

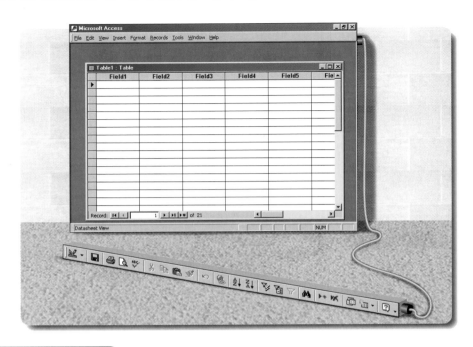

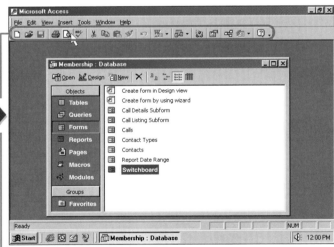

1 To display the name
of a toolbar button,
position the mouse
over the button.

■ After a few seconds,
the name of the button
appears in a yellow box.
The button name can
help you determine the
task the button performs.

2 To use a toolbar button
to select a command, click
the button.

Access offers several toolbars that you can display or hide at any time. Each toolbar contains buttons that help you quickly perform common tasks.

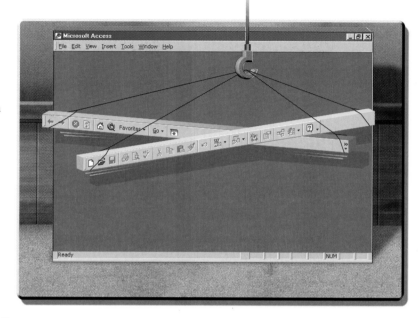

The available toolbars depend on the task you are performing.

DISPLAY OR HIDE A TOOLBAR

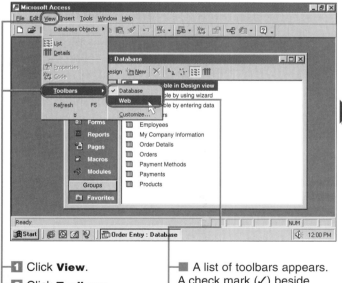

■1 Click **View**.

■2 Click **Toolbars**.

■ A list of toolbars appears. A check mark (✓) beside the name of a toolbar tells you the toolbar is currently displayed.

■3 Click the name of the toolbar you want to display or hide.

■ Access displays or hides the toolbar you selected.

OPEN A DATABASE

You can open
a database you
previously created
and display it on
your screen. This
lets you review
and make changes
to the database.

You can have only one
database open at a time.
Access will close a
database displayed on
your screen when you
open another database.

OPEN A DATABASE

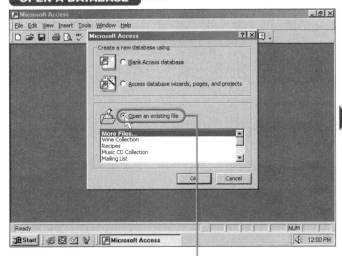

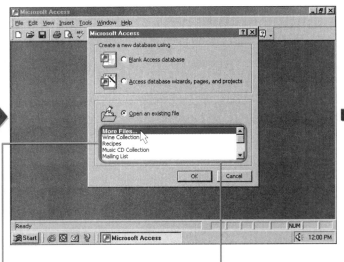

■ The Microsoft
Access dialog box
appears each time
you start Access.

1 Click this option to
open an existing database
(○ changes to ◉).

■ This area displays the
names of the last databases
you worked with. To open
one of these databases,
double-click the name of
the database.

*Note: The names of sample
databases may also appear
in the list.*

2 If the database you
want to open is not
listed, double-click
More Files.

■ The Open dialog
box appears.

24

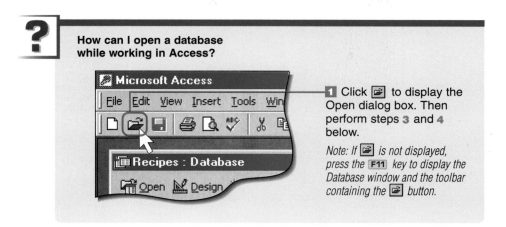

How can I open a database while working in Access?

1 Click 🖼 to display the Open dialog box. Then perform steps **3** and **4** below.

Note: If 🖼 is not displayed, press the F11 key to display the Database window and the toolbar containing the 🖼 button.

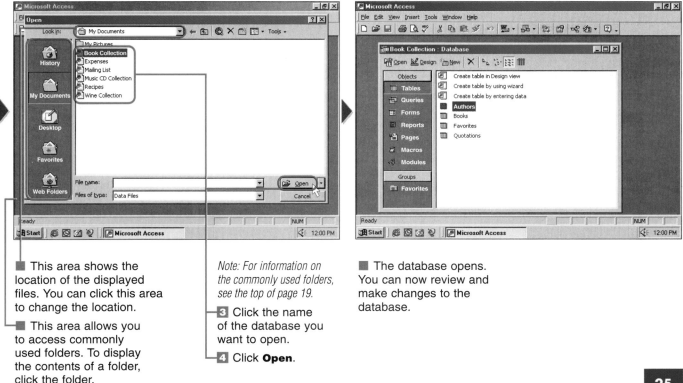

■ This area shows the location of the displayed files. You can click this area to change the location.

■ This area allows you to access commonly used folders. To display the contents of a folder, click the folder.

Note: For information on the commonly used folders, see the top of page 19.

3 Click the name of the database you want to open.

4 Click **Open**.

■ The database opens. You can now review and make changes to the database.

USING THE DATABASE WINDOW

You can use the
Database window
to open and work
with objects in
your database.

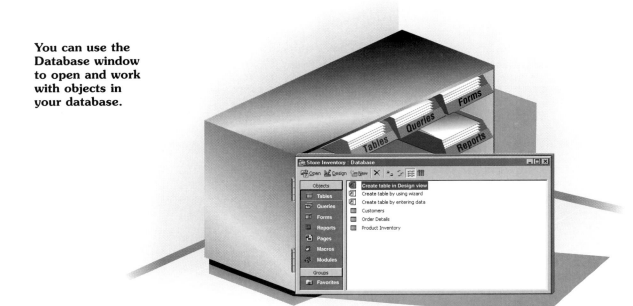

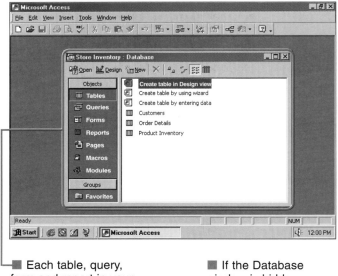

■ Each table, query,
form and report in your
database appears in the
Database window.

■ If the Database
window is hidden
behind other windows,
press the **F11** key to
display the window.

■ This area displays
the types of objects
in your database.

1 Click the type of
object you want to
work with.

■ This area displays all
the objects for the type
you selected.

2 Double-click an object
to open the object.

26

What types of objects will I find in the Database window?

Tables

Contain information about a specific topic, such as a mailing list.

Queries

Allow you to find information of interest in your database.

Forms

Provide a quick way to view, enter and change data in your database.

Reports

Summarize the data from your database in professional-looking documents.

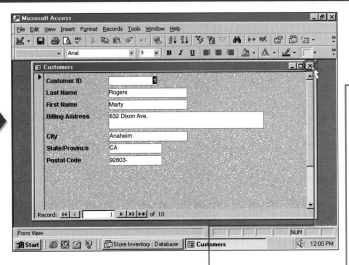

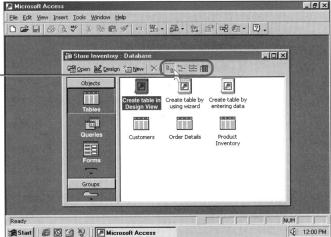

■ Access opens the object and displays its contents on your screen.

3 When you finish working with the object, click ☒ to close the object and return to the Database window.

CHANGE APPEARANCE OF OBJECTS

1 Click one of these buttons to change the appearance of the objects in the Database window.

▣ Large Icons

▣ Small Icons

▤ List

▦ Details

SWITCH BETWEEN WINDOWS

Access allows you to have more than one window open at a time. You can easily switch from one open window to another.

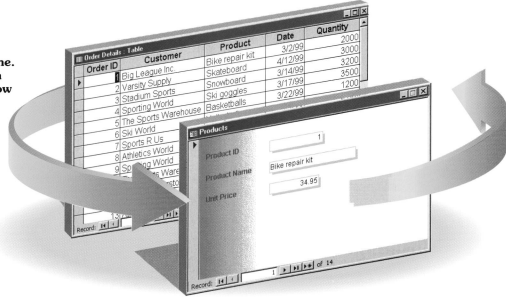

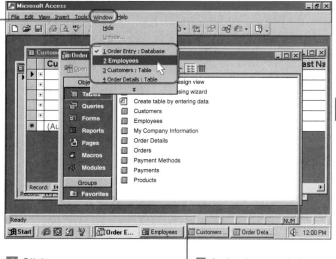

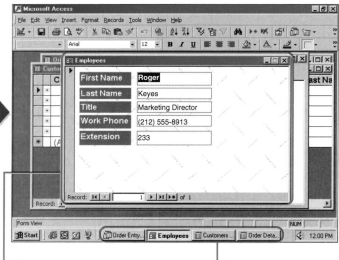

◼1 Click **Window** to display a list of all the windows you have open.

◼ A check mark (✓) appears beside the name of the window that is currently in front of all other windows.

◼2 Click the name of the window you want to switch to.

◼ The window you selected appears in front of all other windows.

◼ The taskbar displays a button for each open window. You can also switch to a window by clicking its button on the taskbar.

28

When you finish
using Access,
you can exit the
program.

You should exit
all programs
before turning off
your computer.

EXIT ACCESS

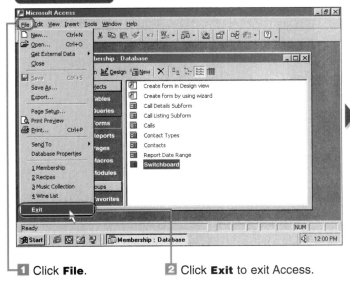

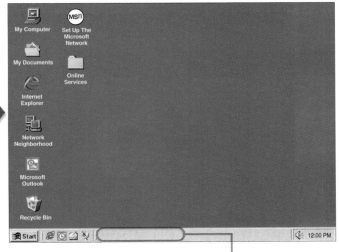

■1 Click **File**.

■2 Click **Exit** to exit Access.

■ The Microsoft Access
window disappears from
your screen.

■ The button for the
program disappears
from the taskbar.

GETTING HELP

If you do not know how to perform a task, you can ask the Office Assistant for help.

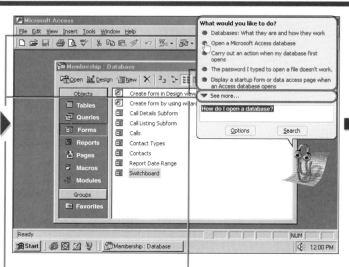

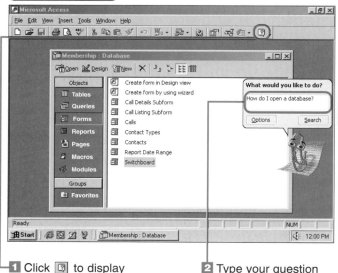

◼ Click 📳 to display the Office Assistant.

2 Type your question and then press the **Enter** key.

Note: If the question area does not appear, click the Office Assistant.

◼ A list of help topics related to your question appears.

◼ If more help topics exist, you can click **See more** to view the additional topics.

Note: If you do not see a help topic of interest, try rephrasing your question.

3 Click a help topic of interest.

Why do some words in the Help window appear in blue?

> **What do you want to do?**
>
> Create all tables, forms, and reports in one operation
>
> Choose fields for a new table from existing tables
>
> Create tables automatically from your data
>
> Create a table from scratch
>
> Create a new table from existing data

> **Create a table**
>
> Microsoft Access provides two ways to create a table. You can create a blank (empty) table for entering your own data, or you can create a table using existing data from another source.

You can click a word or phrase that appears in blue with an underline to display a related help topic.

You can click a word or phrase that appears in blue without an underline to display a definition of the text. To hide the definition, click anywhere on your screen.

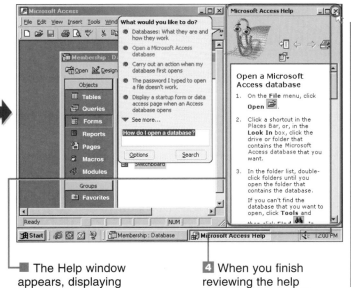

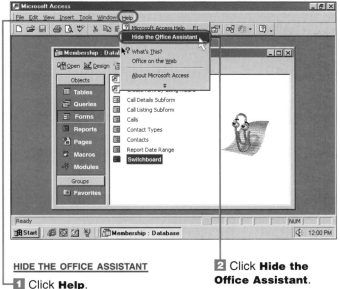

■ The Help window appears, displaying information about the help topic.

4 When you finish reviewing the help information, click ✕ to close the Help window.

HIDE THE OFFICE ASSISTANT

1 Click **Help**.

2 Click **Hide the Office Assistant**.

RECIPE

Recipe ID	Recipe Name	...ation Time
1	Chicken Stir-fry	...nutes
2	Omelet	...tes
3	Veggie Pizza	
4	Lasagna	
5	Pancakes	
6	Pork Chops	
7	Garden Salad	
8	Fruit Salad	
9	Sirloin	
10	Roast Pork	45 minutes

Meal

Dinner
Breakfast
Lunch
Dinner
Breakfast
Dinner
Lunch
Breakfast
Dinner
Dinner

Database

UNDER CONSTRUCTION

VT100

CHAPTER 2

Create Tables

Are you wondering how to create tables in your database? Learn how in this chapter.

Customer ID	Company Name	Billing Address	City	State/Province

CREATE A TABLE IN THE DATASHEET VIEW

A table stores a collection
of information about a
specific topic, such as a
list of addresses. You can
create a table to store
new information in
your database.

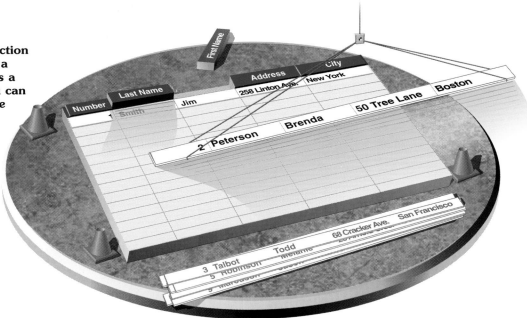

CREATE A TABLE IN THE DATASHEET VIEW

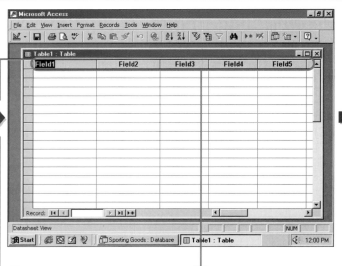

1 Click **Tables** in the
Database window.

2 Double-click **Create
table by entering data**.

■ A blank table appears.

■ This area displays
the field names for
each field in your table.

3 To change a field
name, double-click the
field name to highlight
the name.

34

? **What are the parts of a table?**

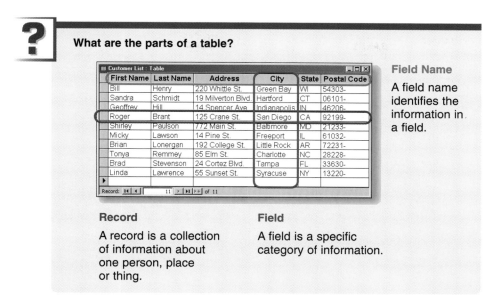

Field Name

A field name identifies the information in a field.

Record

A record is a collection of information about one person, place or thing.

Field

A field is a specific category of information.

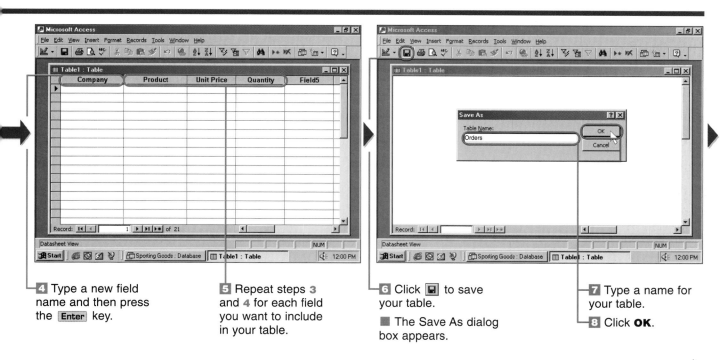

◢4 Type a new field name and then press the Enter key.

◢5 Repeat steps 3 and 4 for each field you want to include in your table.

◢6 Click 🖫 to save your table.

■ The Save As dialog box appears.

◢7 Type a name for your table.

◢8 Click **OK**.

CONTINUED ▶

CREATE A TABLE IN THE DATASHEET VIEW

You can have Access create a primary key for your table. A primary key is one or more fields that uniquely identifies each record in a table, such as a field containing ID numbers.

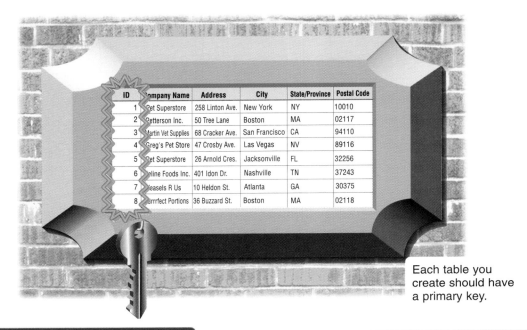

ID	Company Name	Address	City	State/Province	Postal Code
1	Pet Superstore	258 Linton Ave.	New York	NY	10010
2	Petterson Inc.	50 Tree Lane	Boston	MA	02117
3	Martin Vet Supplies	68 Cracker Ave.	San Francisco	CA	94110
4	Greg's Pet Store	47 Crosby Ave.	Las Vegas	NV	89116
5	Pet Superstore	26 Arnold Cres.	Jacksonville	FL	32256
6	Feline Foods Inc.	401 Idon Dr.	Nashville	TN	37243
7	Weasels R Us	10 Heldon St.	Atlanta	GA	30375
8	Purrrfect Portions	36 Buzzard St.	Boston	MA	02118

Each table you create should have a primary key.

CREATE A TABLE IN THE DATASHEET VIEW (CONTINUED)

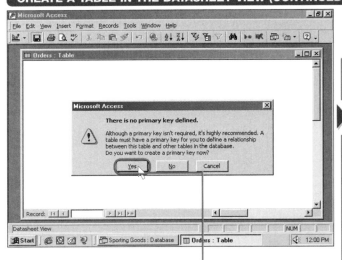

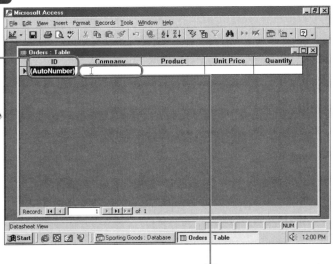

■ A dialog box appears, stating that your table does not have a primary key.

9 To have Access create a primary key for you, click **Yes**.

Note: You can later change the primary key. To change the primary key, see page 126.

■ Access removes the rows and columns that do not contain data.

■ If you selected **Yes** in step **9**, Access adds an ID field to your table to serve as the primary key. This field will automatically display a number for each record you add to your table.

10 To enter the data for a record, click the first empty cell in the row.

36

Why do I need to create a primary key in my table?

Access uses the primary key to establish relationships between the tables in your database. Relationships allow Access to bring together related information stored in the tables in your database. For more information on relationships, see page 128.

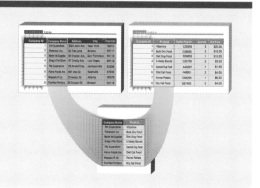

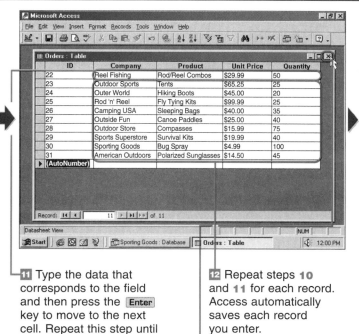

11 Type the data that corresponds to the field and then press the **Enter** key to move to the next cell. Repeat this step until you finish entering all the data for the record.

12 Repeat steps **10** and **11** for each record. Access automatically saves each record you enter.

13 When you finish entering records, click ☒ to close your table.

■ The name of your table appears in the Database window.

CREATE A TABLE USING THE TABLE WIZARD

You can use the Table Wizard to help you create a table that suits your needs. The wizard asks you a series of questions and then sets up a table based on your answers.

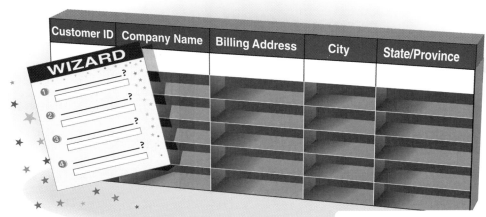

The wizard can help you create a table for business or personal use. The wizard offers tables such as Expenses, Investments, Mailing List, Orders and Recipes.

CREATE A TABLE USING THE TABLE WIZARD

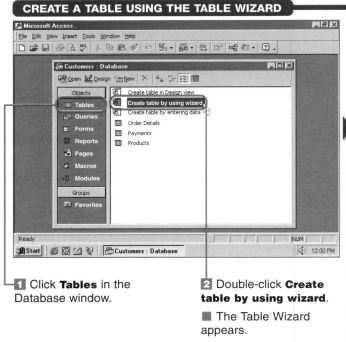

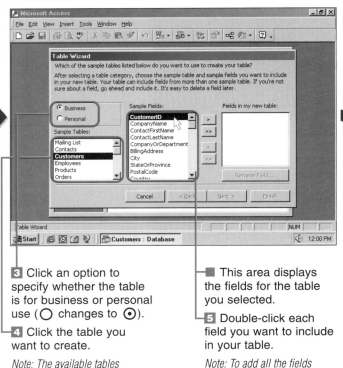

■1 Click **Tables** in the Database window.

■2 Double-click **Create table by using wizard**.

■ The Table Wizard appears.

■3 Click an option to specify whether the table is for business or personal use (○ changes to ⊙).

■4 Click the table you want to create.

Note: The available tables depend on the option you selected in step 3.

■ This area displays the fields for the table you selected.

■5 Double-click each field you want to include in your table.

Note: To add all the fields at once, click >> .

What is a primary key?

A primary key is one or more fields that uniquely identifies each record in a table, such as a field containing ID numbers. When creating a table using the wizard, you can have Access set a primary key for you. Access will create a field that automatically numbers each record in your table. To later change the primary key, see page 126.

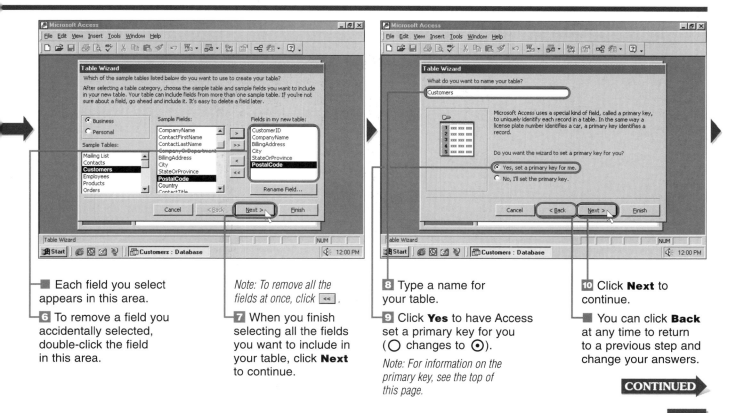

■ Each field you select appears in this area.

6 To remove a field you accidentally selected, double-click the field in this area.

Note: To remove all the fields at once, click ⟪ *.*

7 When you finish selecting all the fields you want to include in your table, click **Next** to continue.

8 Type a name for your table.

9 Click **Yes** to have Access set a primary key for you (○ changes to ⊙).

Note: For information on the primary key, see the top of this page.

10 Click **Next** to continue.

■ You can click **Back** at any time to return to a previous step and change your answers.

CONTINUED

CREATE A TABLE USING THE TABLE WIZARD

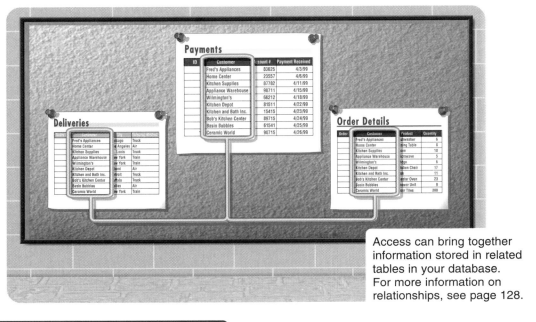

The Table Wizard shows how your new table relates to the other tables in your database.

Access can bring together information stored in related tables in your database. For more information on relationships, see page 128.

CREATE A TABLE USING THE TABLE WIZARD (CONTINUED)

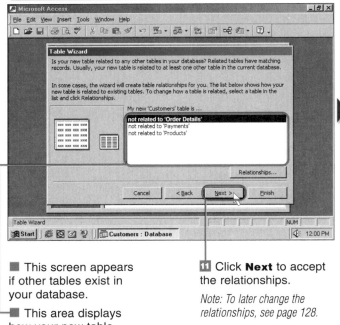

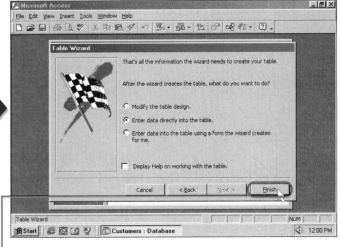

■ This screen appears if other tables exist in your database.

■ This area displays how your new table relates to the other tables in your database.

11 Click **Next** to accept the relationships.

Note: To later change the relationships, see page 128.

12 Click **Finish** to create your table.

Can I rename a field in my table?

Yes. Double-click the name of the field you want to change and then type a new name. For more information on renaming fields, see page 44.

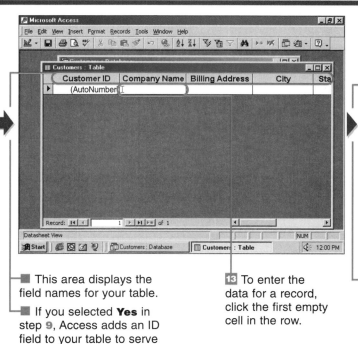

■ This area displays the field names for your table.

■ If you selected **Yes** in step 9, Access adds an ID field to your table to serve as the primary key. This field will automatically display a number for each record you add to the table.

13 To enter the data for a record, click the first empty cell in the row.

14 Type the data that corresponds to the field and then press the `Enter` key to move to the next cell. Repeat this step until you finish entering all the data for the record.

15 Repeat steps 13 and 14 for each record. Access automatically saves each record you enter.

16 When you finish entering records, click ⨉ to close your table.

OPEN A TABLE

You can open a table to display its contents on your screen. This lets you review and make changes to the table.

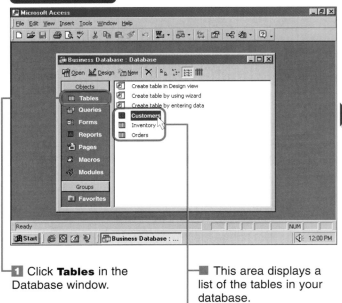

1 Click **Tables** in the Database window.

■ This area displays a list of the tables in your database.

2 Double-click the table you want to open.

■ The table opens. You can now review and make changes to the table.

■ When you finish working with the table, click ⊠ to close the table.

■ A dialog box will appear if you did not save changes you made to the layout of the table. Click **Yes** to save the changes.

42

CHANGE COLUMN WIDTH

You can change the width of a column in your table. Increasing the width of a column lets you view data that is too long to display in the column.

Address	First Na	Last Na	Address	City	State/Pr	Postal
1	Jim	Schmith	258 Linton Ave.	New Yor	NY	100
2	Brenda	Peterson	50 Tree Lane	Boston	MA	021
3	Todd	Talbot	68 Cracker Ave.	San Fran	CA	941
4	Chuck	Dean	47 Crosby Ave.	Las Vega	NV	891
5	Melanie	Robinson	26 Arnold Cres.	Jacksonv	FL	322
6	Susan	Hughes	401 Idon Dr.	Nashville	TN	372
7	Allen	Toppins	10 Heldon St.	Atlanta	GA	303
8	Greg	Kilkenny	36 Buzzard St.	Boston	MA	021

Reducing the width of a column allows you to display more fields on your screen at once.

CHANGE COLUMN WIDTH

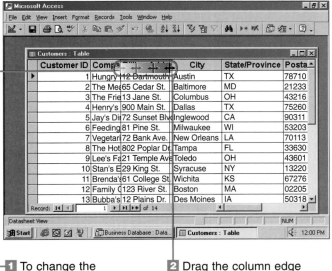

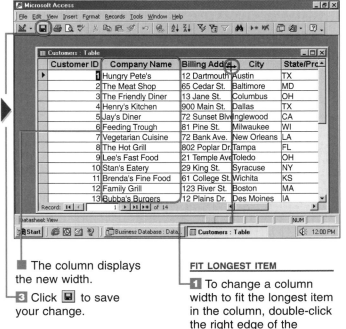

◼1 To change the width of a column, position the mouse ⬚ over the right edge of the column heading (⬚ changes to ✛).

◼2 Drag the column edge until the line displays the column width you want.

◼ The column displays the new width.

◼3 Click 🖬 to save your change.

FIT LONGEST ITEM

◼1 To change a column width to fit the longest item in the column, double-click the right edge of the column heading.

RENAME A FIELD

You can give a field a
different name to more
accurately describe the
contents of the field.

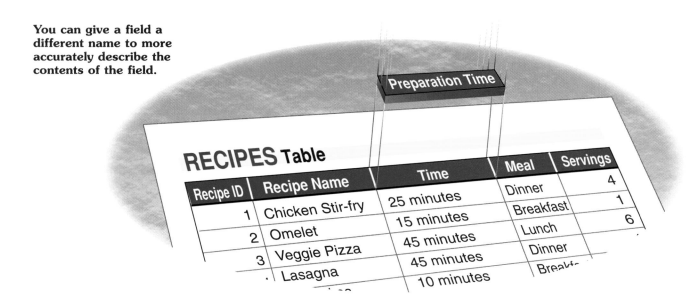

RECIPES Table

Recipe ID	Recipe Name	Time	Meal	Servings
1	Chicken Stir-fry	25 minutes	Dinner	4
2	Omelet	15 minutes	Breakfast	1
3	Veggie Pizza	45 minutes	Lunch	6
.	Lasagna	45 minutes	Dinner	
		10 minutes	Break...	

RENAME A FIELD

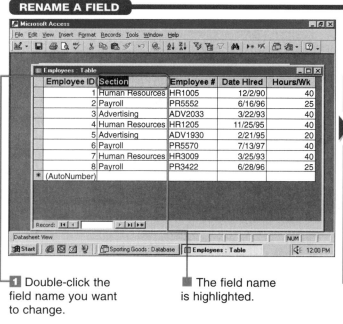

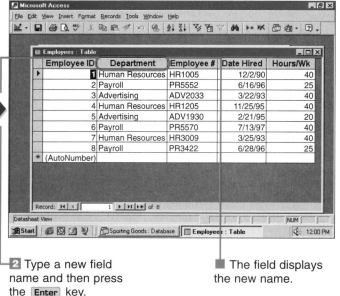

1 Double-click the
field name you want
to change.

■ The field name
is highlighted.

2 Type a new field
name and then press
the Enter key.

■ The field displays
the new name.

REARRANGE FIELDS

You can change
the order of fields
to better organize
the information in
your table.

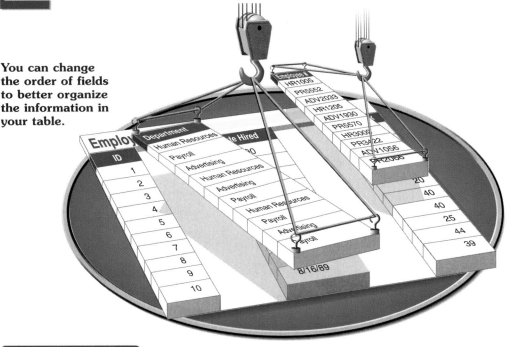

Rearranging fields in the
Datasheet view will not
affect how the fields appear
in the Design view or
in other objects in the
database, such as a form
or report. For information
on the Datasheet and
Design views, see page 76.

REARRANGE FIELDS

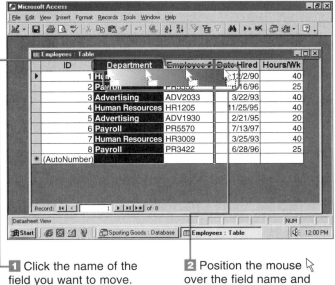

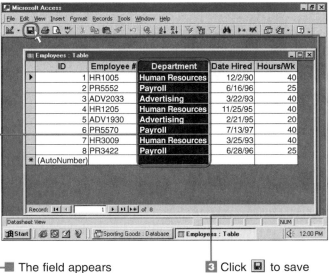

1 Click the name of the
field you want to move.
The field is highlighted.

2 Position the mouse ⌖
over the field name and
then drag the field to a
new location.

■ A thick line shows
where the field will appear.

■ The field appears
in the new location.

3 Click 🖫 to save
your change.

ADD A FIELD

You can add a field to your table when you want to include an additional category of information.

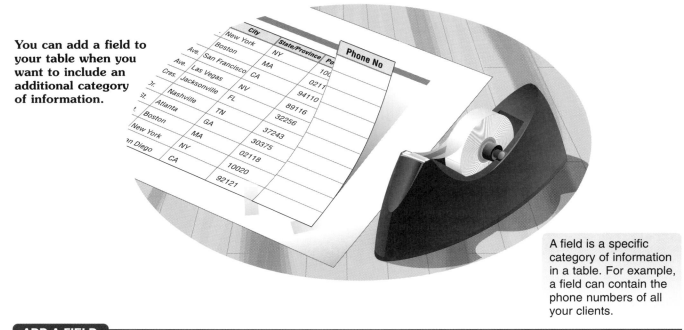

A field is a specific category of information in a table. For example, a field can contain the phone numbers of all your clients.

ADD A FIELD

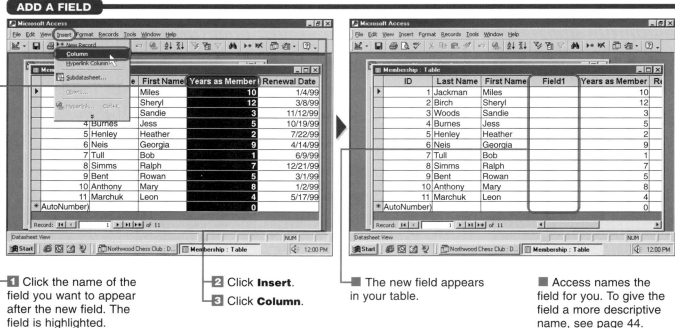

1 Click the name of the field you want to appear after the new field. The field is highlighted.

2 Click **Insert**.

3 Click **Column**.

■ The new field appears in your table.

■ Access names the field for you. To give the field a more descriptive name, see page 44.

DELETE A FIELD

If you no longer need a field, you can permanently delete the field from your table.

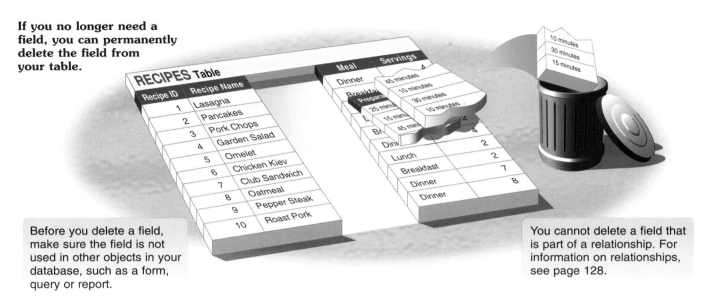

Before you delete a field, make sure the field is not used in other objects in your database, such as a form, query or report.

You cannot delete a field that is part of a relationship. For information on relationships, see page 128.

DELETE A FIELD

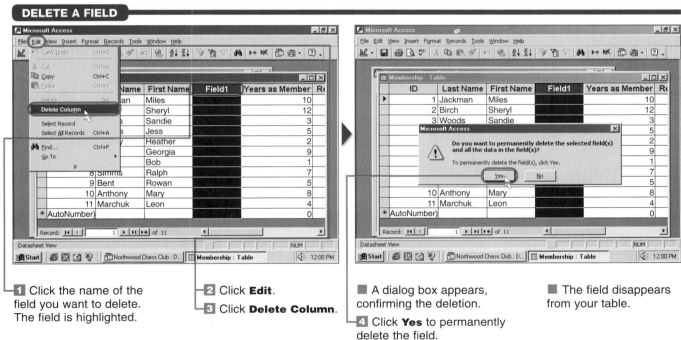

◾1 Click the name of the field you want to delete. The field is highlighted.

◾2 Click **Edit**.

◾3 Click **Delete Column**.

■ A dialog box appears, confirming the deletion.

◾4 Click **Yes** to permanently delete the field.

■ The field disappears from your table.

RENAME A TABLE

You can change the
name of a table to
better describe the
information stored
in the table.

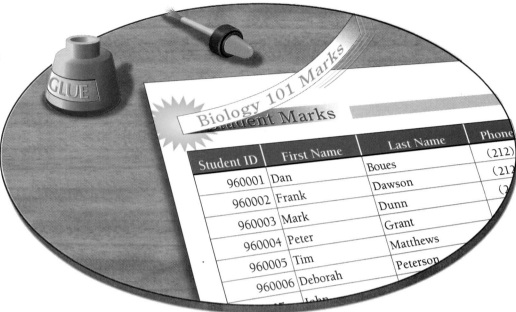

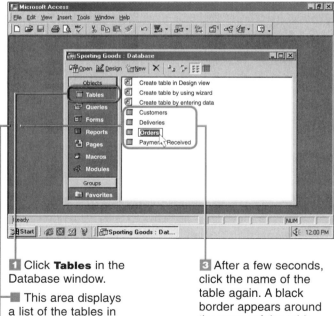

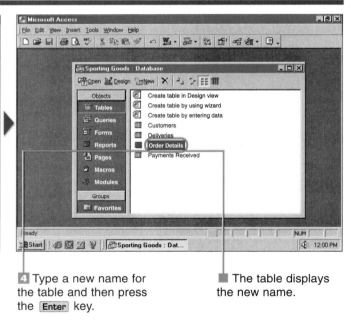

1 Click **Tables** in the
Database window.

■ This area displays
a list of the tables in
your database.

2 Click the name of the
table you want to rename.

3 After a few seconds,
click the name of the
table again. A black
border appears around
the name of the table.

*Note: If you accidentally
double-click the name of the
table, the table will open.*

4 Type a new name for
the table and then press
the **Enter** key.

■ The table displays
the new name.

48

DELETE A TABLE

If you no longer need the information stored in a table, you can permanently delete the table from your database.

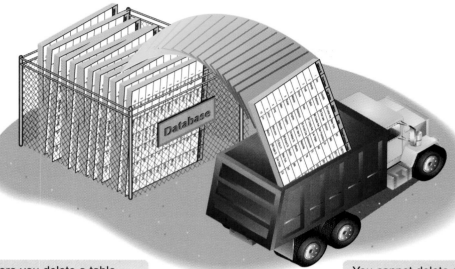

Before you delete a table, make sure other objects in your database, such as a form or report, do not use the table.

You cannot delete a table that is related to another table in your database. For information on relationships, see page 128.

DELETE A TABLE

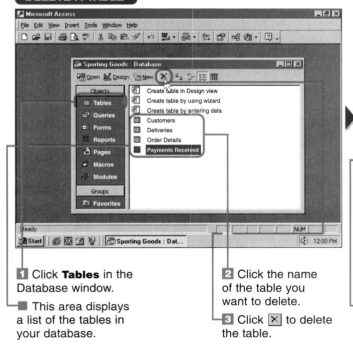

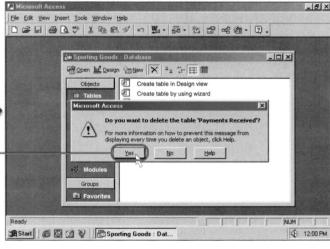

■1 Click **Tables** in the Database window.

■ This area displays a list of the tables in your database.

■2 Click the name of the table you want to delete.

■3 Click ✕ to delete the table.

■ A dialog box appears, confirming the deletion.

■4 Click **Yes** to permanently delete the table.

■ The table disappears from the Database window.

First Name	Last Name	Address	City	State/Province	Postal Code
Jim	Schmith	258 Linton Ave.	New York	NY	10010
Brenda	Peterson	50 Tree Lane	Boston	MA	02117
Todd	Talbot	8 Cracker Ave.	San Francisco	CA	94110
Chuck	Dean	47 Crosby Ave.	Las Vegas	NV	89116
Melanie	Robinson	26 Arnold Cres.	Jacksonville	FL	32256
					30375
Allen	Toppins	10 Heldon St.	Atlanta	GA	
Greg			Boston	MA	02118

Kilkenny

36 Buzzard St.

CHAPTER 3

Edit Tables

Do you want to make changes to your tables? In this chapter you will learn how to edit data, add a new record, change the appearance of your tables and more.

MOVE THROUGH DATA

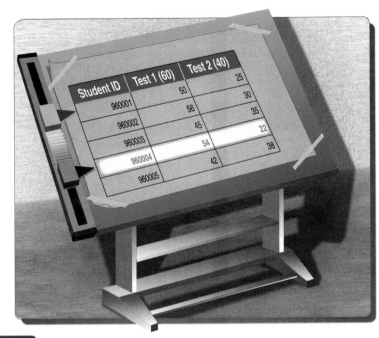

You can move through the data in your table to review and edit information.

If your table contains a lot of data, your computer screen may not be able to display all the data at once. You can scroll through fields and records to display data that does not appear on your screen.

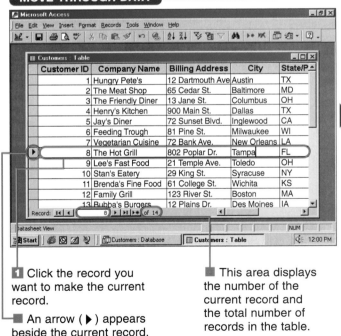

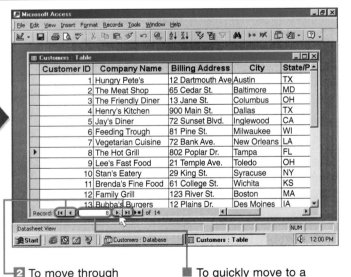

■1 Click the record you want to make the current record.

■ An arrow (▶) appears beside the current record.

■ This area displays the number of the current record and the total number of records in the table.

■2 To move through the records, click one of the following buttons.

◄◄	First record
◄	Previous record
►	Next record
►►	Last record

■ To quickly move to a specific record, double-click this area and then type the number of the record you want to display. Then press the **Enter** key.

How do I use my keyboard to move through data in a table?

Press on Keyboard	Description
Page Up	Move up one screen of records
Page Down	Move down one screen of records
Tab	Move to the next field in the current record
↑	Move up one record in the same field
↓	Move down one record in the same field

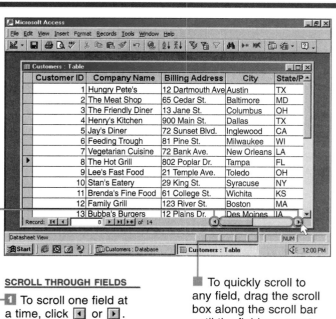

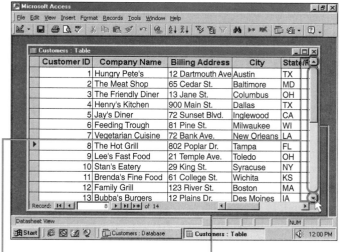

SCROLL THROUGH FIELDS

◼ 1 To scroll one field at a time, click ◀ or ▶.

Note: You cannot scroll through fields if all the fields appear on your screen.

◼ To quickly scroll to any field, drag the scroll box along the scroll bar until the field you want to view appears.

SCROLL THROUGH RECORDS

◼ 1 To scroll one record at a time, click ▲ or ▼.

Note: You cannot scroll through records if all the records appear on your screen.

◼ To quickly scroll to any record, drag the scroll box along the scroll bar until a yellow box displays the number of the record you want to view.

SELECT DATA

Before performing many tasks in a table, you must select the data you want to work with. Selected data appears highlighted on your screen.

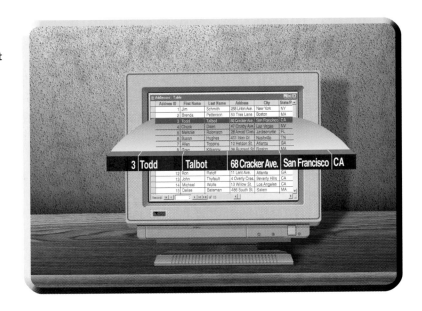

To deselect data in a table, click anywhere in the table.

SELECT DATA

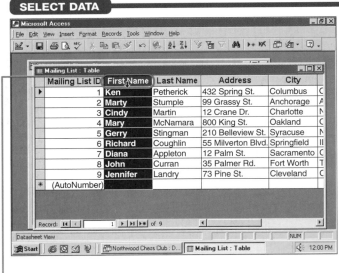

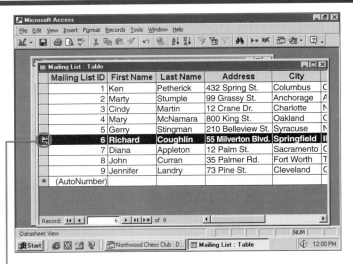

SELECT A FIELD

1 Position the mouse ⩗ over the name of the field you want to select (⩗ changes to ↓) and then click to select the field.

■ To select multiple fields, position the mouse ⩗ over the name of the first field (⩗ changes to ↓). Then drag the mouse ↓ until you highlight all the fields you want to select.

SELECT A RECORD

1 Position the mouse ⩗ over the area to the left of the record you want to select (⩗ changes to →) and then click to select the record.

■ To select multiple records, position the mouse I over the area to the left of the first record (I changes to →). Then drag the mouse → until you highlight all the records you want to select.

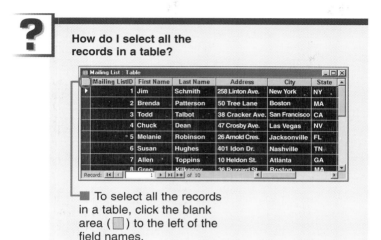

How do I select all the records in a table?

■ To select all the records in a table, click the blank area (☐) to the left of the field names.

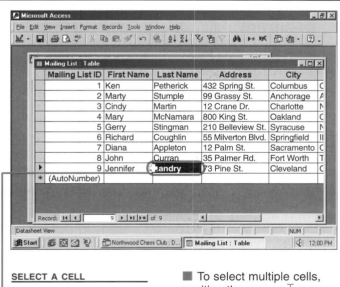

SELECT A CELL

1 Position the mouse I over the left edge of the cell you want to select (I changes to ⇩) and then click to select the cell.

■ To select multiple cells, position the mouse I over the left edge of the first cell (I changes to ⇩). Then drag the mouse ⇩ until you highlight all the cells you want to select.

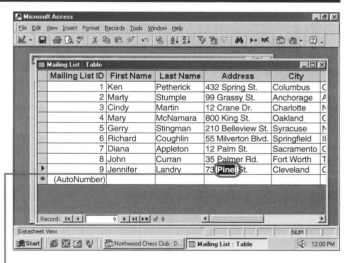

SELECT DATA IN A CELL

1 Position the mouse I over the left edge of the data and then drag the mouse I until you highlight all the data you want to select.

■ To quickly select a word, double-click the word.

EDIT DATA

You can edit the data in a table to correct a mistake or update the data.

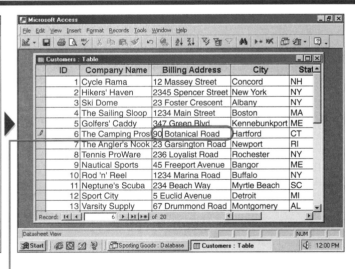

Recipe ID	Recipe	Meal	Vegetarian
1	Chicken St...	Dinner	No
2	Omelet	Breakfast	Yes
3	Veggie Pizza	...nch	Yes
4	Lasagna		No
5	Pancakes	...ast	Yes
6	Pork Chops	Dinner	No
7	Garden Salad	Lunch	Yes
8	Fruit Salad	Breakfast	Yes

Access automatically saves the changes you make to the data in a table.

EDIT DATA

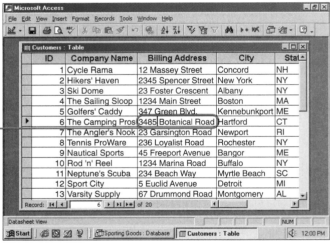

1 Click the location in the cell where you want to edit data.

■ A flashing insertion point appears in the cell.

Note: You can press the ← or → key to move the insertion point to where you want to edit data.

2 To remove the character to the left of the insertion point, press the ◆Backspace key.

3 To insert data where the insertion point flashes on your screen, type the data.

4 When you finish making changes to the data, press the Enter key.

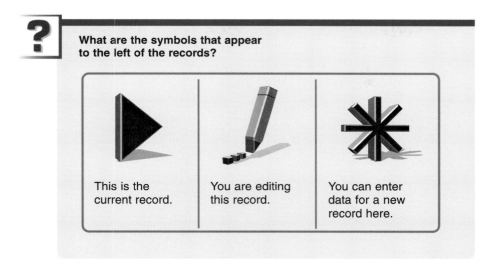

What are the symbols that appear to the left of the records?

This is the current record.

You are editing this record.

You can enter data for a new record here.

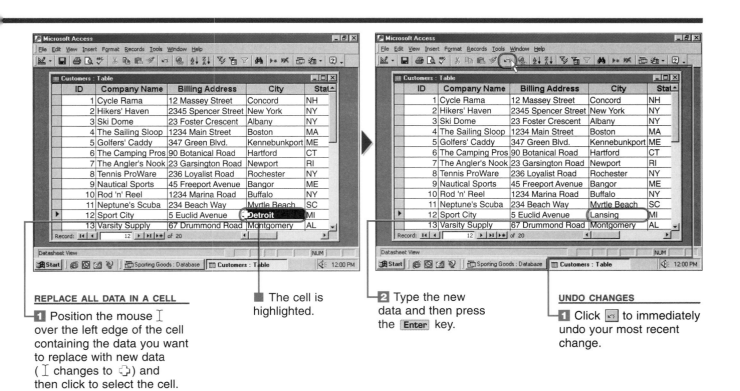

REPLACE ALL DATA IN A CELL

1 Position the mouse I over the left edge of the cell containing the data you want to replace with new data (I changes to ⇨) and then click to select the cell.

■ The cell is highlighted.

2 Type the new data and then press the **Enter** key.

UNDO CHANGES

1 Click ⟲ to immediately undo your most recent change.

ZOOM INTO A CELL

You can zoom into any
cell in a table to make
the contents of the cell
easier to review and edit.

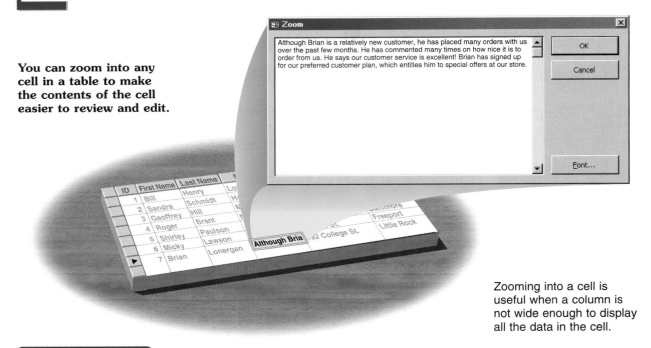

Zooming into a cell is
useful when a column is
not wide enough to display
all the data in the cell.

ZOOM INTO A CELL

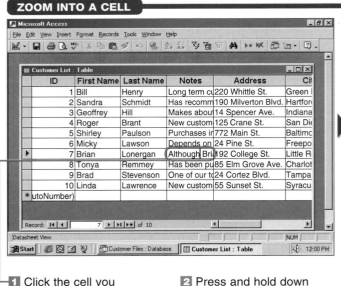

1 Click the cell you
want to zoom into.

2 Press and hold down
the **Shift** key as you
press the **F2** key.

■ The Zoom dialog
box appears.

■ This area displays all
the data in the cell. You
can review and edit the
data. To edit data, see
page 56.

3 When you finish
reviewing and editing
the data, click **OK** to
close the dialog box.

■ The table will
display any changes
you made to the data.

58

When viewing the records in a table, you can display a subdatasheet to view and edit related data from another table.

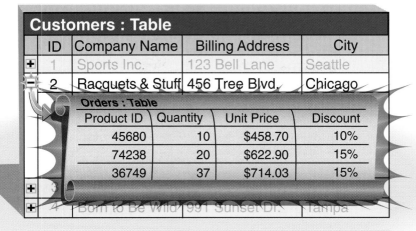

For example, in a table containing customer information, you can display a subdatasheet to view the orders for a customer.

You can only display a subdatasheet when the table you are working with is related to another table. For information on relationships, see page 128.

DISPLAY A SUBDATASHEET

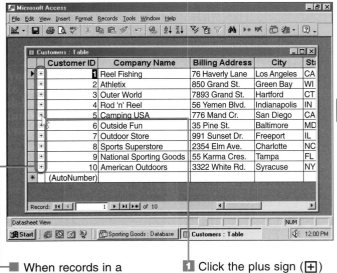

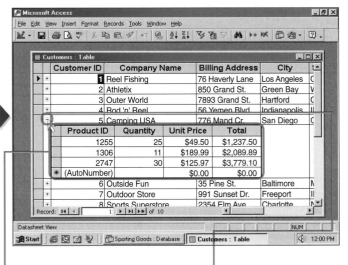

■ When records in a table relate to data in another table, a plus sign (⊞) appears beside each record.

1 Click the plus sign (⊞) beside a record to display the related data from the other table (⊞ changes to ⊟).

■ The related data from the other table appears. You can review and edit the data. To edit data, see page 56.

2 To once again hide the related data, click the minus sign (⊟) beside the record.

CHECK SPELLING

You can find and correct all the spelling errors in your table.

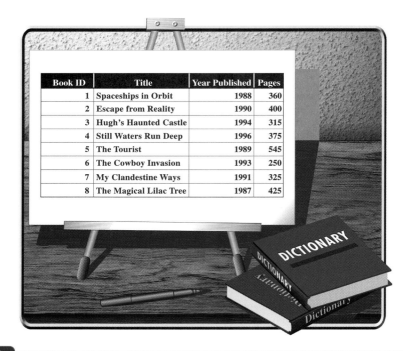

Book ID	Title	Year Published	Pages
1	Spaceships in Orbit	1988	360
2	Escape from Reality	1990	400
3	Hugh's Haunted Castle	1994	315
4	Still Waters Run Deep	1996	375
5	The Tourist	1989	545
6	The Cowboy Invasion	1993	250
7	My Clandestine Ways	1991	325
8	The Magical Lilac Tree	1987	425

Access compares every word in your table to words in its dictionary. If a word in your table does not exist in the dictionary, Access considers the word misspelled.

CHECK SPELLING

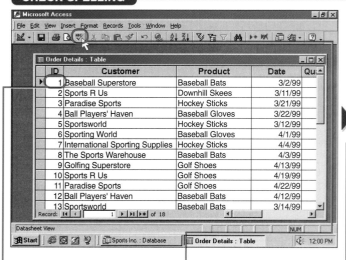

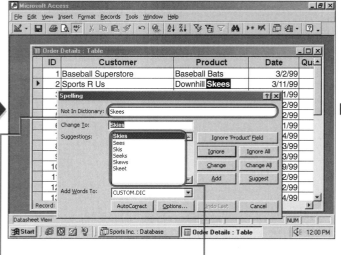

1 To start the spell check at the beginning of your table, click the first cell in the table.

■ To spell check a single field or record, select the field or record in the table. To select a field or record, see page 54.

2 Click 📝 to start the spell check.

■ The Spelling dialog box appears if Access finds a misspelled word in your table.

■ This area displays the misspelled word.

■ This area displays suggestions for correcting the word.

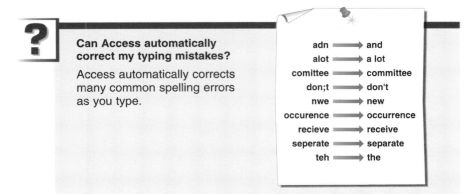

Can Access automatically correct my typing mistakes?

Access automatically corrects many common spelling errors as you type.

adn	➡	and
alot	➡	a lot
comittee	➡	committee
don;t	➡	don't
nwe	➡	new
occurence	➡	occurrence
recieve	➡	receive
seperate	➡	separate
teh	➡	the

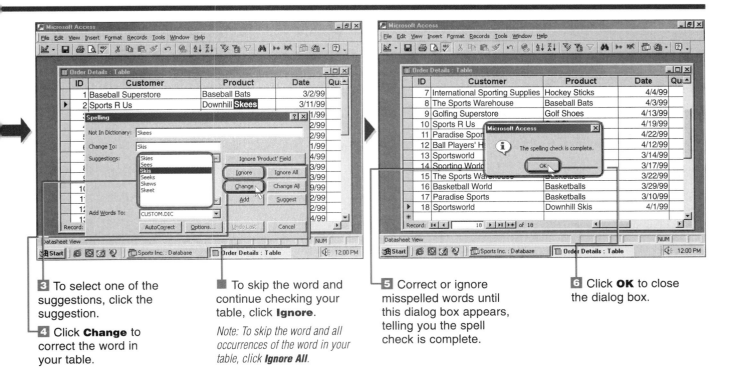

3 To select one of the suggestions, click the suggestion.

4 Click **Change** to correct the word in your table.

■ To skip the word and continue checking your table, click **Ignore**.

Note: To skip the word and all occurrences of the word in your table, click Ignore All.

5 Correct or ignore misspelled words until this dialog box appears, telling you the spell check is complete.

6 Click **OK** to close the dialog box.

MOVE OR COPY DATA

You can move or copy data to a new location in your table.

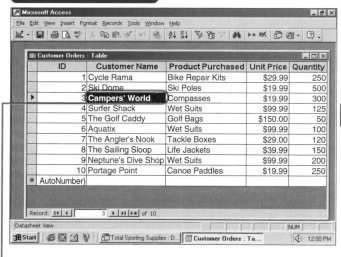

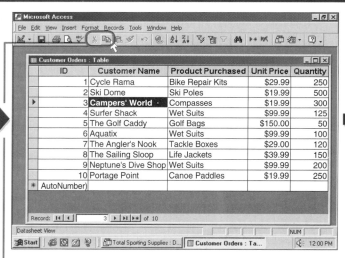

■1 To copy data, select the cell(s) containing the data. To select cells, see page 55.

■ To move data, drag the mouse I over the data until you highlight the data.

■2 Click one of the following buttons.

✂ Move data

🖺 Copy data

Note: The Clipboard toolbar may appear. To hide the Clipboard toolbar, click ☒ on the toolbar.

62

What is the difference between moving and copying data?

Moving data

Moving data allows you to rearrange data in your table. When you move data, the data disappears from its original location.

Copying data

Copying data allows you to repeat data in your table without having to retype the data. When you copy data, the data appears in both the original and new locations.

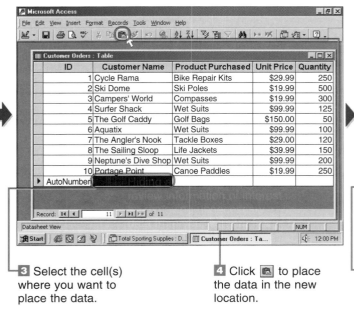

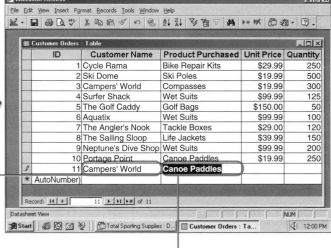

3 Select the cell(s) where you want to place the data.

4 Click [image] to place the data in the new location.

■ The data appears in the new location.

COPY DATA DOWN ONE CELL

1 Click the cell below the data you want to copy. Then press and hold down the **Ctrl** key as you press the [image] key.

■ Access copies the data to the cell.

ADD A RECORD

You can add a record to insert new information into your table. For example, you may want to add information about a new customer.

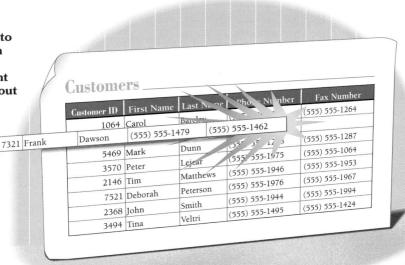

Access automatically saves each new record you add to a table.

ADD A RECORD

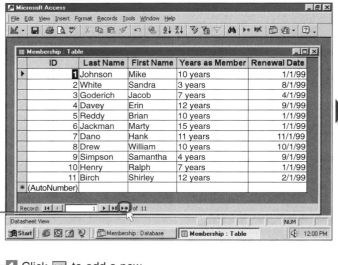

1 Click ►* to add a new record to your table.

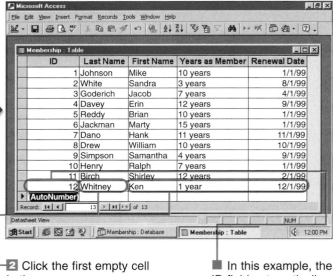

2 Click the first empty cell in the row.

3 Type the data that corresponds to the field and then press the **Enter** key to move to the next cell. Repeat this step until you finish entering all the data for the record.

■ In this example, the ID field automatically displays a number for the new record.

DELETE A RECORD

You can delete a record to permanently remove information you no longer need from a table. For example, you may want to remove information about a product you no longer offer.

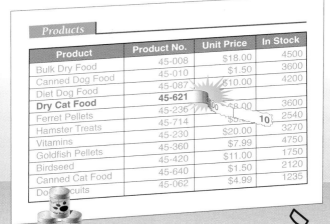

Deleting records saves storage space on your computer and reduces clutter in your database.

DELETE A RECORD

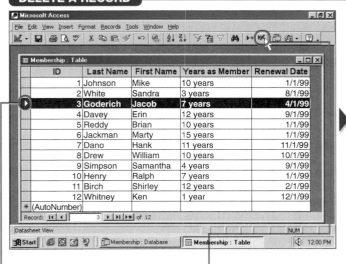

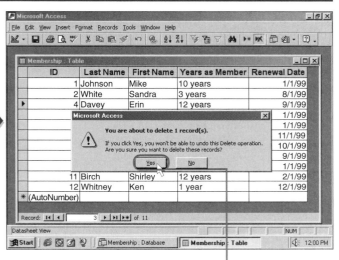

1 Position the mouse ⤢ over the area to the left of the record you want to delete (⤢ changes to ➡) and then click to select the record.

2 Click 🔀 to delete the record.

■ The record disappears.

■ A warning dialog box appears, confirming the deletion.

3 Click **Yes** to permanently delete the record.

CHANGE FONT OF DATA

You can change the font, style, size and color of data to enhance the appearance of your table.

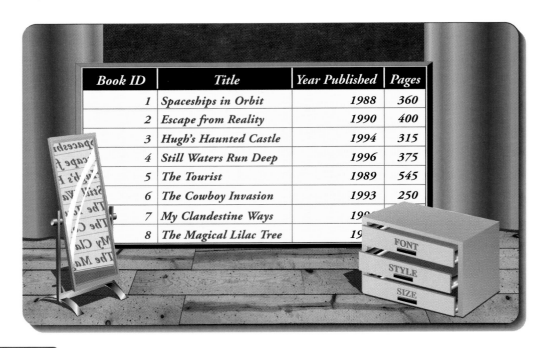

CHANGE FONT OF DATA

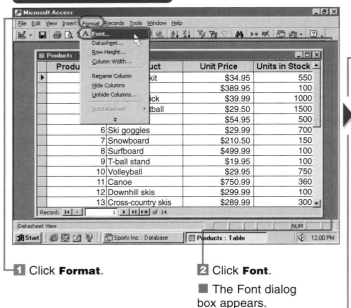

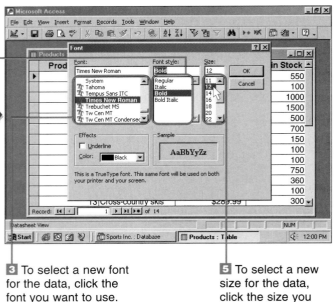

1 Click **Format**.

2 Click **Font**.

■ The Font dialog box appears.

3 To select a new font for the data, click the font you want to use.

4 To select a new style for the data, click the style you want to use.

5 To select a new size for the data, click the size you want to use.

66

What determines which fonts are available on my computer?

The fonts available on your computer may be different from the fonts on other computers. The available fonts depend on your printer and the setup of your computer.

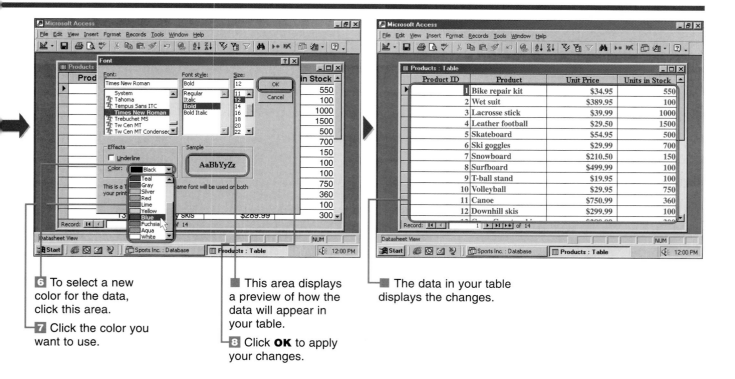

■ **6** To select a new color for the data, click this area.

■ **7** Click the color you want to use.

■ This area displays a preview of how the data will appear in your table.

■ **8** Click **OK** to apply your changes.

■ The data in your table displays the changes.

CHANGE APPEARANCE OF TABLE

You can add cell effects and colors to a table to enhance the appearance of the table.

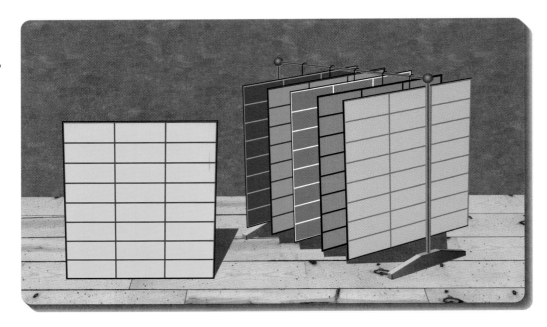

CHANGE APPEARANCE OF TABLE

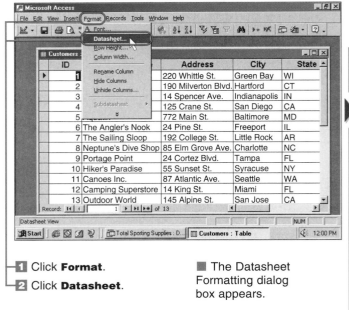

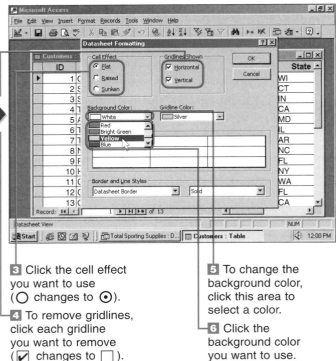

■1 Click **Format**.

■2 Click **Datasheet**.

■ The Datasheet Formatting dialog box appears.

■3 Click the cell effect you want to use (○ changes to ⊙).

■4 To remove gridlines, click each gridline you want to remove (☑ changes to ☐).

■5 To change the background color, click this area to select a color.

■6 Click the background color you want to use.

I cannot remove gridlines or change the colors for my table. What is wrong?

If you selected the **Raised** or **Sunken** cell effect in step 3 below, Access automatically displays all gridlines and sets the background color and gridline color for you.

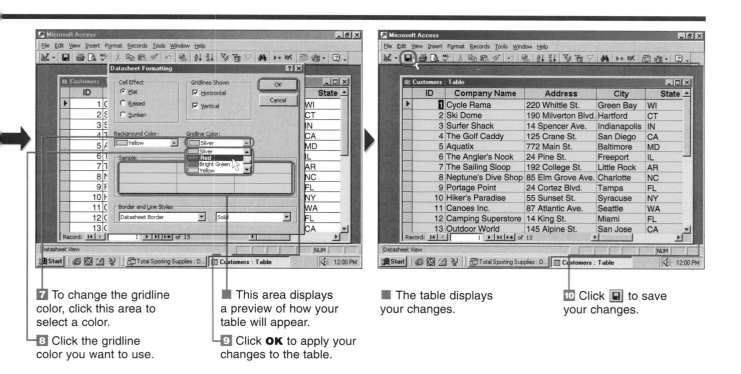

7 To change the gridline color, click this area to select a color.

8 Click the gridline color you want to use.

■ This area displays a preview of how your table will appear.

9 Click **OK** to apply your changes to the table.

■ The table displays your changes.

10 Click 🖫 to save your changes.

HIDE A FIELD

You can temporarily hide a field in your table to reduce the amount of information displayed on your screen.

When you hide a field, Access does not delete the field. You can redisplay the field at any time.

HIDE A FIELD

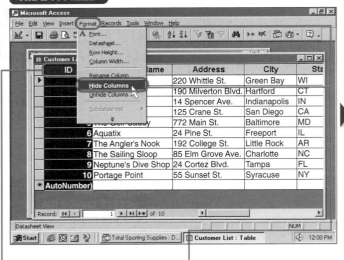

■1 Click the name of the field you want to hide. The field is highlighted.

Note: To hide more than one field, select the fields you want to hide. To select multiple fields, see page 54.

■2 Click **Format**.

■3 Click **Hide Columns**.

■ The field disappears from your table.

When would I hide a field?

Hiding a field can help you review information of interest by removing unnecessary data from your screen. For example, if you want to browse through the names and telephone numbers of your customers, you can hide fields displaying other information.

First Name	Last Name	Phone No.	Add
Sue	Jones	(512) 555-8973	65 A
Matt	Andrews	(305) 555-9822	4 St
Jim	Smith	(213) 555-0231	8910
Karen	Taylor	(215) 555-4520	21 Kirk
Mandy	Roberts	(501) 555-8203	44 Sun

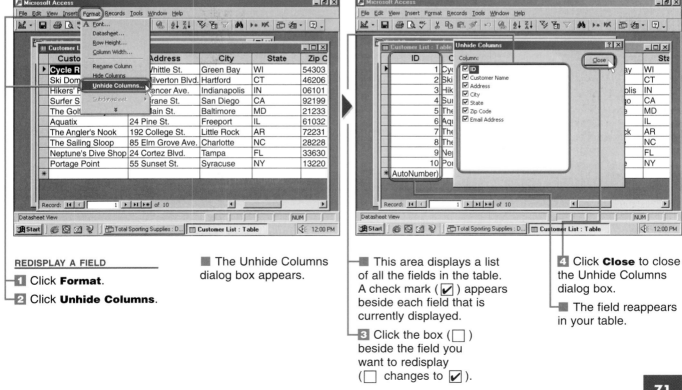

REDISPLAY A FIELD

◼ Click **Format**.

◼ Click **Unhide Columns**.

◼ The Unhide Columns dialog box appears.

◼ This area displays a list of all the fields in the table. A check mark (✔) appears beside each field that is currently displayed.

◼ Click the box (☐) beside the field you want to redisplay (☐ changes to ✔).

◼ Click **Close** to close the Unhide Columns dialog box.

◼ The field reappears in your table.

FREEZE A FIELD

You can freeze a field in
your table so the field
will remain on your
screen at all times.

FREEZE A FIELD

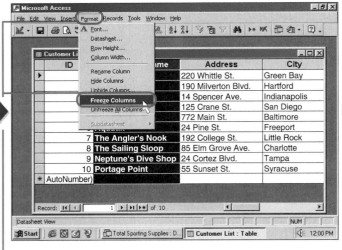

■1 Click the name of the
field you want to freeze.
The field is highlighted.

*Note: To freeze more than one
field, select the fields you want
to freeze. To select multiple
fields, see page 54.*

■2 Click **Format**.

■3 Click **Freeze Columns**.

*Note: If Freeze Columns does not
appear on the menu, position the
mouse ⌖ over the bottom of the
menu to display all the menu
commands.*

When would I freeze a field?

Freezing a field allows you to keep important data displayed on your screen as you move through data in a large table. For example, you can freeze a field containing product numbers so the numbers will remain on your screen while you scroll through the product information.

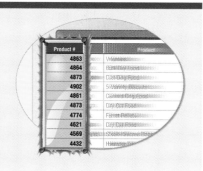

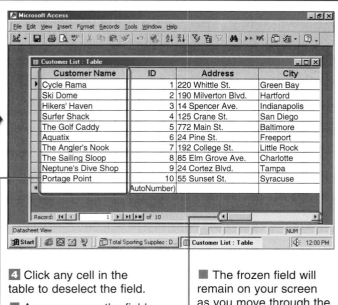

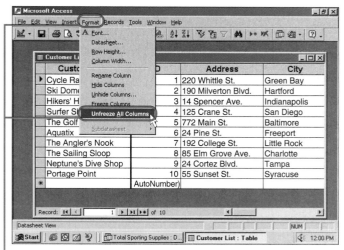

■ **4** Click any cell in the table to deselect the field.

■ Access moves the field to the left side of the table. The vertical line to the right of the field indicates the field is frozen.

■ The frozen field will remain on your screen as you move through the other fields in the table.

■ You can use this scroll bar to move through the fields in the table.

UNFREEZE A FIELD

1 Click **Format**.

2 Click **Unfreeze All Columns**.

Note: If Unfreeze All Columns does not appear on the menu, position the mouse ↕ over the bottom of the menu to display all the menu commands.

■ When you unfreeze a field, Access does not return the field to its original location in the table. To rearrange fields in a table, see page 45.

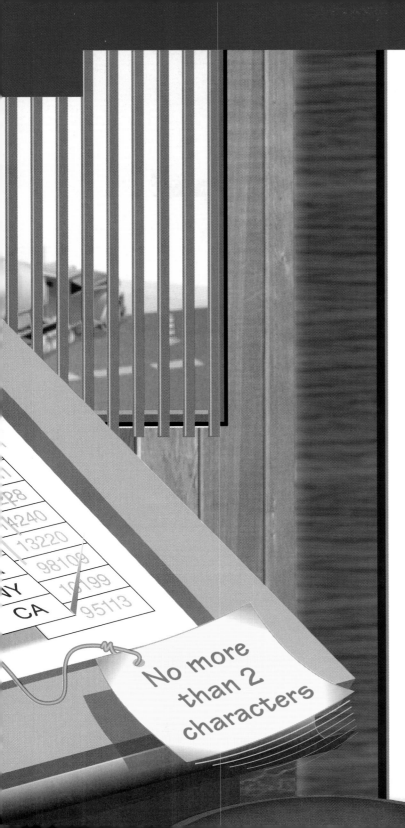

CHAPTER 4

Design Tables

Would you like to customize your tables to better suit your needs? In this chapter you will learn how to specify the type of data a field can contain, set a default value for a field and much more.

CHANGE VIEW OF TABLE

There are two
ways you can
view a table.
Each view allows
you to perform
different tasks.

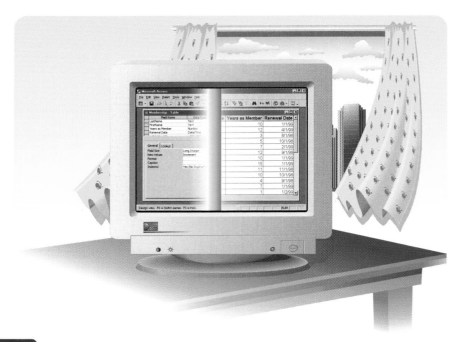

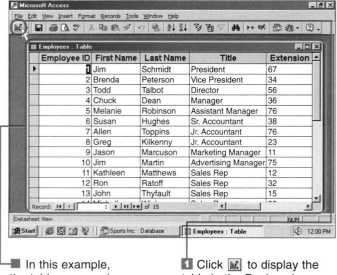

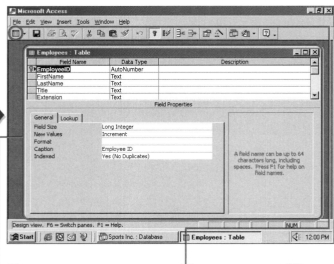

■ In this example,
the table appears in
the Datasheet view.

1 Click  to display the
table in the Design view.

■ The table appears
in the Design view.

■ The View button ![view]
changes to ![datasheet]. You can
click the View button to
quickly switch between
the Datasheet (![datasheet]) and
Design (![design]) views.

THE TABLE VIEWS

DATASHEET VIEW

The Datasheet view displays all the records in a table. You can enter, edit and review records in this view.

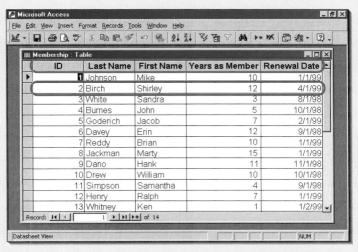

Field Name

A field name identifies the information within a field.

Record

A record is a collection of information about one person, place or thing.

DESIGN VIEW

The Design view allows you to change the structure of a table. You can change the settings in this view to specify the kind of information you can enter in a table.

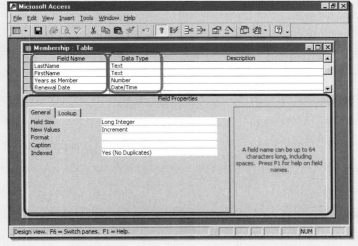

Field Name

A field name identifies the information within a field.

Data Type

The data type determines the type of information you can enter in a field, such as text, numbers or dates. For example, you cannot enter text in a field with the Number data type.

Field Properties

The field properties are a set of characteristics that provide additional control over the information you can enter in a field. For example, you can specify the maximum number of characters a field will accept.

ADD A FIELD

You can add a field to
your table when you
want to include an
additional category
of information.

For example, you can
add a field to store the
phone numbers of all
your customers.

ADD A FIELD

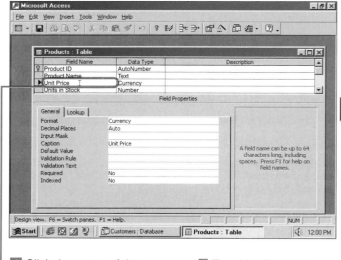

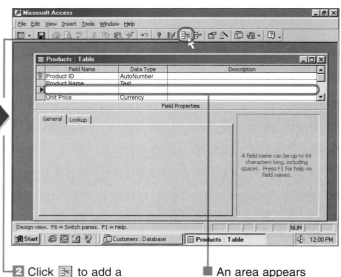

–1 Click the name of the
field you want to appear
after the new field.

■ To add a field to the
end of your table, click
the area directly below
the last field name.
Then skip to step **3**.

–2 Click 🖹 to add a
field to your table.

■ An area appears
where you can enter
information for the
new field.

What should I consider when adding fields to my table?

Make sure each field you add relates directly to the subject of your table. You should also try to keep the number of fields in your table to a minimum. Tables with many fields increase the time it takes Access to process information.

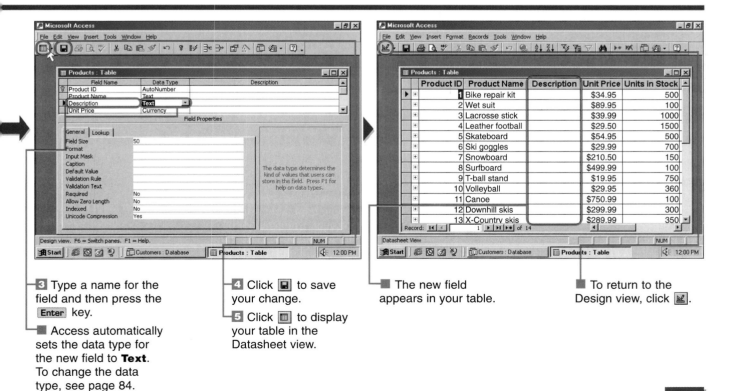

3 Type a name for the field and then press the **Enter** key.

■ Access automatically sets the data type for the new field to **Text**. To change the data type, see page 84.

4 Click 🖫 to save your change.

5 Click 🖩 to display your table in the Datasheet view.

■ The new field appears in your table.

■ To return to the Design view, click 🖳.

DELETE A FIELD

If you no longer need a field, you can permanently delete the field from your table.

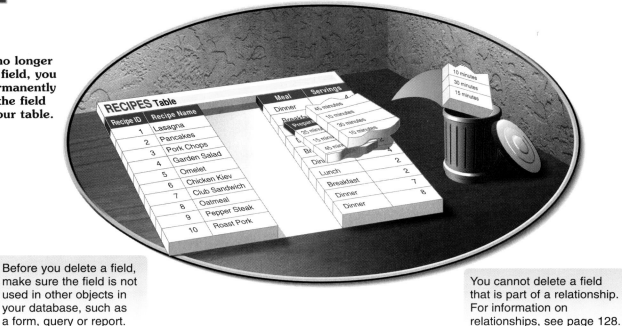

Before you delete a field, make sure the field is not used in other objects in your database, such as a form, query or report.

You cannot delete a field that is part of a relationship. For information on relationships, see page 128.

For information on relationships, see page 128.

DELETE A FIELD

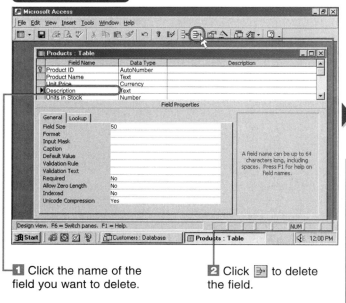

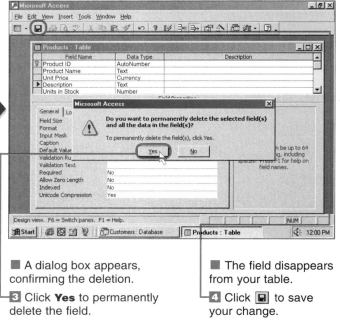

1 Click the name of the field you want to delete.

2 Click 🗈 to delete the field.

■ A dialog box appears, confirming the deletion.

3 Click **Yes** to permanently delete the field.

■ The field disappears from your table.

4 Click 🖫 to save your change.

You can change the
order of fields to better
organize the information
in your table.

When you rearrange
fields in the Design view,
Access also displays the
changes in the Datasheet
view. To change the view,
see page 76.

REARRANGE FIELDS

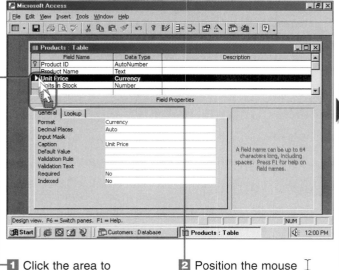

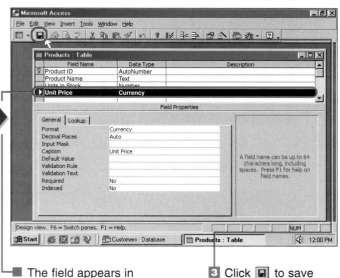

1 Click the area to
the left of the field you
want to move. The
field is highlighted.

2 Position the mouse I
over the area to the left of
the field (I changes to ▷)
and then drag the field to
a new location.

■ A thick line shows where
the field will appear.

■ The field appears in
the new location.

3 Click 🔲 to save
your change.

DISPLAY FIELD PROPERTIES

You can display the properties for each field in your table. The field properties are a set of characteristics that control the information you can enter in a field.

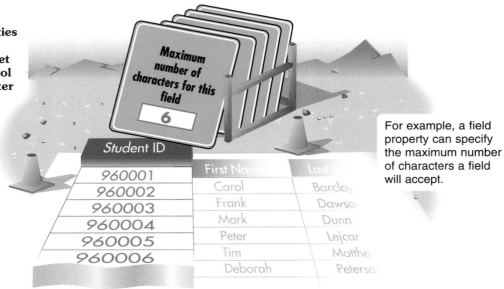

For example, a field property can specify the maximum number of characters a field will accept.

DISPLAY FIELD PROPERTIES

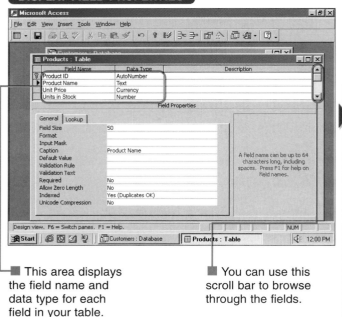

■ This area displays the field name and data type for each field in your table.

■ You can use this scroll bar to browse through the fields.

■1 Click the name of a field to display the properties for the field.

■ A triangle (▶) appears beside the field name.

■ This area displays the properties for the field. The available properties depend on the data type of the field.

ADD A FIELD DESCRIPTION

You can add a description to a field to help you determine the kind of information you should enter in the field.

ADD A FIELD DESCRIPTION

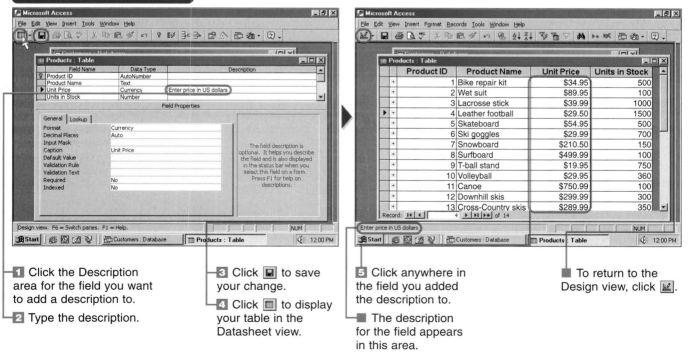

1 Click the Description area for the field you want to add a description to.

2 Type the description.

3 Click 🖫 to save your change.

4 Click 🏢 to display your table in the Datasheet view.

5 Click anywhere in the field you added the description to.

■ The description for the field appears in this area.

■ To return to the Design view, click 🔟.

CHANGE A DATA TYPE

You can change
the type of
data you can
enter in a field.

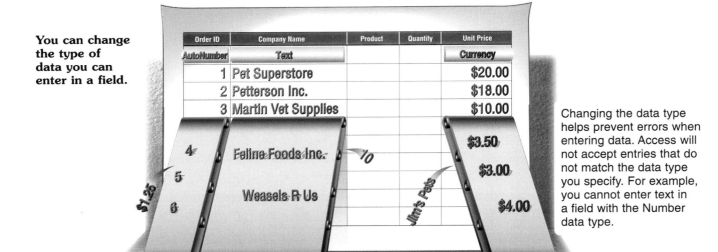

Changing the data type
helps prevent errors when
entering data. Access will
not accept entries that do
not match the data type
you specify. For example,
you cannot enter text in
a field with the Number
data type.

CHANGE A DATA TYPE

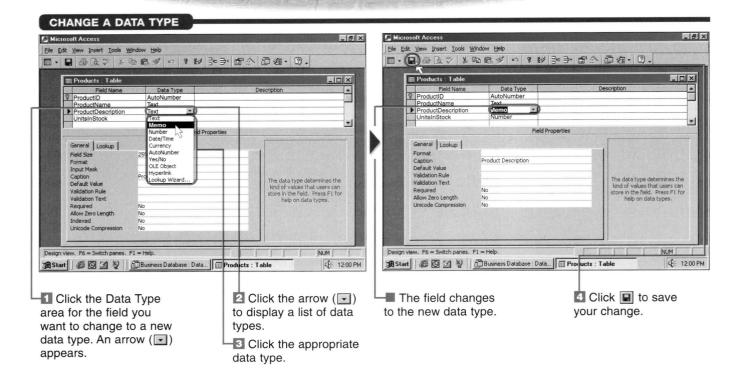

1 Click the Data Type
area for the field you
want to change to a new
data type. An arrow (▼)
appears.

2 Click the arrow (▼)
to display a list of data
types.

3 Click the appropriate
data type.

■ The field changes
to the new data type.

4 Click 🔲 to save
your change.

DATA TYPES

Text

Accepts entries up to 255 characters long that include any combination of text and numbers, such as a name or address. Make sure you use this data type for numbers you will not use in calculations, such as phone numbers and zip codes.

AutoNumber

Automatically numbers each record for you.

Memo

Accepts entries up to 65,535 characters long that include any combination of text and numbers, such as notes, comments and lengthy descriptions.

Yes/No

Accepts only one of two values–Yes/No, True/False or On/Off.

Number

Accepts numbers you want to use in calculations.

OLE Object

Accepts OLE objects. An OLE object is an object created in another program, such as a document, spreadsheet or picture.

Date/Time

Accepts only dates and times.

Hyperlink

Accepts hyperlinks you can select to jump to a document or Web page.

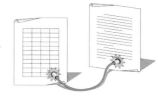

Currency

Accepts only monetary values.

Lookup Wizard

Starts the Lookup Wizard so you can create a list of items to choose from when entering data in a field. For more information on the Lookup Wizard, see page 108.

SELECT A FORMAT

You can select a format to customize the way information appears in a field. For example, you can select the way you want dates to appear.

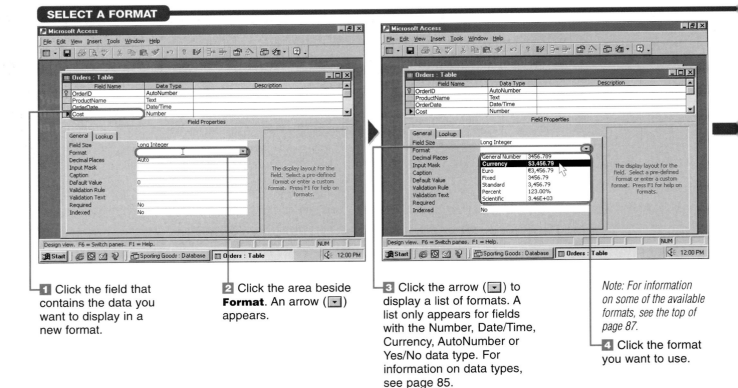

1 Click the field that contains the data you want to display in a new format.

2 Click the area beside **Format**. An arrow (🔽) appears.

3 Click the arrow (🔽) to display a list of formats. A list only appears for fields with the Number, Date/Time, Currency, AutoNumber or Yes/No data type. For information on data types, see page 85.

Note: For information on some of the available formats, see the top of page 87.

4 Click the format you want to use.

What formats are available?

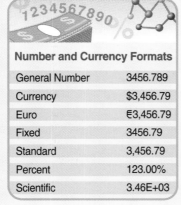

Number and Currency Formats	
General Number	3456.789
Currency	$3,456.79
Euro	€3,456.79
Fixed	3456.79
Standard	3,456.79
Percent	123.00%
Scientific	3.46E+03

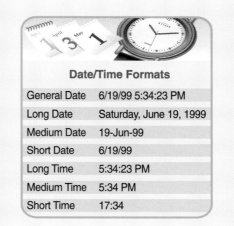

Date/Time Formats	
General Date	6/19/99 5:34:23 PM
Long Date	Saturday, June 19, 1999
Medium Date	19-Jun-99
Short Date	6/19/99
Long Time	5:34:23 PM
Medium Time	5:34 PM
Short Time	17:34

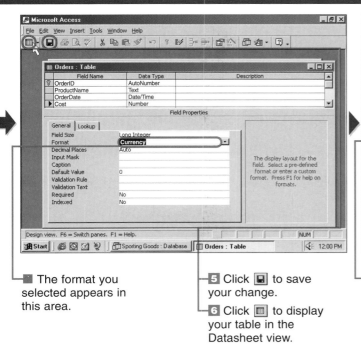

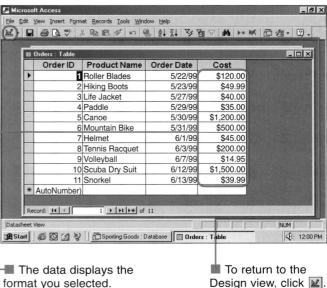

■ The format you selected appears in this area.

5 Click 🖫 to save your change.

6 Click 🏢 to display your table in the Datasheet view.

■ The data displays the format you selected.

■ Access will automatically change any data you enter in the field to the new format. For example, Access will automatically change 1234 to $1,234.00.

■ To return to the Design view, click 🖾.

CHANGE THE FIELD SIZE

You can reduce errors by changing the size of a text or number field. Access can process smaller field sizes more quickly.

You can change the size of a text field to specify the maximum number of characters the field will accept. You can change the size of a number field to specify the type of number the field will accept.

For example, if you set the size of a text field to 2, you can enter CA but not California.

TEXT FIELDS

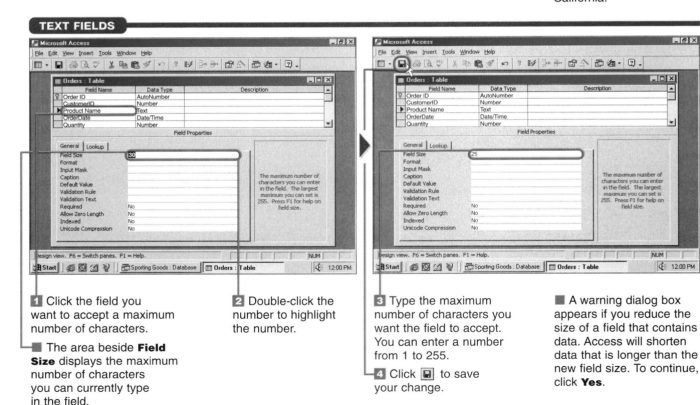

1 Click the field you want to accept a maximum number of characters.

■ The area beside **Field Size** displays the maximum number of characters you can currently type in the field.

2 Double-click the number to highlight the number.

3 Type the maximum number of characters you want the field to accept. You can enter a number from 1 to 255.

4 Click 🖫 to save your change.

■ A warning dialog box appears if you reduce the size of a field that contains data. Access will shorten data that is longer than the new field size. To continue, click **Yes**.

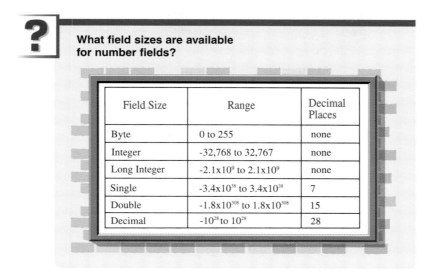

What field sizes are available for number fields?

Field Size	Range	Decimal Places
Byte	0 to 255	none
Integer	-32,768 to 32,767	none
Long Integer	-2.1×10^9 to 2.1×10^9	none
Single	-3.4×10^{38} to 3.4×10^{38}	7
Double	-1.8×10^{308} to 1.8×10^{308}	15
Decimal	-10^{28} to 10^{28}	28

NUMBER FIELDS

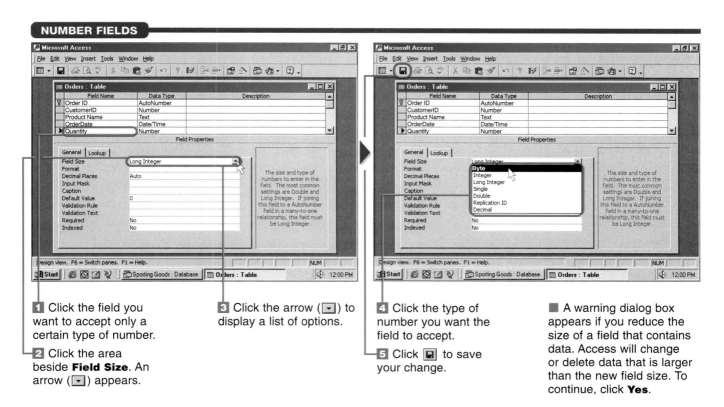

1 Click the field you want to accept only a certain type of number.

2 Click the area beside **Field Size**. An arrow ( ) appears.

3 Click the arrow ( ) to display a list of options.

4 Click the type of number you want the field to accept.

5 Click to save your change.

■ A warning dialog box appears if you reduce the size of a field that contains data. Access will change or delete data that is larger than the new field size. To continue, click **Yes**.

CHANGE NUMBER OF DECIMAL PLACES

You can specify how
many decimal places
you want numbers in
a field to display.

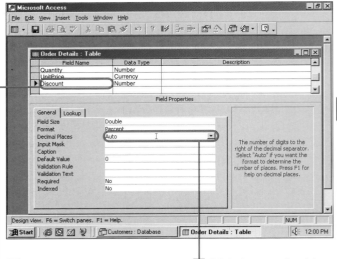

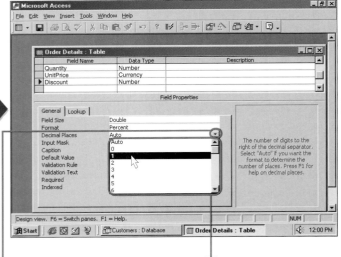

1 Click the field that
contains the data you
want to display a specific
number of decimal places.

2 Click the area beside
Decimal Places. An
arrow (▼) appears.

3 Click the arrow (▼)
to display a list of
decimal place options.

4 Click the number
of decimal places you
want the data in the
field to display.

Why doesn't my data display the number of decimal places I specified?

Changing the number of decimal places will not change the appearance of data if the Format property of the field is blank or set to General Number. To change the Format property of a field, see page 86.

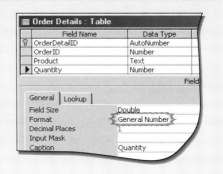

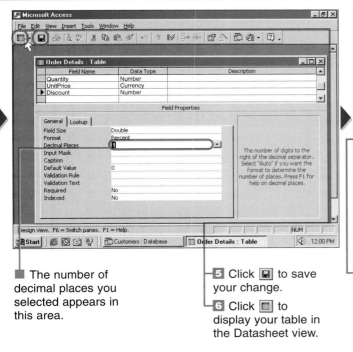

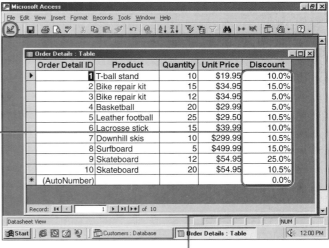

■ The number of decimal places you selected appears in this area.

5 Click 🖫 to save your change.

6 Click 🖼 to display your table in the Datasheet view.

■ The data displays the number of decimal places you specified.

■ Access will automatically display any data you enter in the field with the correct number of decimal places.

Note: If Access changes decimal places you type to zeros (example: 12.34 changes to 12.00), you need to change the field size. To change the field size, see page 88.

■ To return to the Design view, click 🖾.

ADD A CAPTION

You can add a caption to a field. The caption will appear as the heading for the field instead of the field name.

A caption can be longer and more descriptive than a field name.

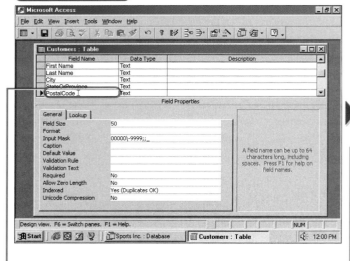

1 Click the field you want to add a caption to.

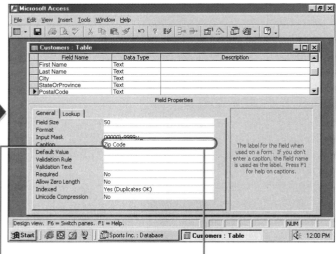

2 Click the area beside **Caption**.

Note: If a caption already exists, drag the mouse ⊥ over the caption to highlight the text.

3 Type the text for the caption.

Will other objects in my database display the caption I added to a field?

After adding a caption to a field, any forms, reports or queries you create that include the field will display the caption instead of the field name.

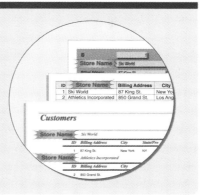

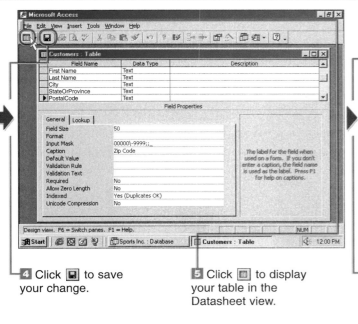

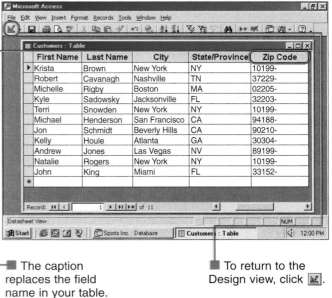

4 Click 🔲 to save your change.

5 Click 📄 to display your table in the Datasheet view.

■ The caption replaces the field name in your table.

■ To return to the Design view, click 🔲.

SET A DEFAULT VALUE

You can specify a value
that you want to appear
automatically in a field
each time you add a new
record. This saves you
from having to repeatedly
type the same data.

For example, if most of
your customers live in
California, you can set
"California" as the default
value for the State field.

SET A DEFAULT VALUE

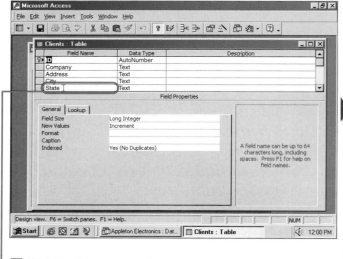

1 Click the field you want
to have a default value.

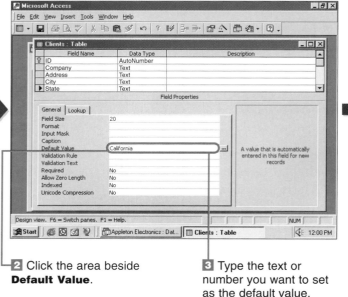

2 Click the area beside
Default Value.

3 Type the text or
number you want to set
as the default value.

?

Can I set the current date as the default value for a field?

You can have Access automatically add the current date to a field each time you add a new record. This is useful for fields containing invoice or shipping dates. Perform the steps below, typing **=Date()** in step **3**.

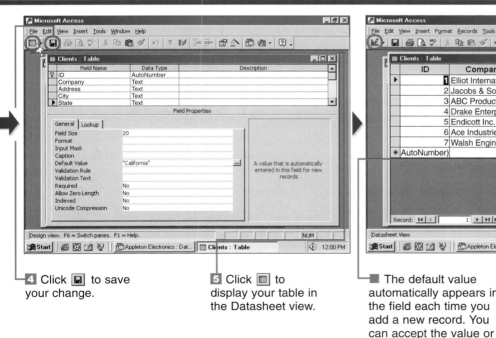

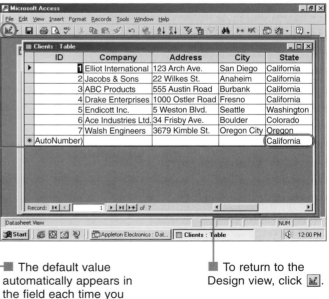

4 Click 🖫 to save your change.

5 Click 📖 to display your table in the Datasheet view.

■ The default value automatically appears in the field each time you add a new record. You can accept the value or type another value.

■ To return to the Design view, click 🖳.

DATA ENTRY REQUIRED

You can specify that a field must contain data for each record. This prevents you from leaving out important information when entering data.

Orders	Qty	Amount	Invoice #
Tennis Balls	505	$3.00	**16437**
Golf Clubs	736	$550.95	**16438**
Biking Shorts	377	$34.99	**16439**
Running Shoes	638	$99.49	**16440**
Hats	894	$15.99	**16441**

Data Required ←

For example, a table containing invoice information can require data in the Invoice Number field.

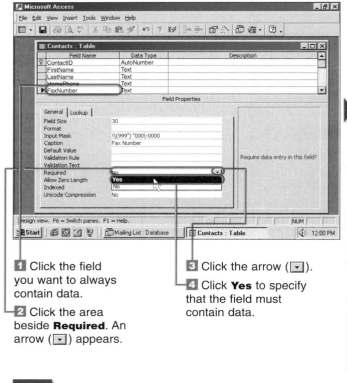

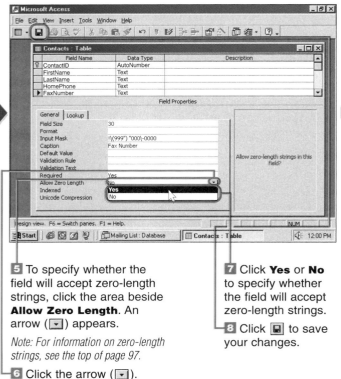

1 Click the field you want to always contain data.

2 Click the area beside **Required**. An arrow (▾) appears.

3 Click the arrow (▾).

4 Click **Yes** to specify that the field must contain data.

5 To specify whether the field will accept zero-length strings, click the area beside **Allow Zero Length**. An arrow (▾) appears.

Note: For information on zero-length strings, see the top of page 97.

6 Click the arrow (▾).

7 Click **Yes** or **No** to specify whether the field will accept zero-length strings.

8 Click 🖫 to save your changes.

What is a zero-length string?

A zero-length string is an entry that contains no characters. A zero-length string is useful if you must enter data in a field, but no data exists. For example, if the Fax Number field must contain data, but a customer does not have a fax machine, you can enter a zero-length string in the field.

To enter a zero-length string, type "" in the cell. The cell will appear empty.

ID	First Name	Last Name	Phone	Fax
1	Theresa	Garcia	555-4433	555-4434
2	Daniel	Goodland	555-1234	
3	Susan	Hughes	555-6677	555-6678
4	Greg	Kilkenny	555-1215	555-1216
5	Stephen	MacDonald	555-2200	
6	Jim	Smith	555-1543	555-1550
7	Allen	Toppins	555-6235	555-6236
8	Linda	Vieira	555-8976	

CAN CONTAIN
ZERO-LENGTH
STRINGS

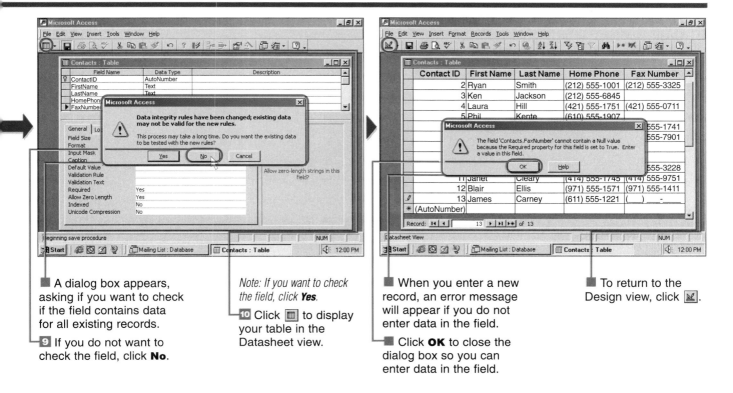

■ A dialog box appears, asking if you want to check if the field contains data for all existing records.

■9 If you do not want to check the field, click **No**.

*Note: If you want to check the field, click **Yes**.*

■10 Click 🔲 to display your table in the Datasheet view.

■ When you enter a new record, an error message will appear if you do not enter data in the field.

■ Click **OK** to close the dialog box so you can enter data in the field.

■ To return to the Design view, click 🔲.

ADD A VALIDATION RULE

You can add a validation rule to a field to help reduce errors when entering data. A field that uses a validation rule can only accept data that meets the requirements you specify.

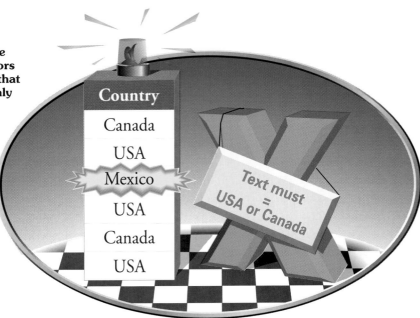

ADD A VALIDATION RULE

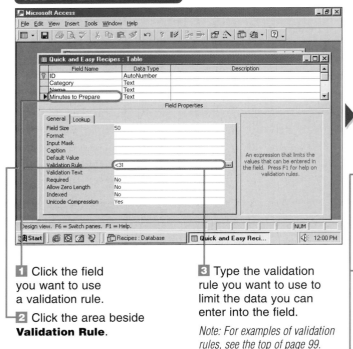

1 Click the field you want to use a validation rule.

2 Click the area beside **Validation Rule**.

3 Type the validation rule you want to use to limit the data you can enter into the field.

Note: For examples of validation rules, see the top of page 99.

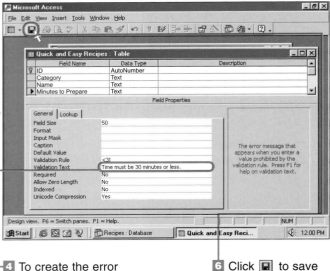

4 To create the error message you want to appear when you enter incorrect data, click the area beside **Validation Text**.

5 Type the error message you want to appear.

6 Click 🖫 to save your changes.

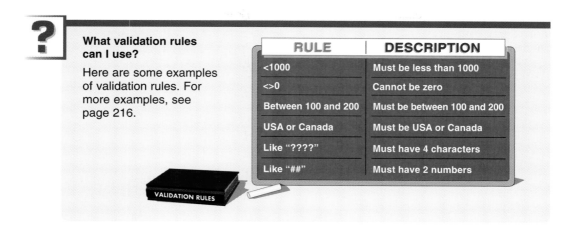

What validation rules can I use?

Here are some examples of validation rules. For more examples, see page 216.

RULE	DESCRIPTION
<1000	Must be less than 1000
<>0	Cannot be zero
Between 100 and 200	Must be between 100 and 200
USA or Canada	Must be USA or Canada
Like "????"	Must have 4 characters
Like "##"	Must have 2 numbers

VALIDATION RULES

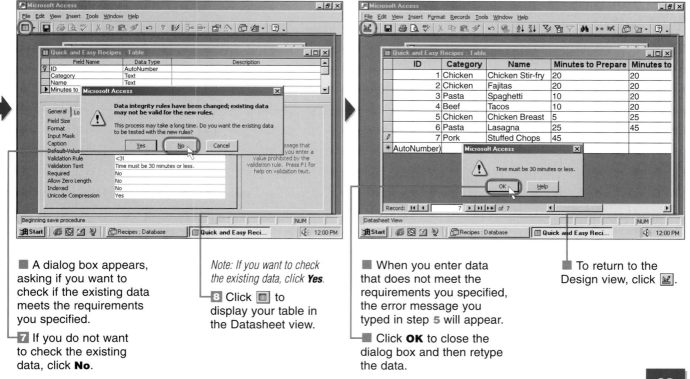

■ A dialog box appears, asking if you want to check if the existing data meets the requirements you specified.

7 If you do not want to check the existing data, click **No**.

*Note: If you want to check the existing data, click **Yes**.*

8 Click 🖿 to display your table in the Datasheet view.

■ When you enter data that does not meet the requirements you specified, the error message you typed in step **5** will appear.

■ Click **OK** to close the dialog box and then retype the data.

■ To return to the Design view, click 🗹.

CREATE AN INDEX

You can create an index for a field to speed up searching and sorting data in the field.

You should index the fields you will frequently search. For example, if you often search for specific last names, you can create an index for the Last Name field.

CREATE AN INDEX

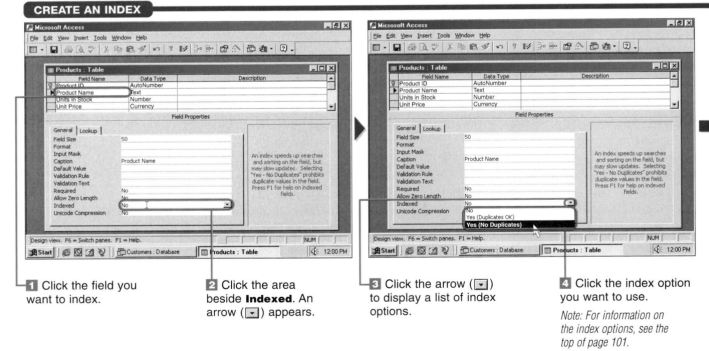

1 Click the field you want to index.

2 Click the area beside **Indexed**. An arrow (▾) appears.

3 Click the arrow (▾) to display a list of index options.

4 Click the index option you want to use.

Note: For information on the index options, see the top of page 101.

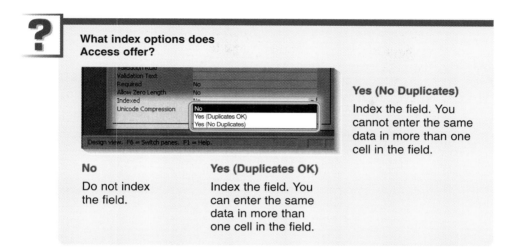

What index options does Access offer?

Yes (No Duplicates)

Index the field. You cannot enter the same data in more than one cell in the field.

No

Do not index the field.

Yes (Duplicates OK)

Index the field. You can enter the same data in more than one cell in the field.

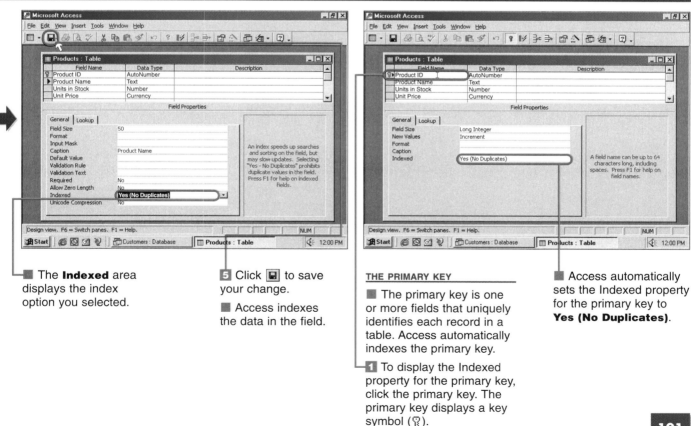

■ The **Indexed** area displays the index option you selected.

5 Click 🖫 to save your change.

■ Access indexes the data in the field.

THE PRIMARY KEY

■ The primary key is one or more fields that uniquely identifies each record in a table. Access automatically indexes the primary key.

1 To display the Indexed property for the primary key, click the primary key. The primary key displays a key symbol (🗝).

■ Access automatically sets the Indexed property for the primary key to **Yes (No Duplicates)**.

CREATE AN INPUT MASK

You can create an input mask to limit the type of information you can enter in a field. Input masks reduce errors and ensure data has a consistent appearance.

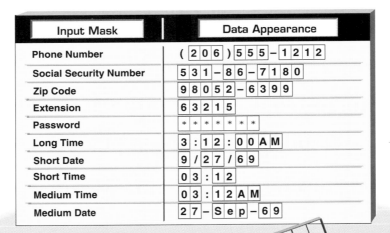

Input Mask	Data Appearance
Phone Number	(2 0 6) 5 5 5 – 1 2 1 2
Social Security Number	5 3 1 – 8 6 – 7 1 8 0
Zip Code	9 8 0 5 2 – 6 3 9 9
Extension	6 3 2 1 5
Password	* * * * * * *
Long Time	3 : 1 2 : 0 0 A M
Short Date	9 / 2 7 / 6 9
Short Time	0 3 : 1 2
Medium Time	0 3 : 1 2 A M
Medium Date	2 7 – S e p – 6 9

The Input Mask Wizard provides common input masks that you can choose from.

CREATE AN INPUT MASK USING THE WIZARD

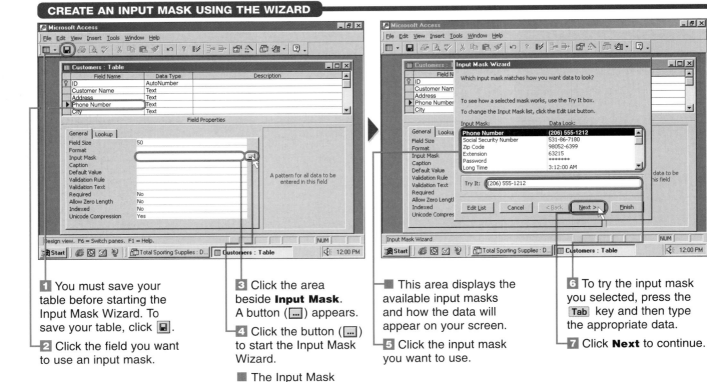

■1 You must save your table before starting the Input Mask Wizard. To save your table, click 🖫.

■2 Click the field you want to use an input mask.

■3 Click the area beside **Input Mask**. A button (⋯) appears.

■4 Click the button (⋯) to start the Input Mask Wizard.

■ The Input Mask Wizard appears.

■ This area displays the available input masks and how the data will appear on your screen.

■5 Click the input mask you want to use.

■6 To try the input mask you selected, press the **Tab** key and then type the appropriate data.

■7 Click **Next** to continue.

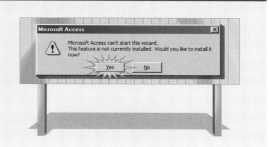

Why does an error message appear when I try to use the Input Mask Wizard?

The Input Mask Wizard is not installed on your computer. Insert the CD-ROM disc you used to install Access into your CD-ROM drive and then click **Yes** to install the wizard.

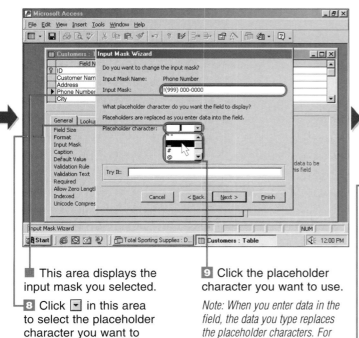

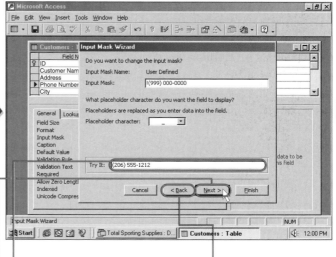

■ This area displays the input mask you selected.

8 Click ▼ in this area to select the placeholder character you want to use for the input mask.

9 Click the placeholder character you want to use.

Note: When you enter data in the field, the data you type replaces the placeholder characters. For example, (___) ___-____ changes to (555) 555-3874.

10 To try the input mask with the placeholder character you selected, press the **Tab** key and then type the appropriate data.

11 Click **Next** to continue.

■ You can click **Back** at any time to return to a previous step and change your answers.

CONTINUED ▶

CREATE AN INPUT MASK

When creating an input mask, the wizard may ask how you want to store the data you enter in the field.

You can store data with or without symbols. Storing data without symbols saves storage space on your computer.

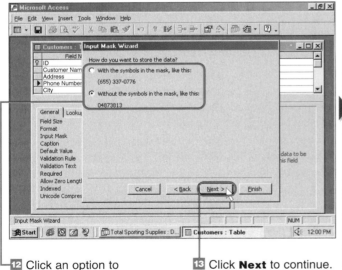

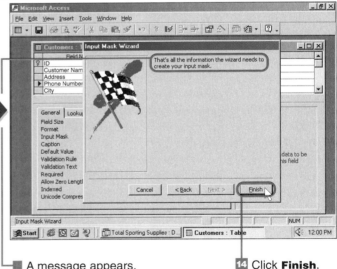

■ Click an option to specify how you want to store the data
(○ changes to ⊙).

Note: This screen does not appear for some input masks.

■ Click **Next** to continue.

■ A message appears, indicating that you have finished creating your input mask.

■ Click **Finish**.

How can an input mask save me time when entering data in a field?

Input masks can save you time by automatically entering characters for you, such as slashes (/) and hyphens (-). For example, when you type **2015551234** in a field that uses the Phone Number input mask, Access will change the data to **(201) 555-1234**.

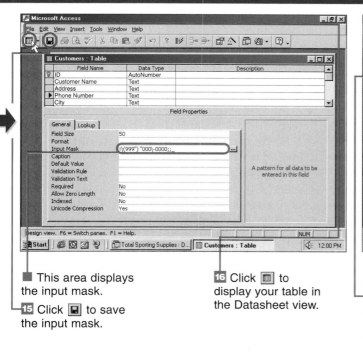

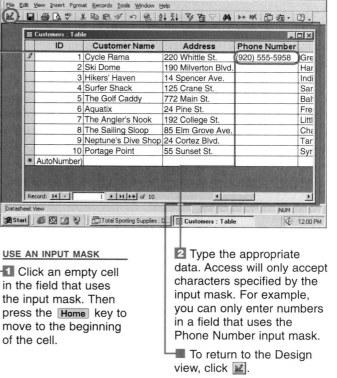

■ This area displays the input mask.

15 Click 🖫 to save the input mask.

16 Click 🔳 to display your table in the Datasheet view.

USE AN INPUT MASK

1 Click an empty cell in the field that uses the input mask. Then press the Home key to move to the beginning of the cell.

2 Type the appropriate data. Access will only accept characters specified by the input mask. For example, you can only enter numbers in a field that uses the Phone Number input mask.

■ To return to the Design view, click 📈.

CREATE AN INPUT MASK

You can create your own input mask to establish a pattern for data you can enter in a field.

Input masks can save you time by automatically entering characters for you. For example, if your invoice numbers always begin with **INV**, you can create an input mask that will automatically enter these characters for you.

CREATE YOUR OWN INPUT MASK

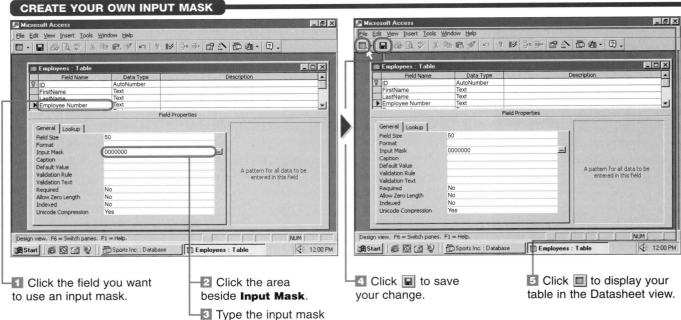

1 Click the field you want to use an input mask.

2 Click the area beside **Input Mask**.

3 Type the input mask you want to use.

4 Click 🖫 to save your change.

5 Click 📱 to display your table in the Datasheet view.

When would I create my own input mask?

You may want to create your own input mask if the Input Mask Wizard does not offer an input mask that suits the data you want to enter in a field. To create an input mask using the wizard, see page 102. Here are some examples of input masks that you can create.

Input Mask	Data Appearance
>LOL OLO	L 4 Z 1 R 9
ISBN 0-#########-0	ISBN 1 - 1 2 3 4 5 - 6 7 8 - 2
	ISBN 0 - 1 2 - 3 4 5 6 7 8 - 3
RBX0000	RBX 1 2 3 4

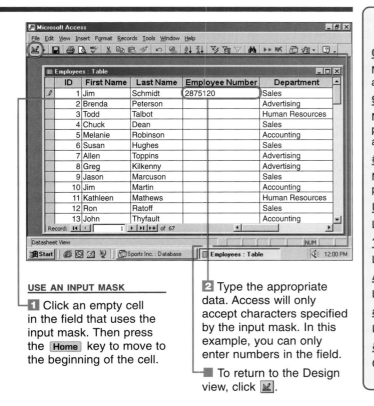

USE AN INPUT MASK

1 Click an empty cell in the field that uses the input mask. Then press the Home key to move to the beginning of the cell.

2 Type the appropriate data. Access will only accept characters specified by the input mask. In this example, you can only enter numbers in the field.

■ To return to the Design view, click ⬚.

You can use these characters to create an input mask.

0
Numbers 0 to 9, required; plus and minus signs not allowed

9
Number or space, optional; plus and minus signs not allowed

#
Number or space, optional; plus and minus signs allowed

L
Letters A to Z, required

?
Letters A to Z, optional

A
Letter or number, required

a
Letter or number, optional

&
Character or space, required

C
Character or space, optional

. , : ; - /
Decimal point and thousands, date and time separators

<
Convert the following characters to lowercase

>
Convert the following characters to uppercase

!
Display characters from right to left, rather than from left to right

****
Display the following input mask character. For example, \& will display &.

Password
Display an asterisk (*) for each character you type

CREATE A LOOKUP COLUMN

You can create a list
of values that you
can choose from
when entering data
in a field.

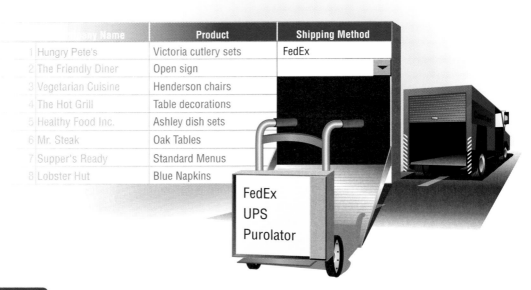

Company Name	Product	Shipping Method
1 Hungry Pete's	Victoria cutlery sets	FedEx
2 The Friendly Diner	Open sign	
3 Vegetarian Cuisine	Henderson chairs	
4 The Hot Grill	Table decorations	
5 Healthy Food Inc.	Ashley dish sets	
6 Mr. Steak	Oak Tables	
7 Supper's Ready	Standard Menus	
8 Lobster Hut	Blue Napkins	

FedEx
UPS
Purolator

CREATE A LOOKUP COLUMN

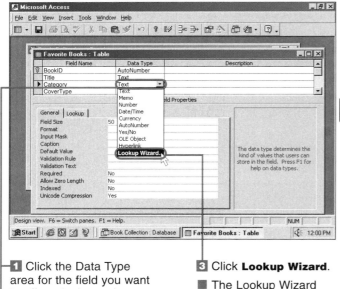

■1 Click the Data Type
area for the field you want
to offer a lookup column.
An arrow (▾) appears.

■2 Click the arrow (▾)
to display a list of
data types.

■3 Click **Lookup Wizard**.

■ The Lookup Wizard
appears.

■4 Click this option to type
the values you want the
lookup column to offer
(○ changes to ⊙).

■5 Click **Next** to continue.

Why would I create a lookup column?

Creating a lookup column is useful if you repeatedly enter the same data in a field. For example, if your customers reside in three states, you can create a lookup column that displays the three states, such as CA, TX and IL.

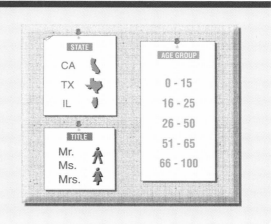

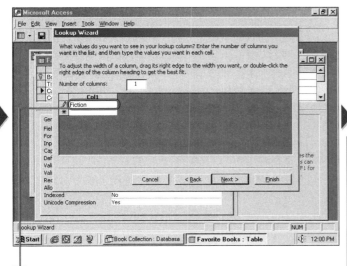

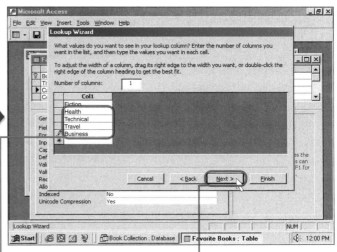

6 Click this area and then type the first value you want to appear in the lookup column.

7 To enter the next value, press the Tab key and then type the value.

8 Repeat step **7** for each value you want to appear in the lookup column.

9 Click **Next** to continue.

CONTINUED

CREATE A LOOKUP COLUMN

When entering data in a field, you can select a value from a lookup column to save time and reduce errors.

Order ID	Company Name	Product	Qty	Ship
1	Hungry Pete's	Victoria cutlery sets	3	Ground
2	The Friendly Diner	Open sign	2	1 Day Air
3	Vegetarian Cuisine	Henderson chairs	4	4 Day Air
4	The Hot Grill	Table decorations	20	4 Day Air
5	Healthy Foods	Ashley dish sets		
6	Mr. Steak	Oak tables		
7	Supper's Ready	Standard Menus		

1 Day Air ▼

Ground
1 Day Air
2 Day Air
4 Day Air

CREATE A LOOKUP COLUMN (CONTINUED)

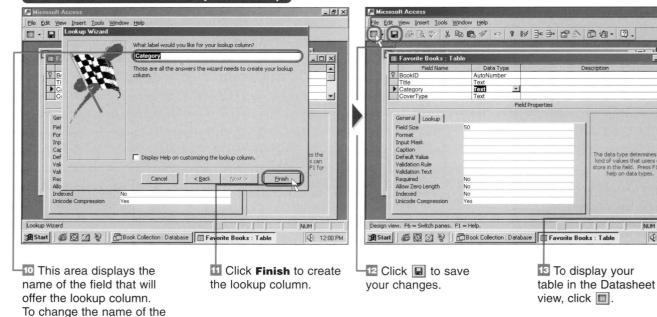

10 This area displays the name of the field that will offer the lookup column. To change the name of the field, type a new name.

11 Click **Finish** to create the lookup column.

12 Click 🔲 to save your changes.

13 To display your table in the Datasheet view, click 🔲.

Do I have to select a value from a lookup column?

No. If a lookup column does not display the value you want to use, you can type a different value. To hide a lookup column you displayed without selecting a value, click outside the lookup column.

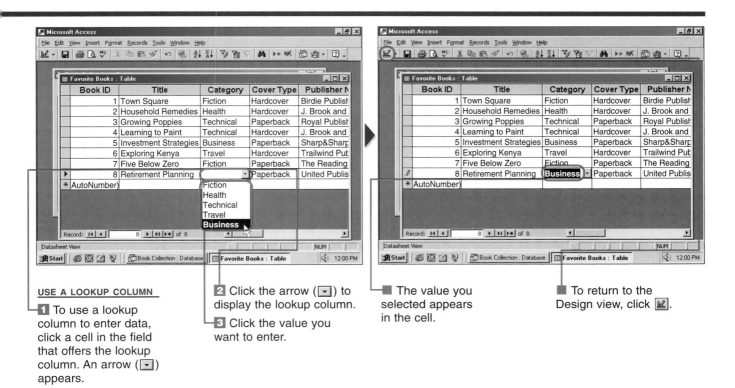

USE A LOOKUP COLUMN

1 To use a lookup column to enter data, click a cell in the field that offers the lookup column. An arrow (▼) appears.

2 Click the arrow (▼) to display the lookup column.

3 Click the value you want to enter.

■ The value you selected appears in the cell.

■ To return to the Design view, click 📐.

CREATE A YES/NO FIELD

You can create a field that accepts only one of two values–Yes/No, True/False or On/Off.

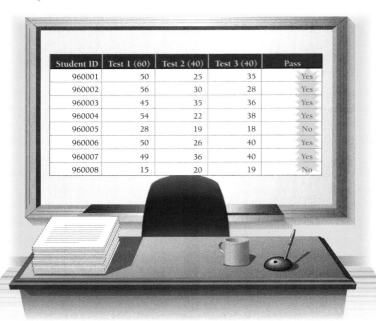

For example, you can create a Yes/No field to specify whether each student passed a course.

CREATE A YES/NO FIELD

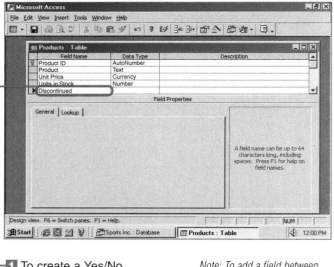

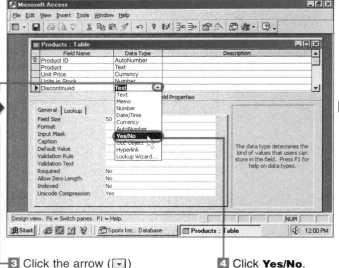

-■1 To create a Yes/No field, click the area directly below the last field name.

-■2 Type a name for the new field and then press the Enter key.

Note: To add a field between existing fields, see page 78.

-■3 Click the arrow (▼) in the Data Type area to select a data type for the new field.

■4 Click **Yes/No**.

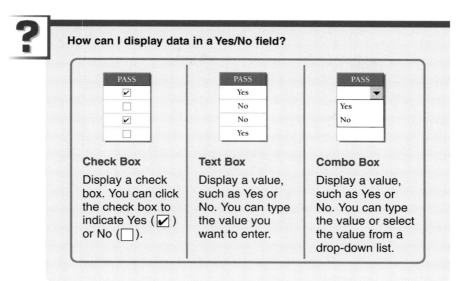

How can I display data in a Yes/No field?

Check Box

Display a check box. You can click the check box to indicate Yes (☑) or No (☐).

Text Box

Display a value, such as Yes or No. You can type the value you want to enter.

Combo Box

Display a value, such as Yes or No. You can type the value or select the value from a drop-down list.

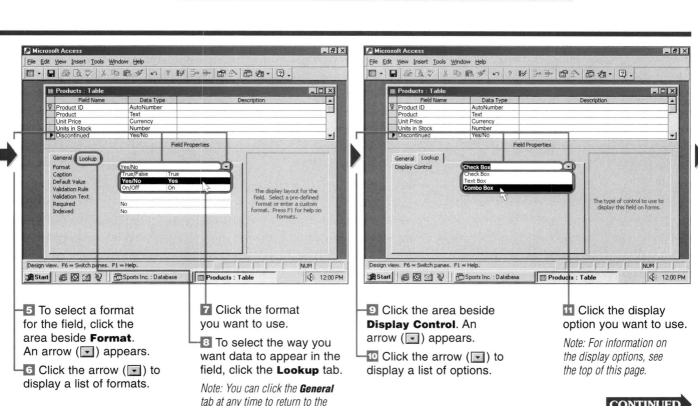

■5 To select a format for the field, click the area beside **Format**. An arrow (▾) appears.

■6 Click the arrow (▾) to display a list of formats.

■7 Click the format you want to use.

■8 To select the way you want data to appear in the field, click the **Lookup** tab.

Note: You can click the General tab at any time to return to the General properties.

■9 Click the area beside **Display Control**. An arrow (▾) appears.

■10 Click the arrow (▾) to display a list of options.

■11 Click the display option you want to use.

Note: For information on the display options, see the top of this page.

CONTINUED ▸

CREATE A YES/NO FIELD

When creating a Yes/No field that uses a Combo Box, you can specify the values you want to appear in the drop-down list for the field.

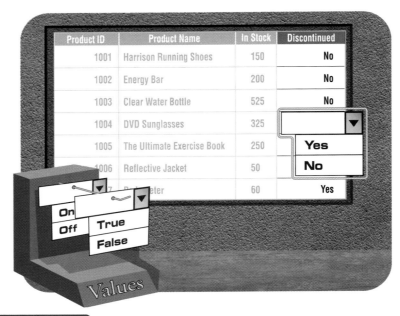

CREATE A YES/NO FIELD (CONTINUED)

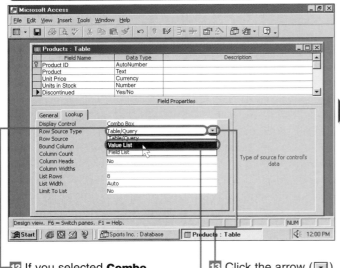

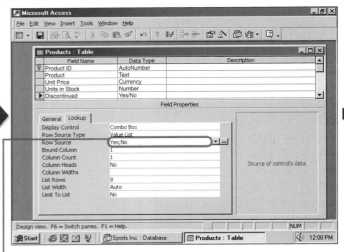

■12 If you selected **Combo Box** in step **11**, click the area beside **Row Source Type**. An arrow (▼) appears.

*Note: If you selected **Check Box** or **Text Box** in step **11**, skip to step **17**.*

■13 Click the arrow (▼) to display the available options.

■14 Click **Value List** to type the values you want to appear in the drop-down list for the field.

■15 Click the area beside **Row Source**.

■16 Type the two values you want to appear in the drop-down list for the field. Separate the values with a semicolon (;).

*Note: The values you type should match the format you selected in step **7**.*

114

How can I speed up entering data in a Yes/No field?

When you add a record to your table, Access automatically displays the **No** value in a Yes/No field. If most of your records require a **Yes** value, you can change the default value to **Yes**. To set the default value for a field, see page 94.

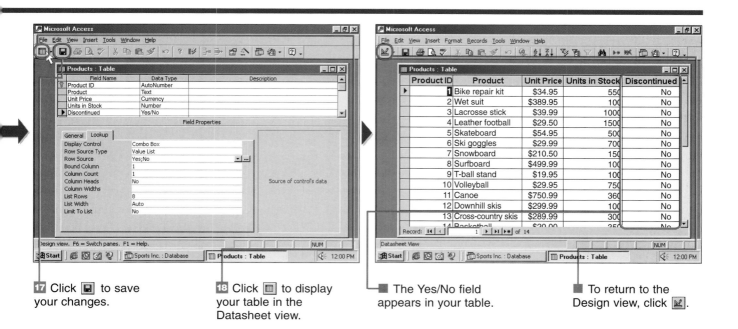

17 Click 🖫 to save your changes.

18 Click 🖩 to display your table in the Datasheet view.

■ The Yes/No field appears in your table.

■ To return to the Design view, click 🖾.

115

ADD PICTURES TO RECORDS

You can add
a picture to
each record
in your table.

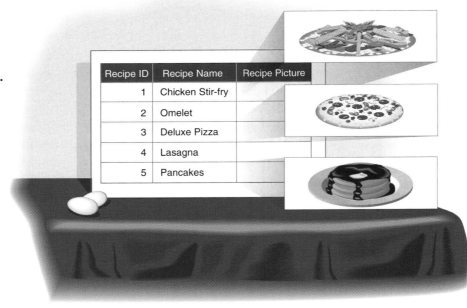

Recipe ID	Recipe Name	Recipe Picture
1	Chicken Stir-fry	
2	Omelet	
3	Deluxe Pizza	
4	Lasagna	
5	Pancakes	

For example, you
can add pictures of
employees, houses
for sale, artwork,
recipes or products.

ADD PICTURES TO RECORDS

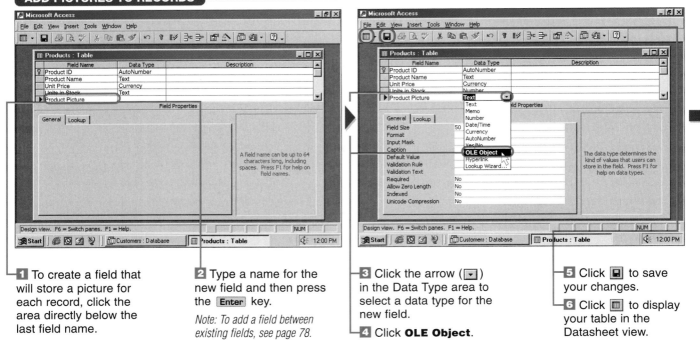

■1 To create a field that
will store a picture for
each record, click the
area directly below the
last field name.

■2 Type a name for the
new field and then press
the Enter key.

*Note: To add a field between
existing fields, see page 78.*

■3 Click the arrow (▾)
in the Data Type area to
select a data type for the
new field.

■4 Click **OLE Object**.

■5 Click 🔲 to save
your changes.

■6 Click 🔳 to display
your table in the
Datasheet view.

What other types of objects can I add to my table?

You can add objects such as Word documents, Excel worksheets, sound files and video clips to your table.

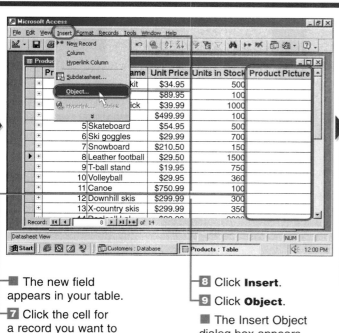

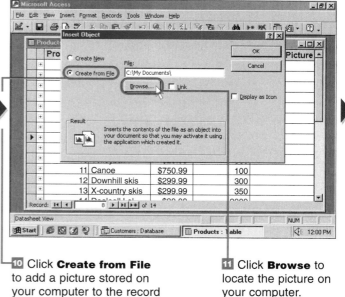

■ The new field appears in your table.

7 Click the cell for a record you want to add a picture to.

8 Click **Insert**.

9 Click **Object**.

■ The Insert Object dialog box appears.

10 Click **Create from File** to add a picture stored on your computer to the record (○ changes to ⊙).

11 Click **Browse** to locate the picture on your computer.

CONTINUED

ADD PICTURES TO RECORDS

When adding a picture
to a record in your table,
you must specify where
the picture is stored
on your computer.

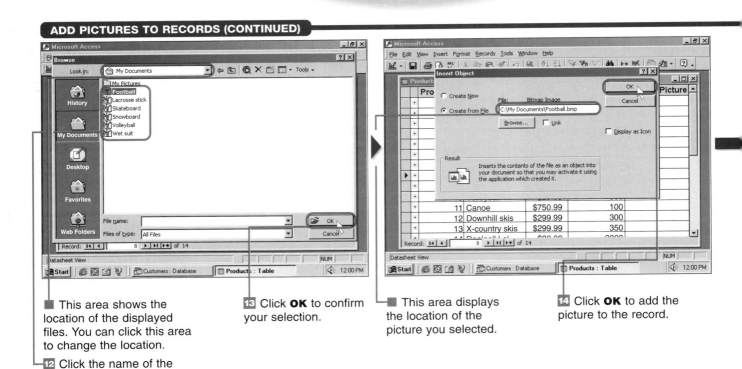

■ This area shows the
location of the displayed
files. You can click this area
to change the location.

12 Click the name of the
picture you want to add
to the record.

13 Click **OK** to confirm
your selection.

■ This area displays
the location of the
picture you selected.

14 Click **OK** to add the
picture to the record.

118

Will the pictures I add to my table appear in a form?

When you create a form using a table that includes pictures, the form will also display the pictures.

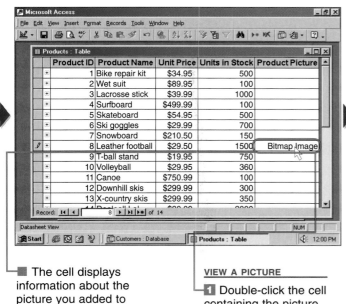

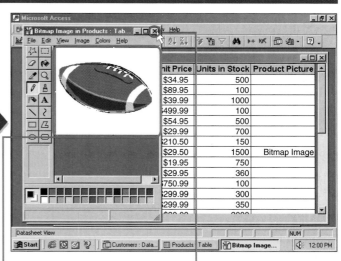

■ The cell displays information about the picture you added to the record.

■ To add pictures to other records, repeat steps **7** to **14** starting on page 117 for each record.

VIEW A PICTURE

1 Double-click the cell containing the picture you want to view.

■ A window appears, displaying the picture.

2 When you finish viewing the picture, click ⊠ to close the picture.

ADD HYPERLINKS TO RECORDS

You can add a hyperlink to each record in your table. A hyperlink allows you to quickly display a document stored on your computer, network, corporate intranet or the Internet.

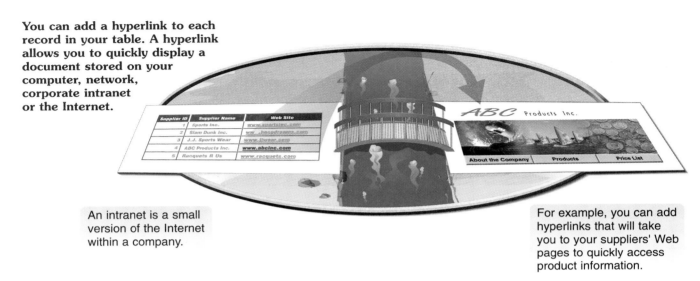

An intranet is a small version of the Internet within a company.

For example, you can add hyperlinks that will take you to your suppliers' Web pages to quickly access product information.

ADD HYPERLINKS TO RECORDS

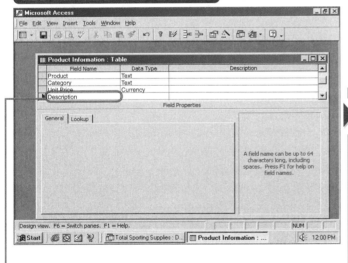

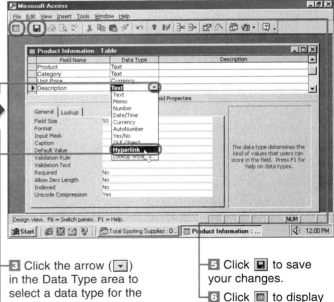

■1 To create a field that will store hyperlinks, click the area directly below the last field name.

■2 Type a name for the new field and then press the Enter key.

Note: To add a field between existing fields, see page 78.

■3 Click the arrow (▼) in the Data Type area to select a data type for the new field.

■4 Click **Hyperlink**.

■5 Click 🔲 to save your changes.

■6 Click 🔲 to display your table in the Datasheet view.

Is there a faster way to add a hyperlink to a record?

When you type a Web page address in a field that stores hyperlinks, Access will automatically change the address to a hyperlink for you.

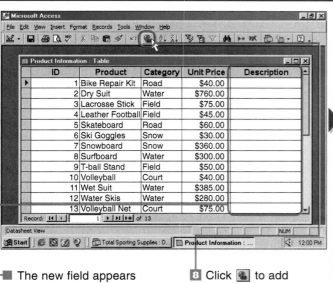

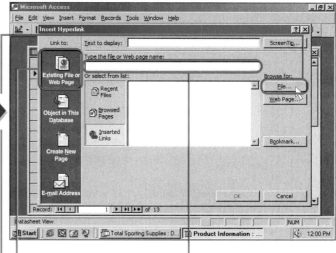

■ The new field appears in your table.

7 Click the cell for a record you want to add a hyperlink to.

8 Click 📷 to add a hyperlink.

■ The Insert Hyperlink dialog box appears.

9 Click **Existing File or Web Page** to create a hyperlink to an existing document.

10 To create a hyperlink to a document on your computer or network, click **File**.

■ To create a hyperlink to a page on the Web, click this area and then type the Web page address (example: www.maran.com). Then skip to step **13** on page 122.

CONTINUED

ADD HYPERLINKS TO RECORDS

You can easily identify hyperlinks in your table. Hyperlinks appear underlined and in color.

Company ID	Company Name	Web Site
1	Sports Inc.	www.sportsinc.com
2	Slam Dunk Inc.	www.slamdunk.com
3	J.J. Sports Wear	www.jjsportswear.com
4	Total Sports Inc.	www.totalsports.com
5	Racquets R Us	www.racquets.com

ADD HYPERLINKS TO RECORDS (CONTINUED)

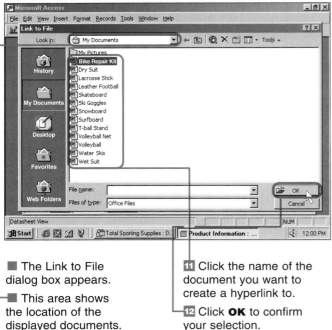

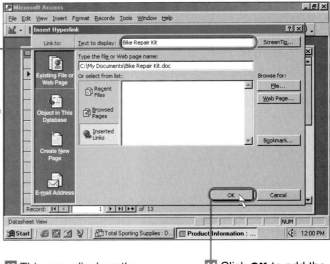

■ The Link to File dialog box appears.

■ This area shows the location of the displayed documents. You can click this area to change the location.

11 Click the name of the document you want to create a hyperlink to.

12 Click **OK** to confirm your selection.

13 This area displays the text that will appear in your table. To change the text, drag the mouse I over the text until you highlight all the text. Then type the text you want to appear in your table.

14 Click **OK** to add the hyperlink to the record.

Will the hyperlinks I add to my table appear in a form?

When you create a form using a table that contains hyperlinks, the form will also display the hyperlinks. You can select a hyperlink on a form as you would select a hyperlink in a table.

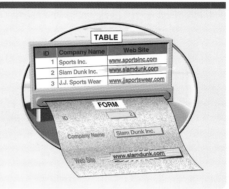

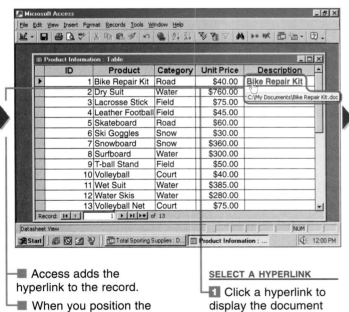

■ Access adds the hyperlink to the record.

■ When you position the mouse 👆 over a hyperlink, a yellow box appears, displaying where the hyperlink will take you.

SELECT A HYPERLINK

■1 Click a hyperlink to display the document or Web page connected to the hyperlink.

■ The document or Web page connected to the hyperlink appears.

■2 When you finish reviewing the document or Web page, click ☒ to close the window.

Unit Price	Units in Stock	Discontinued
	550	No
$34.95	100	No
$389.95	1000	No
$39.95	1500	No
$29.50	500	No
$54.95	700	No
$29.99	150	No
$210.50	100	No
$499.99	100	No
$19.95	750	No
$29.95		

Establish Relationships

Are you ready to establish relationships between the tables in your database? This chapter teaches you how.

SET THE PRIMARY KEY

A primary key is one or more fields that uniquely identifies each record in a table. Each table in your database should have a primary key.

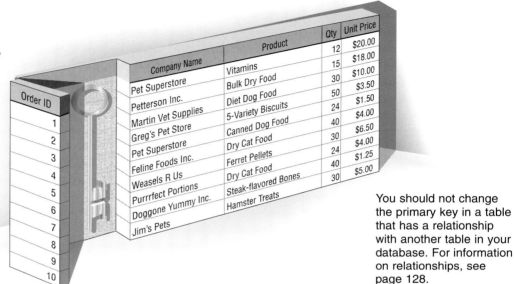

You should not change the primary key in a table that has a relationship with another table in your database. For information on relationships, see page 128.

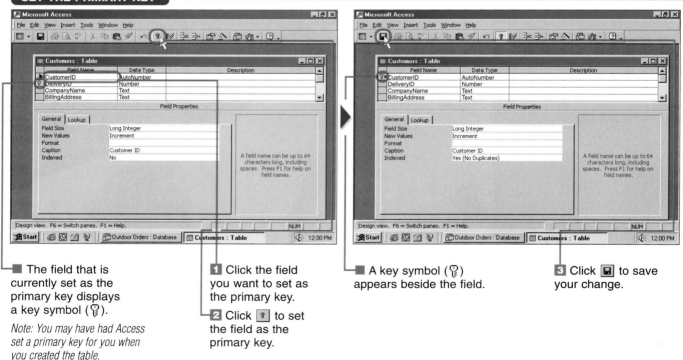

■ The field that is currently set as the primary key displays a key symbol (🔑).

Note: You may have had Access set a primary key for you when you created the table.

1 Click the field you want to set as the primary key.

2 Click 🔑 to set the field as the primary key.

■ A key symbol (🔑) appears beside the field.

3 Click 🖫 to save your change.

126

What types of primary keys can I create?

ID
1
2
3
4

Invoice No
6218
7410
8611
9431

Name	Appt Time
Johnson	9:15 AM
Smith	11:30 AM
Petterson	2:45 PM
Lee	3:30 PM

AutoNumber

A field that automatically assigns a unique number to each record you add. When you create a table, Access can create an AutoNumber primary key for you.

Single-Field

A field that contains a unique value for each record.

Multiple-Field

Two or more fields that together make up a unique value for each record.

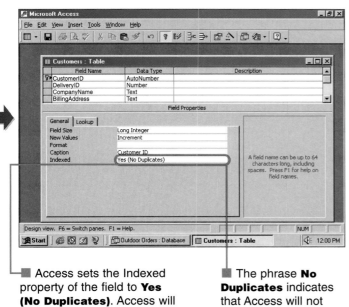

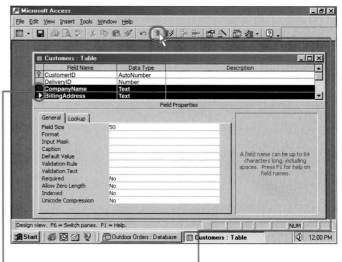

■ Access sets the Indexed property of the field to **Yes (No Duplicates)**. Access will index the data in the field so you can quickly sort and search for data in the field.

■ The phrase **No Duplicates** indicates that Access will not allow you to enter the same value in the field more than once.

You can set more than one field as the primary key.

1 Press and hold down the **Ctrl** key.

2 Still holding down the **Ctrl** key, click the area to the left of each field you want to set as the primary key.

3 Click 🔑 to set the fields as the primary key.

■ A key symbol (🔑) appears beside each field.

CREATE RELATIONSHIPS BETWEEN TABLES

You can create relationships between tables. Relationships allow you to bring together related information in your database.

If you used the Database Wizard to create your database, the wizard automatically created relationships between tables for you. For information on the Database Wizard, see page 12.

CREATE RELATIONSHIPS BETWEEN TABLES

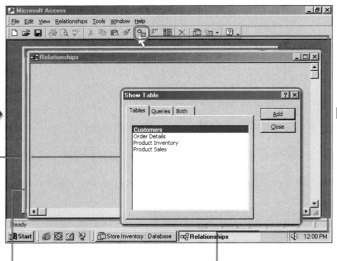

1 Click ⬛ to display the Relationships window.

Note: If ⬛ is not available, display the Database window. To display the Database window, press the **F11** *key.*

■ The Relationships window appears. If any relationships exist between the tables in your database, a box for each table appears in the window.

■ The Show Table dialog box may also appear, listing all the tables in your database.

2 If the Show Table dialog box does not appear, click ⬛ to display the dialog box.

Why do I need to create relationships between the tables in my database?

Relationships between tables are essential for creating a form, report or query that uses information from more than one table in your database.

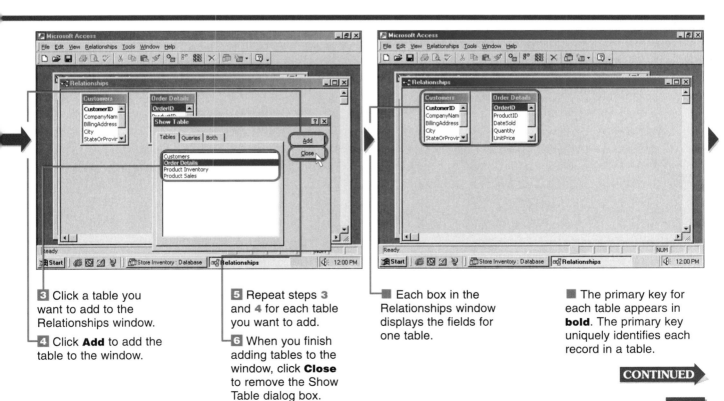

3 Click a table you want to add to the Relationships window.

4 Click **Add** to add the table to the window.

5 Repeat steps **3** and **4** for each table you want to add.

6 When you finish adding tables to the window, click **Close** to remove the Show Table dialog box.

■ Each box in the Relationships window displays the fields for one table.

■ The primary key for each table appears in **bold**. The primary key uniquely identifies each record in a table.

CONTINUED

CREATE RELATIONSHIPS BETWEEN TABLES

You create a relationship between tables by identifying the matching fields in the tables.

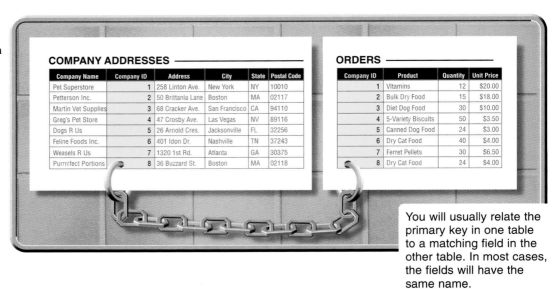

COMPANY ADDRESSES

Company Name	Company ID	Address	City	State	Postal Code
Pet Superstore	1	258 Linton Ave.	New York	NY	10010
Petterson Inc.	2	50 Brittania Lane	Boston	MA	02117
Martin Vet Supplies	3	68 Cracker Ave.	San Francisco	CA	94110
Greg's Pet Store	4	47 Crosby Ave.	Las Vegas	NV	89116
Dogs R Us	5	26 Arnold Cres.	Jacksonville	FL	32256
Feline Foods Inc.	6	401 Idon Dr.	Nashville	TN	37243
Weasels R Us	7	1320 1st Rd.	Atlanta	GA	30375
Purrrrfect Portions	8	36 Buzzard St.	Boston	MA	02118

ORDERS

Company ID	Product	Quantity	Unit Price
1	Vitamins	12	$20.00
2	Bulk Dry Food	15	$18.00
3	Diet Dog Food	30	$10.00
4	5-Variety Biscuits	50	$3.50
5	Canned Dog Food	24	$3.00
6	Dry Cat Food	40	$4.00
7	Ferret Pellets	30	$6.50
8	Dry Cat Food	24	$4.00

You will usually relate the primary key in one table to a matching field in the other table. In most cases, the fields will have the same name.

CREATE RELATIONSHIPS BETWEEN TABLES (CONTINUED)

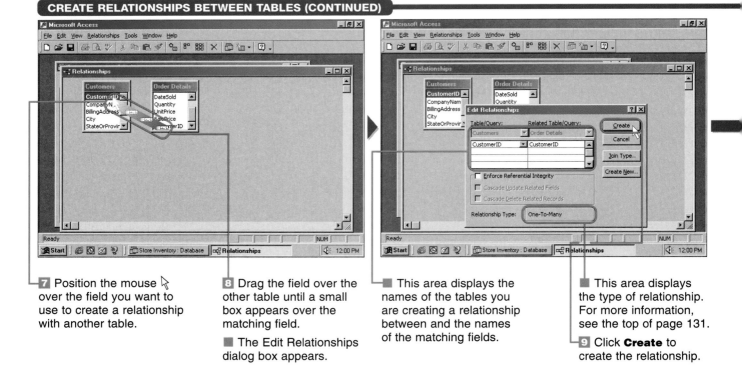

■7 Position the mouse � over the field you want to use to create a relationship with another table.

■8 Drag the field over the other table until a small box appears over the matching field.

■ The Edit Relationships dialog box appears.

■ This area displays the names of the tables you are creating a relationship between and the names of the matching fields.

■ This area displays the type of relationship. For more information, see the top of page 131.

■9 Click **Create** to create the relationship.

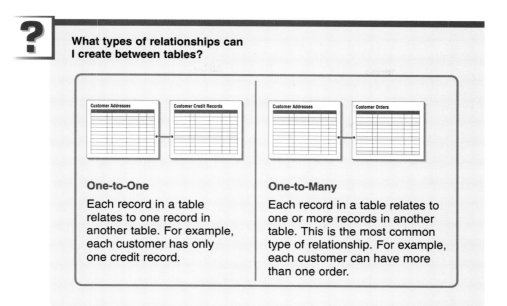

What types of relationships can I create between tables?

One-to-One

Each record in a table relates to one record in another table. For example, each customer has only one credit record.

One-to-Many

Each record in a table relates to one or more records in another table. This is the most common type of relationship. For example, each customer can have more than one order.

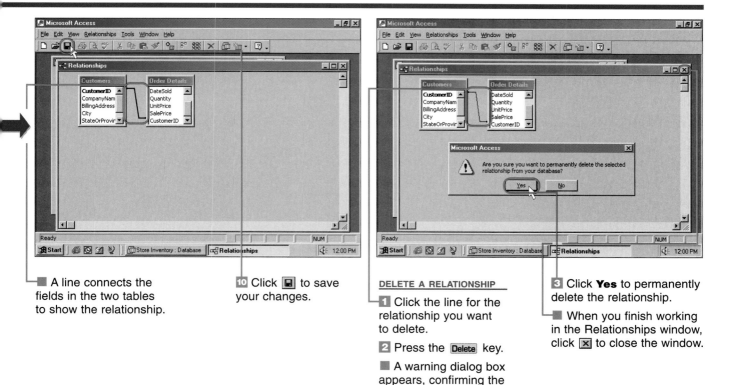

■ A line connects the fields in the two tables to show the relationship.

10 Click 🖫 to save your changes.

DELETE A RELATIONSHIP

1 Click the line for the relationship you want to delete.

2 Press the Delete key.

■ A warning dialog box appears, confirming the deletion.

3 Click **Yes** to permanently delete the relationship.

■ When you finish working in the Relationships window, click ☒ to close the window.

ENFORCE REFERENTIAL INTEGRITY

Referential integrity is a set of rules that prevents you from changing or deleting a record if matching records exist in a related table.

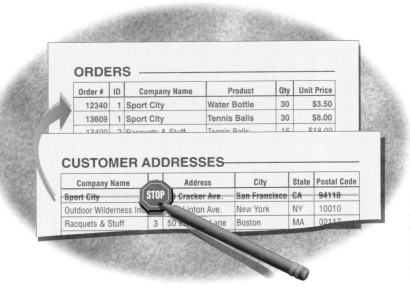

ORDERS

Order #	ID	Company Name	Product	Qty	Unit Price
12340	1	Sport City	Water Bottle	30	$3.50
13609	1	Sport City	Tennis Balls	30	$8.00
12400	2	Racquets & Stuff	Tennis Balls	15	$18.00

CUSTOMER ADDRESSES

Company Name		Address	City	State	Postal Code
Sport City		8 Cracker Ave.	San Francisco	CA	94110
Outdoor Wilderness Inc.		Clinton Ave.	New York	NY	10010
Racquets & Stuff	3	50 B... Lane	Boston	MA	02117

For example, if a table contains orders for a customer, you will not be able to delete the customer from a related table.

ENFORCE REFERENTIAL INTEGRITY

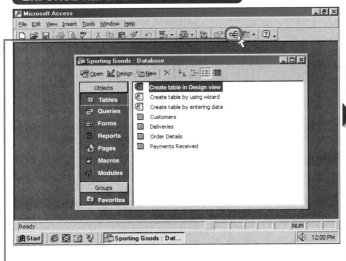

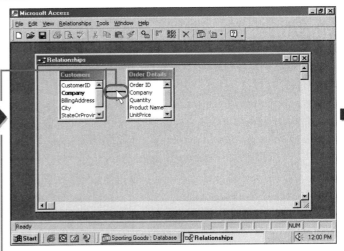

1 Click 🔲 to display the Relationships window.

Note: If 🔲 is not available, display the Database window. To display the Database window, press the **F11** *key.*

■ The Relationships window appears.

2 To enforce referential integrity between two tables, double-click the line showing the relationship between the tables.

Note: If a line does not appear between the tables, you must create a relationship between the tables. To create a relationship, see page 128.

■ The Edit Relationships dialog box appears.

What options can I select when enforcing referential integrity?

Access provides two options that let you override the rules of referential integrity but still protect data from accidental changes or deletions.

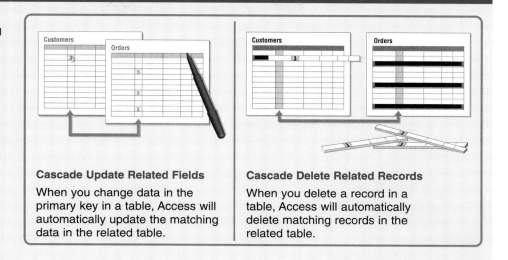

Cascade Update Related Fields

When you change data in the primary key in a table, Access will automatically update the matching data in the related table.

Cascade Delete Related Records

When you delete a record in a table, Access will automatically delete matching records in the related table.

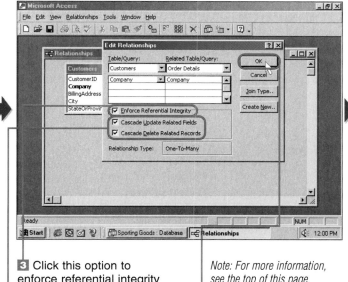

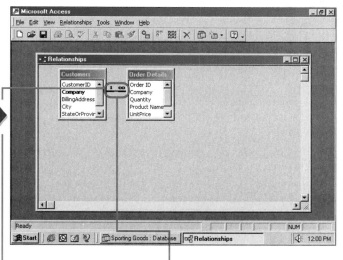

■ **3** Click this option to enforce referential integrity between the tables (☐ changes to ☑).

■ **4** To have Access automatically update related fields or delete related records, click each option you want to use (☐ changes to ☑).

Note: For more information, see the top of this page.

■ **5** Click **OK** to confirm your changes.

■ When you enforce referential integrity, the line showing the relationship between the tables becomes thicker.

■ The symbols above the line indicate the type of relationship. In this example, each record in the Customers table (**1**) relates to one or more records in the Order Details table (**∞**). For information on the types of relationships, see the top of page 131.

Columnar

CustomerID	2
Company Name	Big League Inc.
Billing Address	423 Idon Dr.
City	Nashville
State/Province	TN
Postal Code	37243

Tabular

Customer ID	Company Name	Billing Address	City	State/Pro	Postal Code
2	Big League Inc.	423 Idon Dr.	Nashville	TN	37243-
7	Indoor Sports	4 Overly Rd.	Beverly Hills	CA	90210-
5	Risky Wheelz	23 Bizzo Dr.	New York	NY	10020-
1	Ski World	255 Linton Ave.	New York	NY	10010-
8	Spokes 'n' Stuff	22 Heldon St.	Atlanta	GA	30375-
4	Stadium Sports	54 Arnold Cres.	Jacksonville	FL	32256-
6	Surfers' Apparel	62 Cracker Ave.	San Diego	CA	92129-
3	Varsity Supply	32 Buzzard St.	Boston	MA	02118-
9	Waveriders Inc.	57 Crosby Ave.	Las Vegas	NV	89116-

Datasheet

Customer ID	Company Name	Billing Address	City
2	Big League Inc.	423 Idon Dr.	Nashville
7	Indoor Sports	4 Overly Rd.	Beverly Hills
5	Risky Wheelz	23 Bizzo Dr.	New York
1	Ski World	255 Linton Ave.	New York
8	Spokes 'n' Stuff	22 Heldon St.	Atlanta
4	Stadium Sports	54 Arnold Cres.	Jacksonville
6	Surfers' Apparel	62 Cracker Ave.	San Diego
3	Varsity Supply	32 Buzzard St.	Boston
9	Waveriders Inc.	57 Crosby Ave.	Las Vegas

Create Forms

Would you like to use forms to work with data in your database? This chapter teaches you how to present information in an easy-to-use format so you can quickly view, enter and change data.

Justified

CustomerID	Company Name	
2	Big League Inc.	
Billing Address		
423 Idon Dr.		
City	State/Province	Postal Code
Nashville	TN	37243

CREATE A FORM USING AN AUTOFORM

You can use the AutoForm
Wizard to quickly create
a form that displays the
information from a table
in your database.

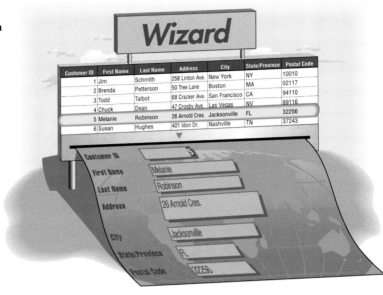

A form presents
data from a table
in an attractive,
easy-to-use format.

CREATE A FORM USING AN AUTOFORM

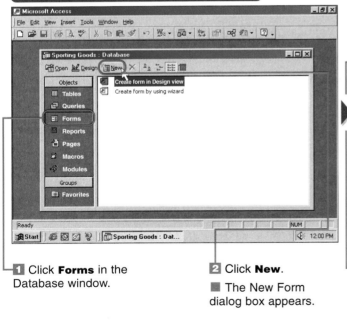

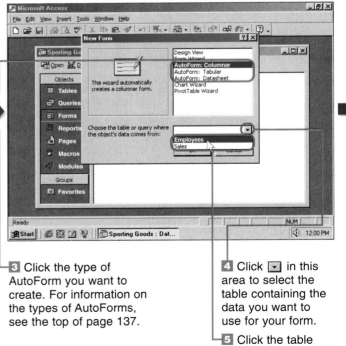

■1 Click **Forms** in the
Database window.

■2 Click **New**.

■ The New Form
dialog box appears.

■3 Click the type of
AutoForm you want to
create. For information on
the types of AutoForms,
see the top of page 137.

■4 Click ▼ in this
area to select the
table containing the
data you want to
use for your form.

■5 Click the table
containing the data.

What types of AutoForms can I create?

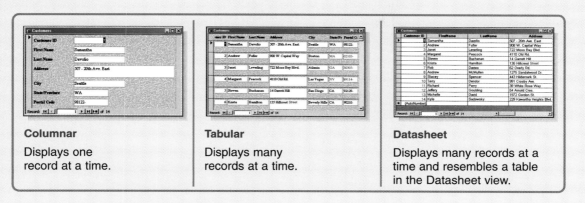

Columnar

Displays one record at a time.

Tabular

Displays many records at a time.

Datasheet

Displays many records at a time and resembles a table in the Datasheet view.

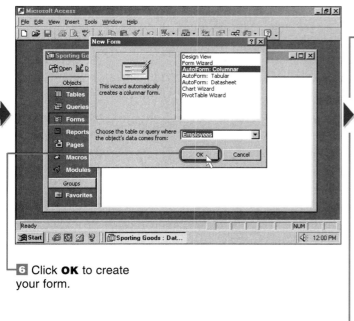

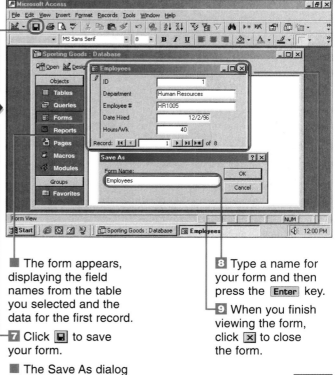

6 Click **OK** to create your form.

■ The form appears, displaying the field names from the table you selected and the data for the first record.

7 Click 🖫 to save your form.

■ The Save As dialog box appears.

8 Type a name for your form and then press the Enter key.

9 When you finish viewing the form, click ✕ to close the form.

CREATE A FORM USING THE FORM WIZARD

You can use the Form
Wizard to help you create
a form. The wizard asks
you a series of questions
and then sets up a form
based on your answers.

CREATE A FORM FROM ONE TABLE

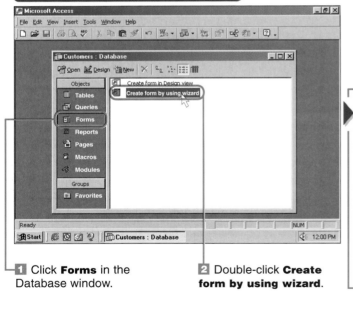

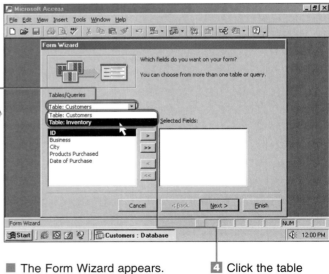

1 Click **Forms** in the
Database window.

2 Double-click **Create
form by using wizard**.

■ The Form Wizard appears.

3 Click ▼ in this area to
select the table containing
the fields you want to
include in your form.

4 Click the table
containing the fields.

How can a form help me work with the data in my database?

A form presents data from a table in an attractive, easy-to-use format. You can use a form to view, enter and change data in a table. Many people find forms easier to work with than tables.

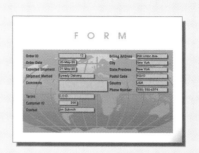

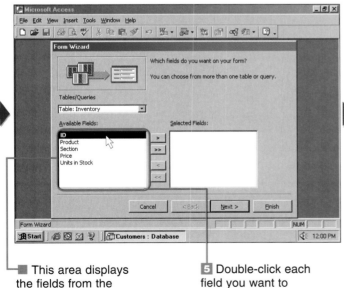

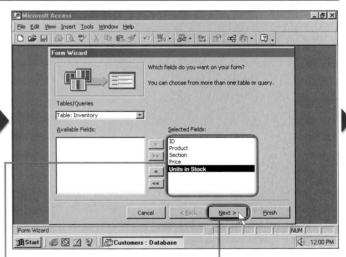

■ This area displays the fields from the table you selected.

5 Double-click each field you want to include in your form.

Note: To add all the fields at once, click >> .

■ Each field you select appears in this area.

6 To remove a field you accidentally selected, double-click the field in this area.

Note: To remove all the fields at once, click << .

7 When you finish selecting all the fields you want to include in your form, click **Next** to continue.

CONTINUED

CREATE A FORM USING THE FORM WIZARD

When creating a form, you can choose from several layouts for the form. The layout of a form determines the arrangement of information on the form.

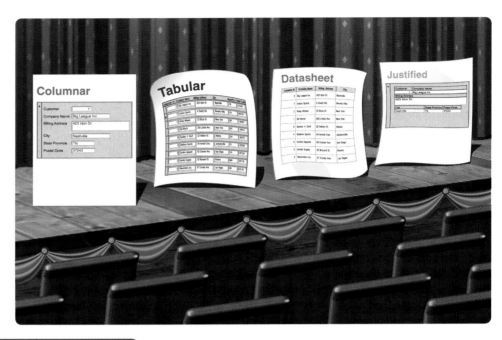

CREATE A FORM FROM ONE TABLE (CONTINUED)

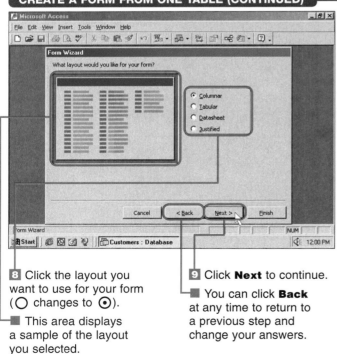

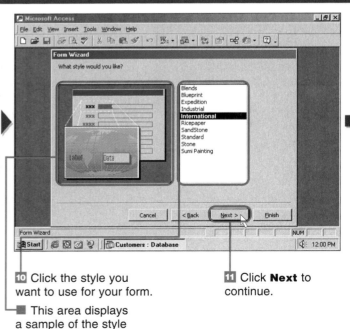

8 Click the layout you want to use for your form (○ changes to ⊙).

■ This area displays a sample of the layout you selected.

9 Click **Next** to continue.

■ You can click **Back** at any time to return to a previous step and change your answers.

10 Click the style you want to use for your form.

■ This area displays a sample of the style you selected.

11 Click **Next** to continue.

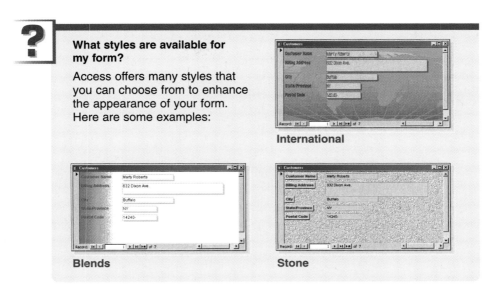

What styles are available for my form?

Access offers many styles that you can choose from to enhance the appearance of your form. Here are some examples:

International

Blends

Stone

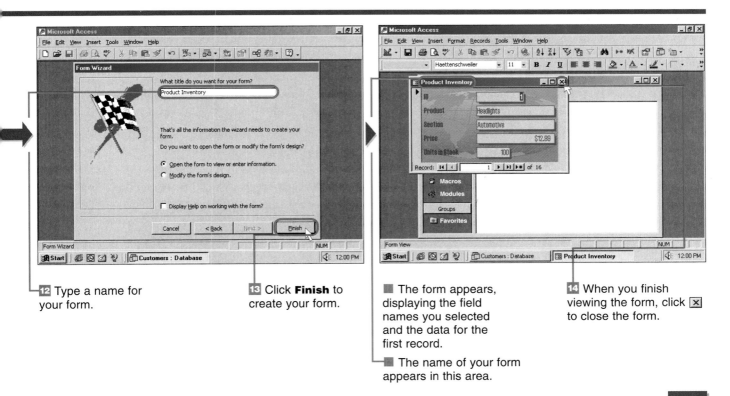

12 Type a name for your form.

13 Click **Finish** to create your form.

■ The form appears, displaying the field names you selected and the data for the first record.

14 When you finish viewing the form, click ✕ to close the form.

■ The name of your form appears in this area.

CREATE A FORM USING THE FORM WIZARD

You can use the Form Wizard to create a form that displays information from more than one table in your database.

CREATE A FORM FROM MULTIPLE TABLES

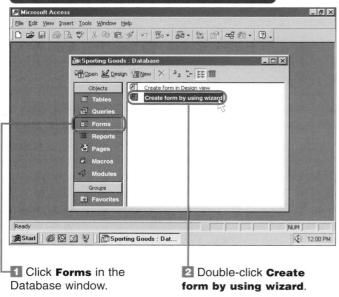

1 Click **Forms** in the Database window.

2 Double-click **Create form by using wizard**.

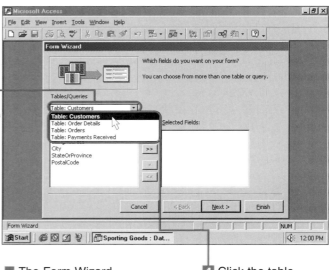

■ The Form Wizard appears.

3 Click ▼ in this area to select a table containing fields you want to include in your form.

4 Click the table containing the fields.

Which tables in my database can I use to create a form?

You can use any table in your database to create a form. To create a form using data from more than one table, relationships must exist between the tables. For information on relationships, see page 128.

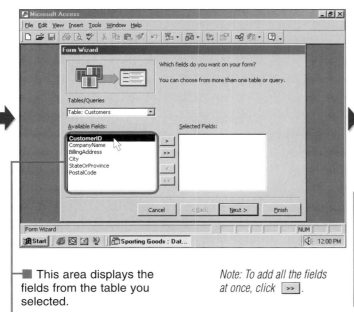

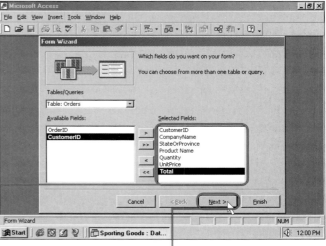

■ This area displays the fields from the table you selected.

5 Double-click each field you want to include in your form.

Note: To add all the fields at once, click ⓘ >> *.*

■ Each field you select appears in this area.

6 To remove a field you accidentally selected, double-click the field in this area.

Note: To remove all the fields at once, click ⓘ << *.*

7 To add fields from other tables, repeat steps **3** to **6** for each table.

8 Click **Next** to continue.

CONTINUED

CREATE A FORM USING THE FORM WIZARD

When creating a form using data from multiple tables, you can choose the way you want to view the data on your form.

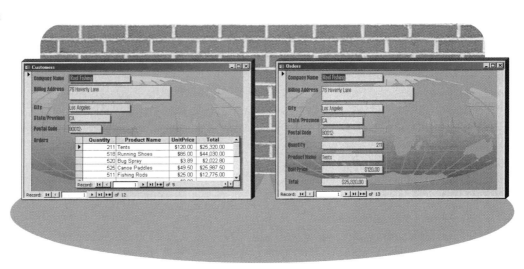

CREATE A FORM FROM MULTIPLE TABLES (CONTINUED)

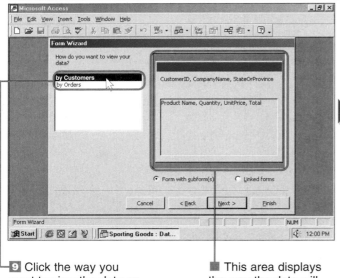

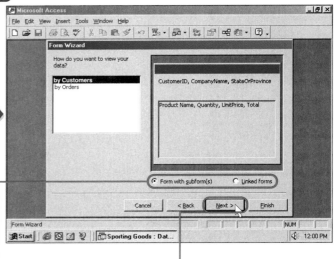

■9 Click the way you want to view the data on your form. You can view the data from each table in separate sections or together in one section.

■ This area displays the way the data will appear on your form.

■10 Click the way you want to organize the data (○ changes to ⊙). For more information, see the top of page 145.

Note: These options are not available if you chose to view the data from each table in one section in step 9.

■11 Click **Next** to continue.

144

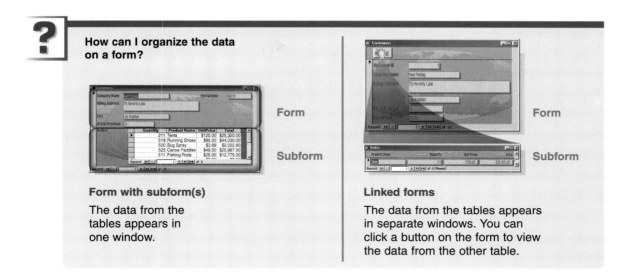

How can I organize the data on a form?

Form

Subform

Form with subform(s)

The data from the tables appears in one window.

Form

Subform

Linked forms

The data from the tables appears in separate windows. You can click a button on the form to view the data from the other table.

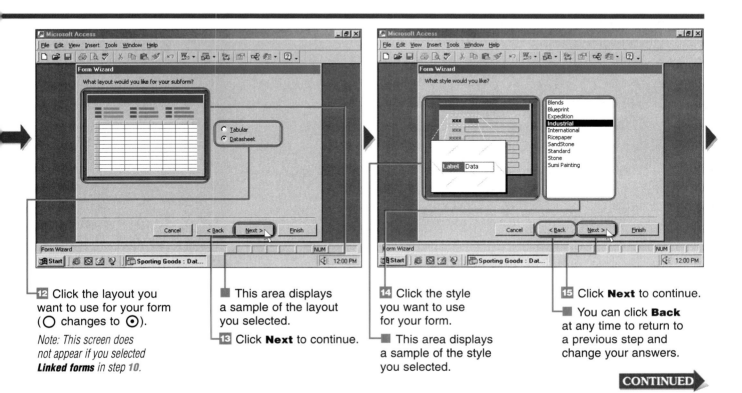

■12 Click the layout you want to use for your form (○ changes to ⊙).

*Note: This screen does not appear if you selected **Linked forms** in step 10.*

■ This area displays a sample of the layout you selected.

■13 Click **Next** to continue.

■14 Click the style you want to use for your form.

■ This area displays a sample of the style you selected.

■15 Click **Next** to continue.

■ You can click **Back** at any time to return to a previous step and change your answers.

CONTINUED

CREATE A FORM USING THE FORM WIZARD

You can give your form a descriptive name. If your form contains a subform, you can also name the subform.

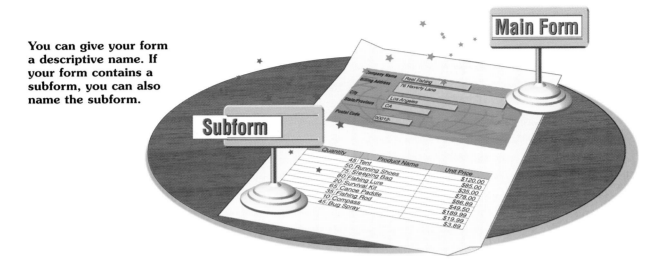

CREATE A FORM FROM MULTIPLE TABLES (CONTINUED)

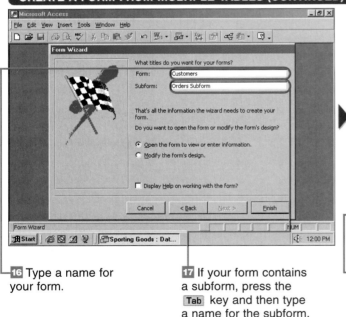

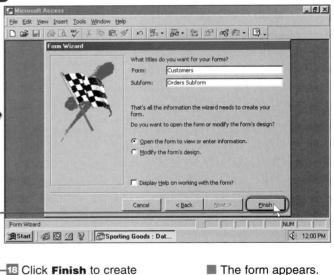

-16 Type a name for your form.

17 If your form contains a subform, press the **Tab** key and then type a name for the subform.

-18 Click **Finish** to create your form.

■ The form appears.

How will my new form appear in the Database window?

If you created a form that contains a subform, both the main form and subform will be listed in the Database window. You must open the main form to work with the contents of both the main form and the subform.

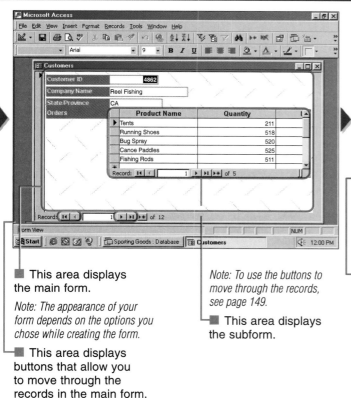

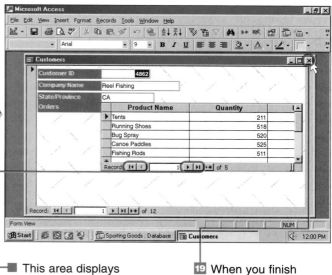

■ This area displays the main form.

Note: The appearance of your form depends on the options you chose while creating the form.

■ This area displays buttons that allow you to move through the records in the main form.

Note: To use the buttons to move through the records, see page 149.

■ This area displays the subform.

■ This area displays buttons that allow you to move through the records in the subform.

■ As you move through the records in the main form, the information in the subform changes. For example, when you display the name and address of a customer, the orders for the customer appear in the subform.

🔢 When you finish viewing the form, click ☒ to close the form.

OPEN A FORM

You can open a form to display its contents on your screen. This lets you review and make changes to the form.

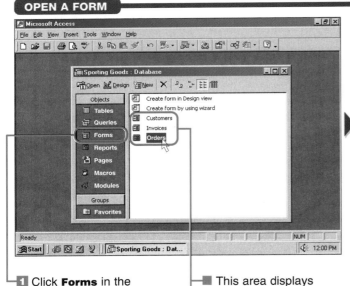

1 Click **Forms** in the Database window.

■ This area displays a list of the forms in your database.

2 Double-click the form you want to open.

■ The form appears. You can now review and make changes to the form.

■ When you finish working with the form, click ☒ to close the form.

■ A dialog box will appear if you did not save changes you made to the design of the form. Click **Yes** to save the changes.

You can move through records in a form to review and edit information.

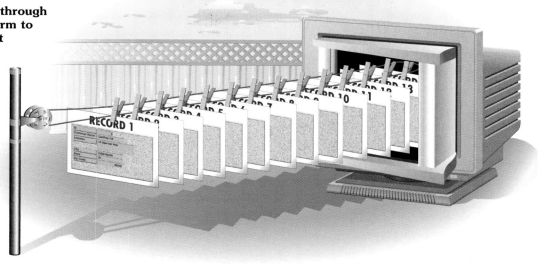

MOVE THROUGH RECORDS

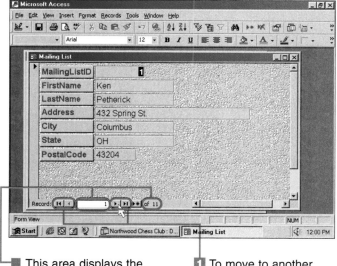

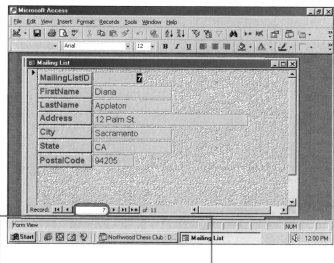

■ This area displays the number of the current record and the total number of records.

1 To move to another record, click one of the following buttons.

   I◄ First record

   ◄ Previous record

   ► Next record

   ►I Last record

MOVE TO A SPECIFIC RECORD

1 Drag the mouse I over the number of the current record. The number is highlighted.

2 Type the number of the record you want to move to and then press the **Enter** key.

EDIT DATA

You can edit the data in a form to correct a mistake or update the data.

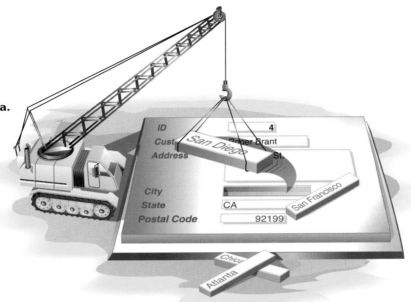

Access automatically saves the changes you make to the data in a form.

When you change data in a form, Access will also change the data in the table you used to create the form.

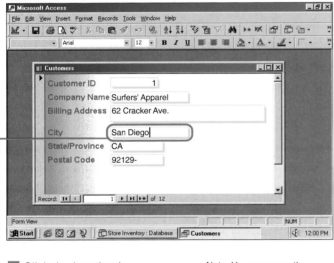

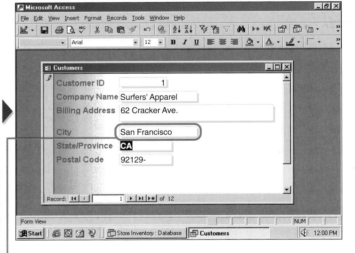

1 Click the location in the cell where you want to edit data.

■ A flashing insertion point appears in the cell.

Note: You can press the ← *or* → *key to move the insertion point to where you want to edit data.*

2 To remove the character to the left of the insertion point, press the **+Backspace** key.

3 To insert data where the insertion point flashes on your screen, type the data.

4 When you finish making changes to the data, press the **Enter** key.

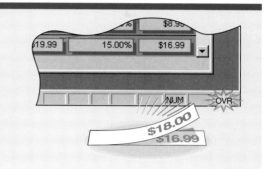

Why does the existing data disappear when I type new data?

When **OVR** appears in **bold** at the bottom of your screen, the Overtype feature is on. When this feature is on, the data you type will replace the existing data. To turn off the Overtype feature, press the `Insert` key.

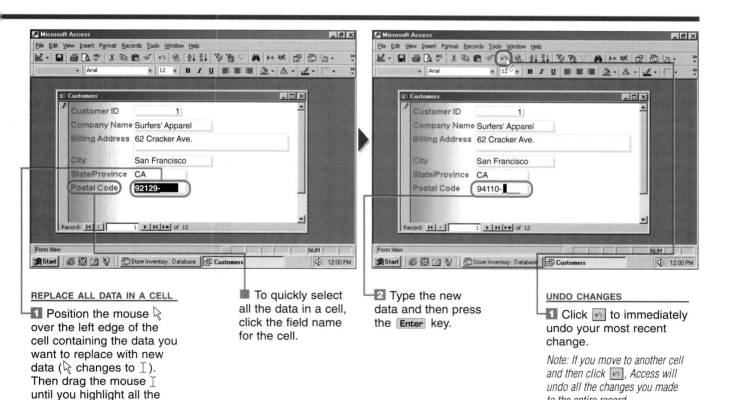

REPLACE ALL DATA IN A CELL

1 Position the mouse ⩗ over the left edge of the cell containing the data you want to replace with new data (⩗ changes to I). Then drag the mouse I until you highlight all the data in the cell.

■ To quickly select all the data in a cell, click the field name for the cell.

2 Type the new data and then press the `Enter` key.

UNDO CHANGES

1 Click 🔙 to immediately undo your most recent change.

Note: If you move to another cell and then click 🔙, Access will undo all the changes you made to the entire record.

151

ADD A RECORD

You can add a record to a form to insert new information into your database. For example, you may want to add information about a new customer.

Access automatically saves each new record you add to a form.

When you add a record to a form, Access also adds the record to the table you used to create the form.

ADD A RECORD

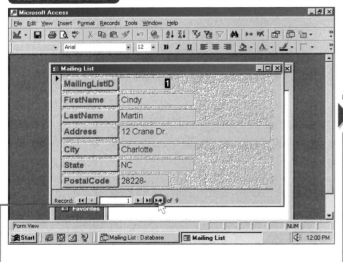

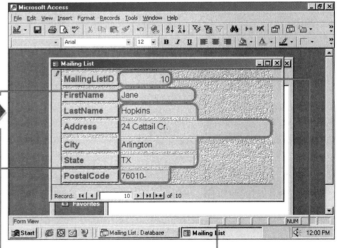

1 Click ▶✱ to add a new record to your form.

■ A blank form appears.

2 Click the first empty field in the form.

3 Type the data that corresponds to the field and then press the Enter key to move to the next field. Repeat this step until you finish entering all the data for the record.

■ In this example, the ID field automatically displays a number for the new record.

152

You can delete a record to permanently remove information you no longer need. For example, you may want to remove information about a customer who no longer orders your products.

When you delete a record from a form, Access also removes the record from the table you used to create the form.

Deleting records saves storage space on your computer and reduces clutter in your database.

DELETE A RECORD

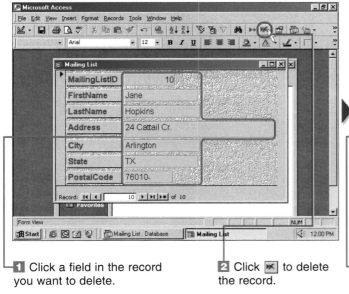

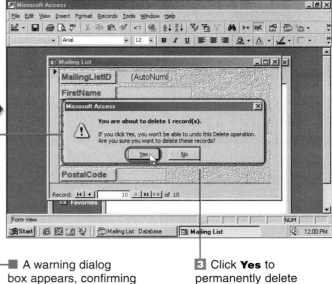

■1 Click a field in the record you want to delete.

■2 Click ⬚ to delete the record.

■ A warning dialog box appears, confirming the deletion.

■3 Click **Yes** to permanently delete the record.

■ The record disappears.

RENAME A FORM

You can change the name of a form to better describe the information the form displays.

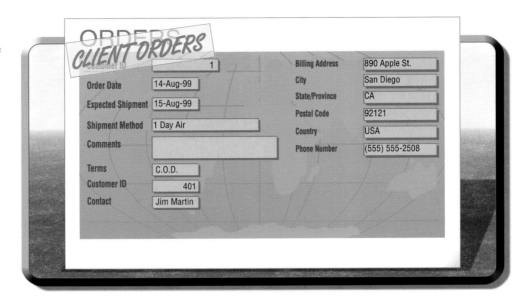

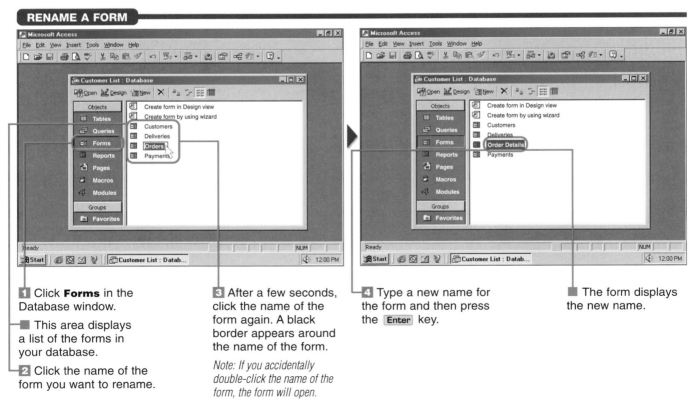

1 Click **Forms** in the Database window.

■ This area displays a list of the forms in your database.

2 Click the name of the form you want to rename.

3 After a few seconds, click the name of the form again. A black border appears around the name of the form.

Note: If you accidentally double-click the name of the form, the form will open.

4 Type a new name for the form and then press the **Enter** key.

■ The form displays the new name.

154

DELETE A FORM

If you no longer
need a form, you
can permanently
delete the form
from your database.

DELETE A FORM

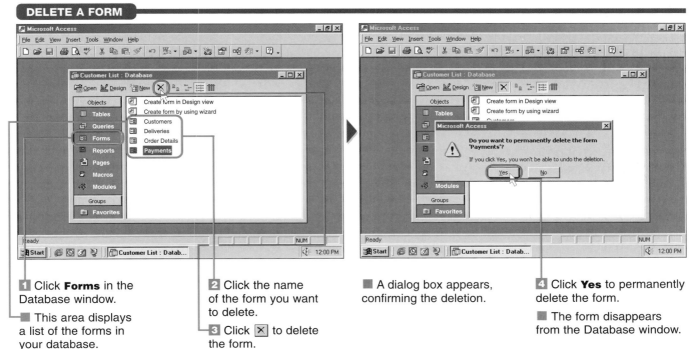

1 Click **Forms** in the
Database window.

■ This area displays
a list of the forms in
your database.

2 Click the name
of the form you want
to delete.

3 Click ☒ to delete
the form.

■ A dialog box appears,
confirming the deletion.

4 Click **Yes** to permanently
delete the form.

■ The form disappears
from the Database window.

CHAPTER 7

Design Forms

Are you interested in customizing the layout and design of your forms? In this chapter you will learn how to move items on a form, change the appearance of text, add a picture and more.

CHANGE VIEW OF FORM

There are three ways
you can view a form.
Each view allows you to
perform different tasks.

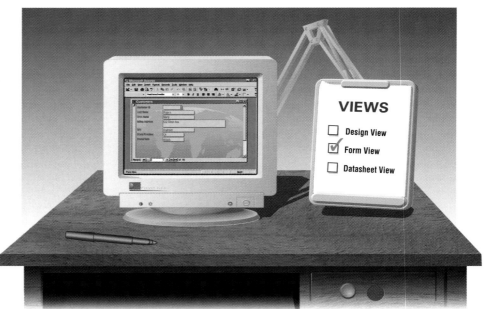

VIEWS

- ☐ Design View
- ☑ Form View
- ☐ Datasheet View

CHANGE VIEW OF FORM

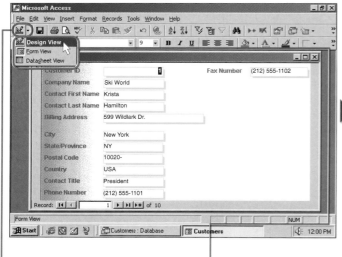

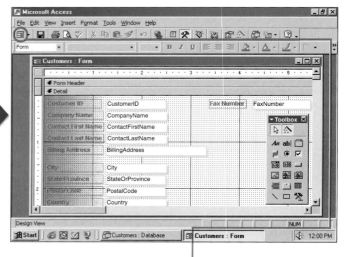

■ In this example, the
form appears in the
Form view.

1 Click ⏷ in this area to
select a different view.

2 Click the view you
want to use.

■ The form appears in
the view you selected.

■ In this example, the View
button 📐 changes to 🖼.
You can click the View
button to quickly switch
between the Form (🖼)
and Design (📐) views.

Design View

The Design view allows you to change the layout and design of a form. You can customize the form to make it easier to use or to enhance the appearance of the form.

You can customize the form to make it easier to use or to enhance the appearance of the form.

Form View

The Form view usually displays one record at a time in an organized and attractive format.

You can use this view to enter, edit and review information.

Datasheet View

The Datasheet view displays all the records in rows and columns. The field names appear across the top of the window.

Each row displays the information for one record. You can enter, edit and review information in this view.

MOVE A CONTROL

You can change the
location of a control
on your form. Moving
a control allows you
to change the order
of information on
the form.

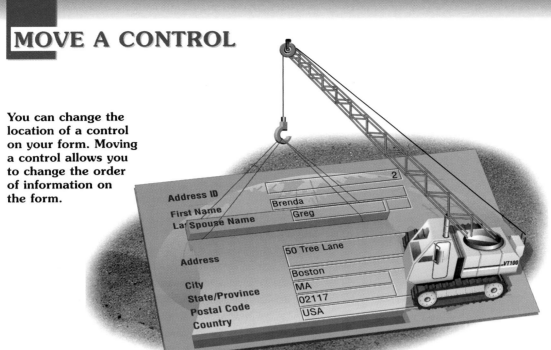

A control is an item on
a form. A control can
be a label that displays
a field name or a text
box that displays data
from a record.

MOVE A CONTROL

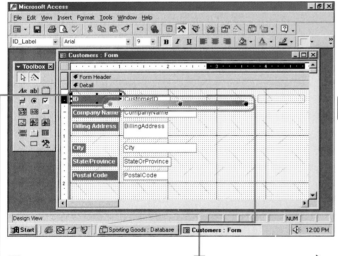

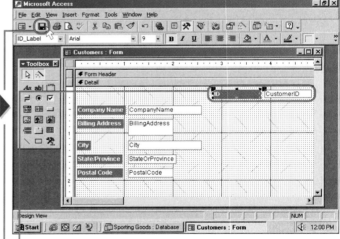

■1 Display the form you
want to change in the
Design view. To change
the view, see page 158.

■2 Click the control you
want to move. Handles (■)
appear around the control.

■3 Position the mouse ⬚
over a border of the
control (⬚ changes to ✋)
and then drag the control
to a new location.

■ In this example, the
label and corresponding
text box appear in the
new location.

■4 Click 🖫 to save
your change.

■ To move a label or text
box individually, perform
steps 1 to 4, except position
the mouse ⬚ over the large
handle (■) at the top left
corner of the control in
step 3 (⬚ changes to ✋).

You can change the
size of a control on
your form. Increasing
the size of a control
allows you to display
more information
in the control.

SIZE A CONTROL

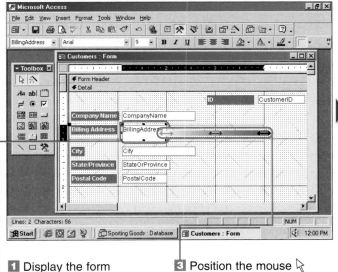

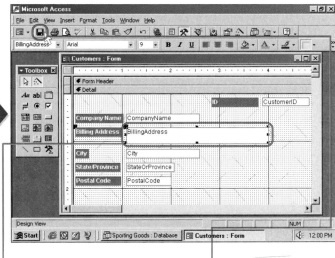

1 Display the form
you want to change
in the Design view.
To change the view,
see page 158.

2 Click the control
you want to size.
Handles (■) appear
around the control.

3 Position the mouse ⌐
over a handle (⌐ changes
to ↔, ↕ or ↘) and then
drag the handle until the
control is the size you want.

■ The control appears
in the new size.

4 Click 🖫 to save
your change.

DELETE A CONTROL

You can delete
a control you
no longer want
to appear on
your form.

A control is an item on a form. A control can be a label that displays a field name or a text box that displays data from a record.

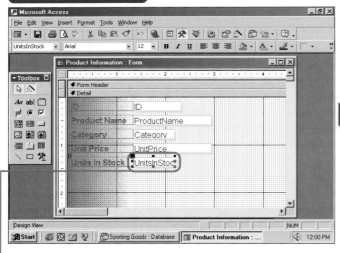

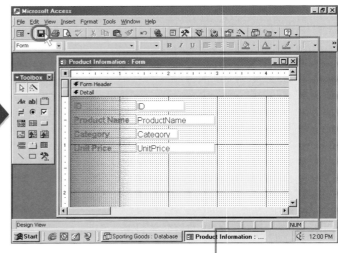

1 Display the form you want to change in the Design view. To change the view, see page 158.

2 Click the control you want to delete. Handles (■) appear around the control.

Note: Selecting a label will delete only the label. Selecting a text box will delete the text box and the corresponding label.

3 Press the Delete key.

■ In this example, the text box and the corresponding label disappear.

4 Click 🖫 to save your change.

You can change the size of your entire form. Increasing the size of a form can give you more room to add information, such as a new field or a picture.

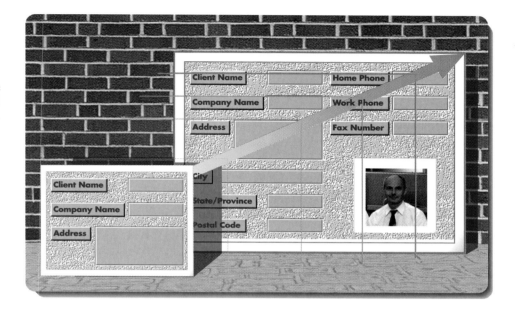

CHANGE SIZE OF FORM

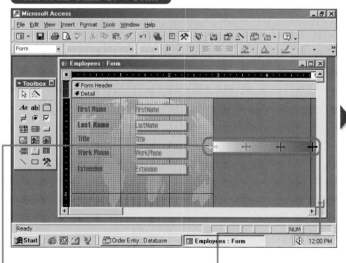

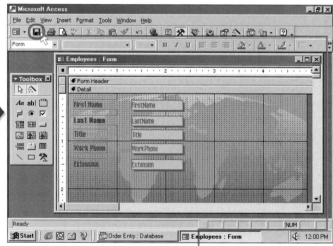

1 Display the form you want to change in the Design view. To change the view, see page 158.

2 Position the mouse ⌖ over the right or bottom edge of the form (⌖ changes to ↔ or ↕).

3 Drag the edge of the form until the form displays the size you want.

■ A line shows the new form size.

■ The form changes to the new size.

4 Click 🔲 to save your change.

ADD A FIELD

You can add a field to your form when you want the form to display additional information.

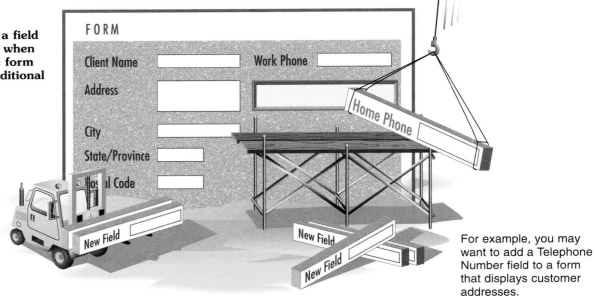

For example, you may want to add a Telephone Number field to a form that displays customer addresses.

ADD A FIELD

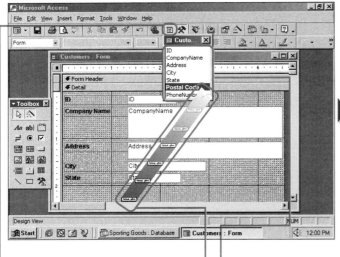

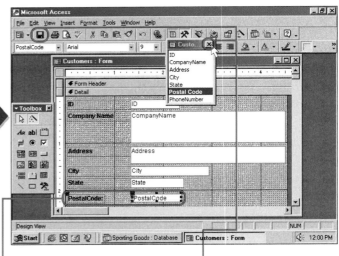

1 Display the form you want to change in the Design view. To change the view, see page 158.

2 Click 🔲 to display a list of fields from the table you used to create your form.

3 Position the mouse ⇧ over the field you want to add to your form.

4 Drag the field to where you want the field to appear on your form.

◼ The label and corresponding text box for the field appear on your form.

Note: To move or size the label or text box, see pages 160 and 161.

5 Click 🔲 to save your change.

6 To hide the list of fields, click ✕.

164

You can add a label that
you want to appear for
each record in your
form. Labels are useful
for displaying important
information.

ADD A LABEL

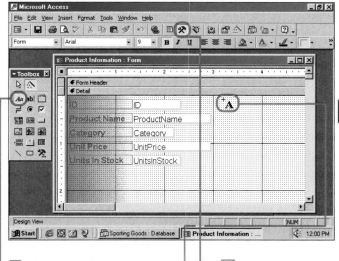

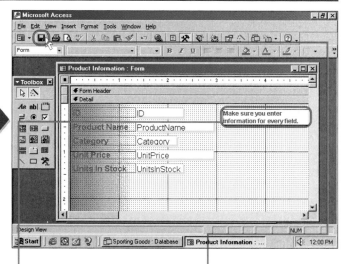

1 Display the form you
want to change in the
Design view. To change
the view, see page 158.

2 Click ![Aa] to add a
label to your form.

■ If ![Aa] is not available,
click ![⚒] to display the
Toolbox toolbar.

3 Click where you
want the top left corner
of the label to appear
on your form.

4 Type the text for
the label and then
press the **Enter** key.

5 Click ![💾] to save
your change.

■ To move or size
the label, see pages
160 and 161.

CHANGE LABEL TEXT

You can change
the text in a label
to make the label
more descriptive.

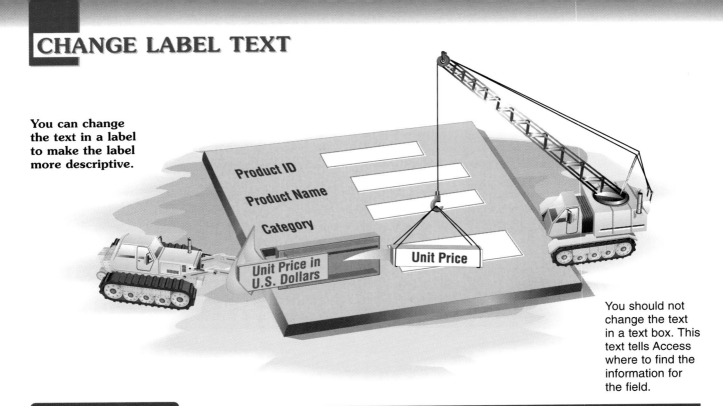

You should not
change the text
in a text box. This
text tells Access
where to find the
information for
the field.

CHANGE LABEL TEXT

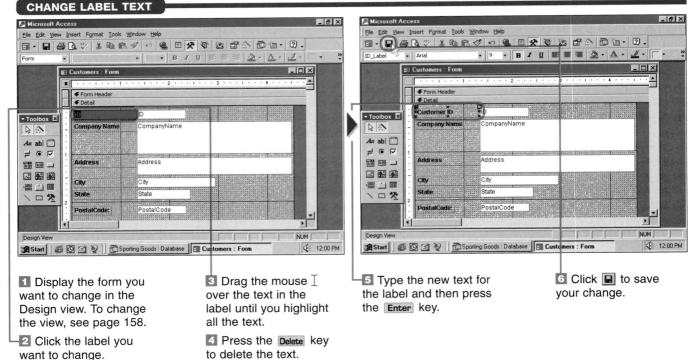

1 Display the form you
want to change in the
Design view. To change
the view, see page 158.

2 Click the label you
want to change.

3 Drag the mouse I
over the text in the
label until you highlight
all the text.

4 Press the Delete key
to delete the text.

5 Type the new text for
the label and then press
the Enter key.

6 Click 🔲 to save
your change.

166

You can use the Bold, Italic
and Underline features to
change the style of text
on your form. This can
help you emphasize
important information.

BOLD, ITALICIZE OR UNDERLINE TEXT

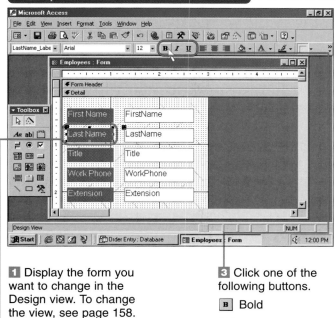

1 Display the form you
want to change in the
Design view. To change
the view, see page 158.

2 Click the control that
displays the text you want
to change to a new style.

3 Click one of the
following buttons.

B Bold

I Italic

U Underline

■ The text changes to
the new style.

*Note: If the control is not large
enough to display all the text,
see page 161 to increase the
size of the control.*

4 Click 🖫 to save
your change.

■ To remove a bold,
italic or underline style,
repeat steps **1** to **4**.

CHANGE FONT OF TEXT

You can change the font
of text in a control to
enhance the appearance
of your form.

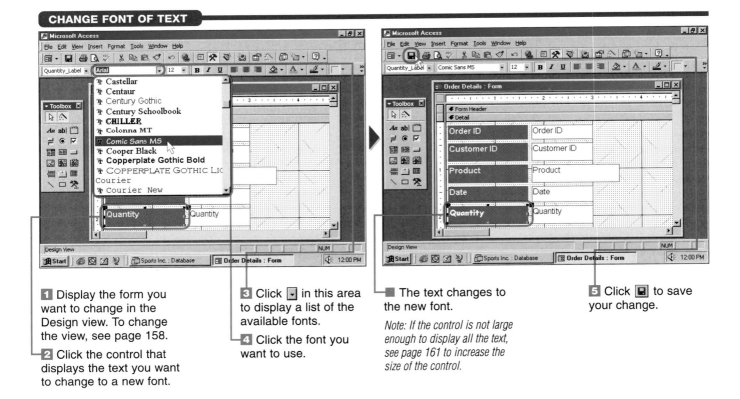

1 Display the form you
want to change in the
Design view. To change
the view, see page 158.

2 Click the control that
displays the text you want
to change to a new font.

3 Click ▼ in this area
to display a list of the
available fonts.

4 Click the font you
want to use.

■ The text changes to
the new font.

*Note: If the control is not large
enough to display all the text,
see page 161 to increase the
size of the control.*

5 Click 🖫 to save
your change.

168

You can increase or
decrease the size of
text in a control.

Access measures
the size of text in
points. There are 72
points in an inch.

CHANGE SIZE OF TEXT

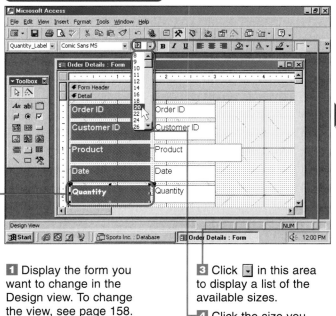

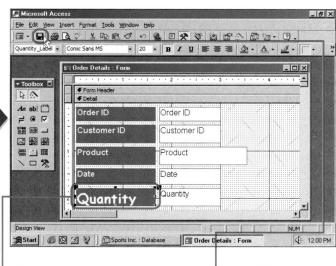

1 Display the form you
want to change in the
Design view. To change
the view, see page 158.

2 Click the control that
displays the text you want
to change to a new size.

3 Click ⯆ in this area
to display a list of the
available sizes.

4 Click the size you
want to use.

■ The text changes
to the new size.

*Note: If the control is not large
enough to display all the text,
see page 161 to increase the
size of the control.*

5 Click 🖫 to save
your change.

CHANGE FORMAT OF FIELD

You can change the
way numbers, dates
and times appear on
your form.

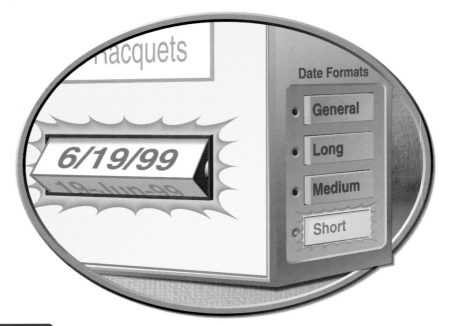

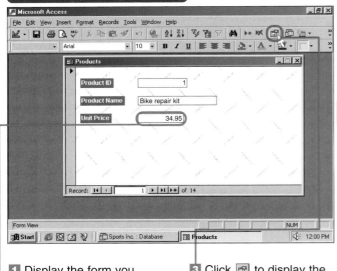

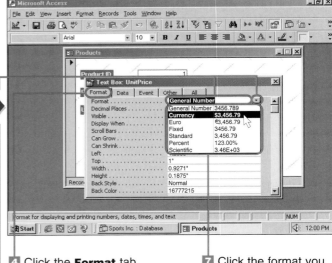

1 Display the form you
want to change in the
Form view. To change
the view, see page 158.

2 Click the field that
contains the data you
want to display in a
new format.

3 Click 🖺 to display the
properties for the field.

■ The Text Box dialog
box appears.

4 Click the **Format** tab.

5 Click the area beside
Format. An arrow (▾)
appears.

6 Click the arrow (▾) to
display a list of formats.

7 Click the format you
want to use.

*Note: The available formats
depend on the data type of
the field you selected. For
information on data types,
see page 85.*

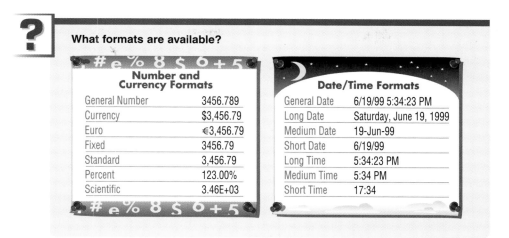

What formats are available?

Number and Currency Formats

General Number	3456.789
Currency	$3,456.79
Euro	€3,456.79
Fixed	3456.79
Standard	3,456.79
Percent	123.00%
Scientific	3.46E+03

Date/Time Formats

General Date	6/19/99 5:34:23 PM
Long Date	Saturday, June 19, 1999
Medium Date	19-Jun-99
Short Date	6/19/99
Long Time	5:34:23 PM
Medium Time	5:34 PM
Short Time	17:34

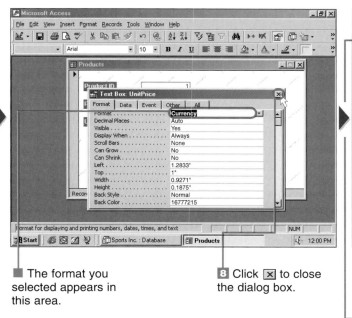

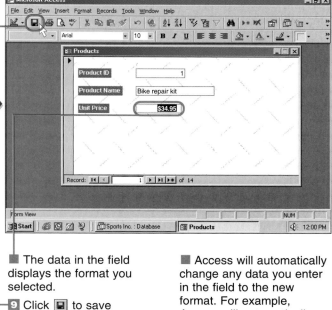

■ The format you selected appears in this area.

8 Click ☒ to close the dialog box.

■ The data in the field displays the format you selected.

9 Click 🖫 to save your change.

■ Access will automatically change any data you enter in the field to the new format. For example, Access will automatically change 1234 to $1,234.00.

CHANGE COLOR OF CONTROL

You can change the background and text color of a control to emphasize information on your form.

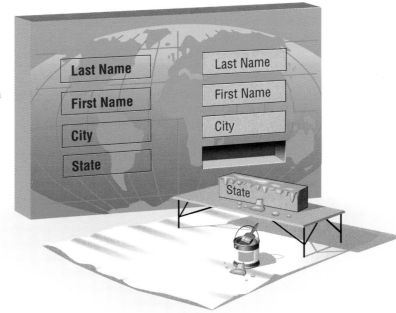

Make sure you select background and text colors that work well together. For example, red text on a blue background can be difficult to read.

CHANGE BACKGROUND COLOR

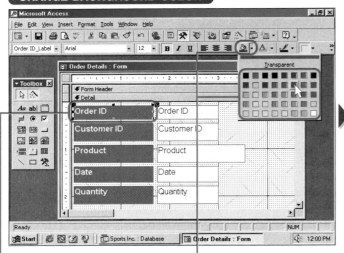

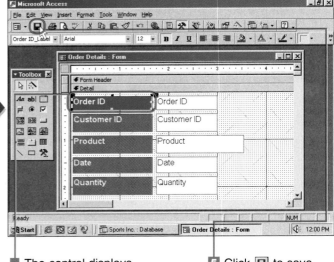

1 Display the form you want to change in the Design view. To change the view, see page 158.

2 Click the control you want to change to a different color.

3 Click ⊡ in this area to display a list of background colors.

4 Click the background color you want to use.

■ The control displays the color you selected.

5 Click 🖫 to save your change.

172

Can I change the color of several controls at once?

Yes. Perform steps 1 to 5 on page 172 or 173, except select all the controls you want to change to a different color in step 2. To select multiple controls, hold down the Shift key as you click each control you want to change.

CHANGE TEXT COLOR

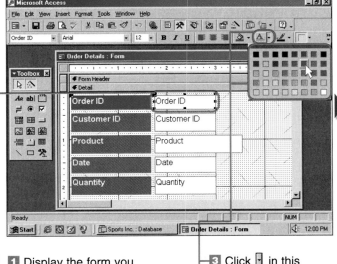

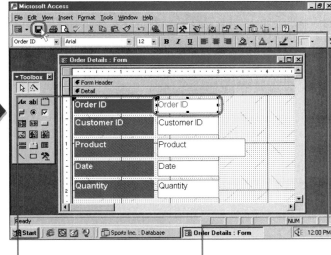

1 Display the form you want to change in the Design view. To change the view, see page 158.

2 Click the control that displays the text you want to change to a different color.

3 Click ⊡ in this area to display a list of text colors.

4 Click the text color you want to use.

■ The text in the control displays the color you selected.

5 Click 🖫 to save your change.

APPLY AN AUTOFORMAT

You can apply an
autoformat to quickly
change the overall
appearance of a form.

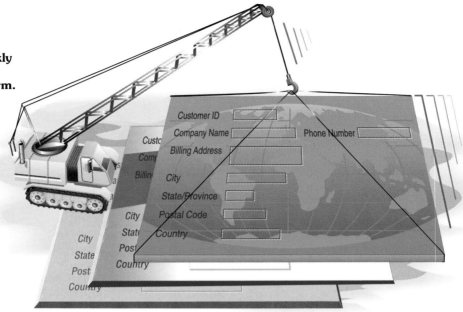

APPLY AN AUTOFORMAT

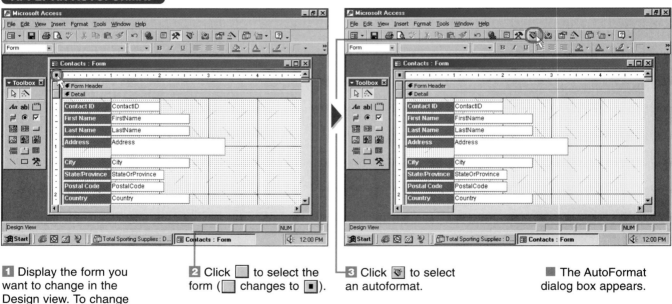

1 Display the form you
want to change in the
Design view. To change
the view, see page 158.

2 Click ☐ to select the
form (☐ changes to ▪).

3 Click ⚘ to select
an autoformat.

■ The AutoFormat
dialog box appears.

174

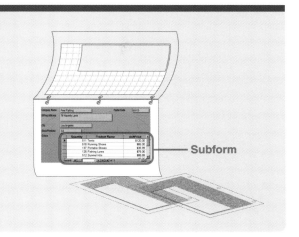

Why didn't my entire form change to the new autoformat?

If your form contains a subform, the appearance of the subform will not change when you apply an autoformat to the form. To change the appearance of the subform, open the subform and then perform steps **1** to **6** below. To open a form, see page 148.

Note: If your subform appears in the Datasheet layout, you cannot change the appearance of the subform. A subform in the Datasheet layout looks like a table.

Subform

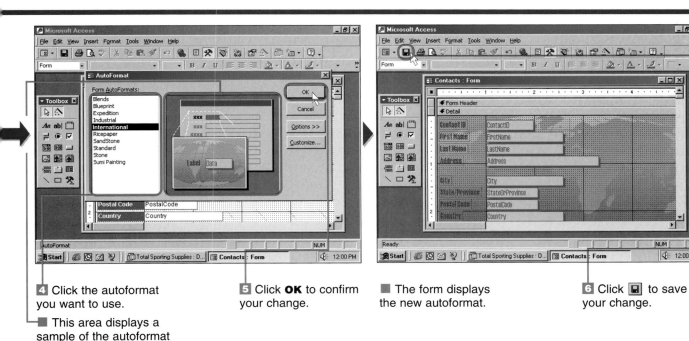

4 Click the autoformat you want to use.

■ This area displays a sample of the autoformat you selected.

5 Click **OK** to confirm your change.

■ The form displays the new autoformat.

6 Click 🖫 to save your change.

ADD A PICTURE

You can add a
picture to your
form to make
the form more
appealing or to
help illustrate
your data.

You can add a picture
such as your company
logo, a colorful design or
a picture of your products.

If you want to display a
different picture for each
record, such as a picture
of each employee, see
page 116.

ADD A PICTURE

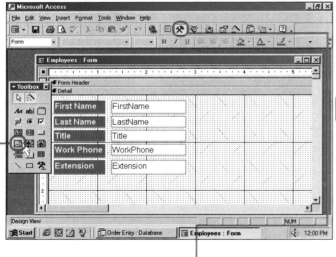

1 Display the form you
want to change in the
Design view. To change
the view, see page 158.

2 Click 🖾 to add a
picture to your form.

■ If 🖾 is not available,
click 🛠 to display the
Toolbox toolbar.

3 Click where you
want the top left corner
of the picture to appear
on your form.

■ The Insert Picture
dialog box appears.

Where can I find pictures that I can use in my forms?

You can use a drawing program to create your own pictures or use a scanner to scan pictures into your computer. You can also buy a collection of pictures, called clip art, at most computer stores. There are many pages on the Web that offer pictures that you can use for free.

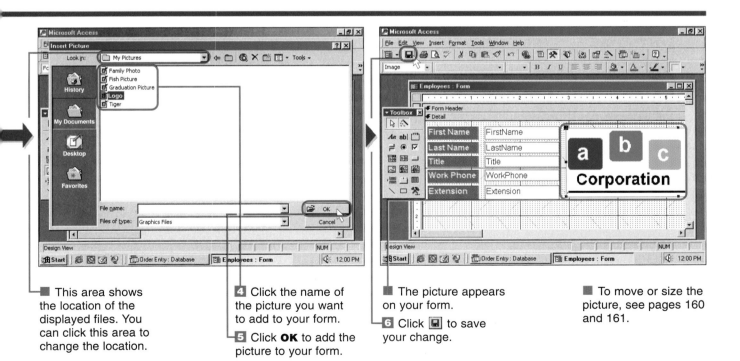

■ This area shows the location of the displayed files. You can click this area to change the location.

■ 4 Click the name of the picture you want to add to your form.

■ 5 Click **OK** to add the picture to your form.

■ The picture appears on your form.

■ 6 Click 🖫 to save your change.

■ To move or size the picture, see pages 160 and 161.

CHAPTER 8

Find Data

Would you like to learn how to find specific data in your database? This chapter teaches you how to find, sort and filter the data in your tables, forms and queries.

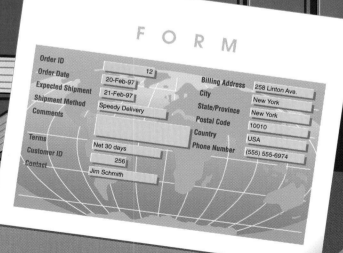

SORT RECORDS

You can change the order of records in a table, query or form. This can help you find, organize and analyze data.

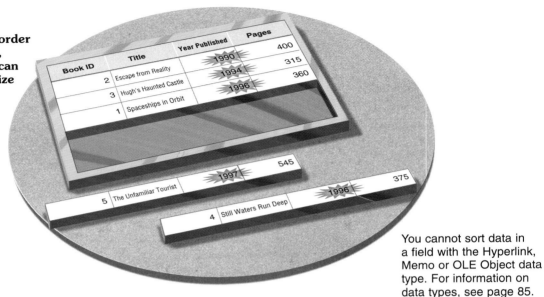

You cannot sort data in a field with the Hyperlink, Memo or OLE Object data type. For information on data types, see page 85.

SORT RECORDS

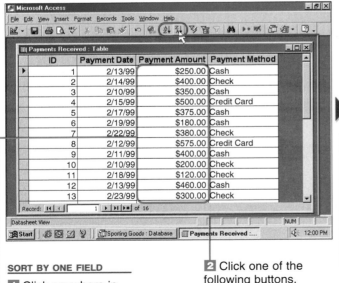

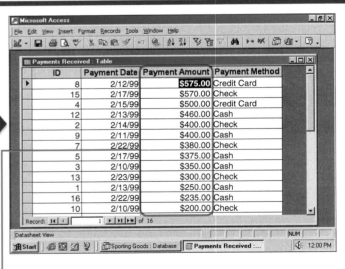

SORT BY ONE FIELD

1 Click anywhere in the field you want to use to sort the records.

2 Click one of the following buttons.

⍋ Sort A to Z, 1 to 9

⍒ Sort Z to A, 9 to 1

■ The records appear in the new order. In this example, the records are sorted by payment amount.

How do I remove a sort from my records?

After sorting records, you can return your records to the original sort order at any time.

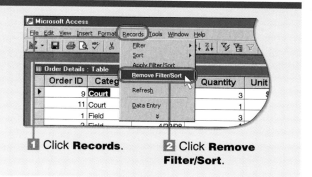

1 Click **Records**.

2 Click **Remove Filter/Sort**.

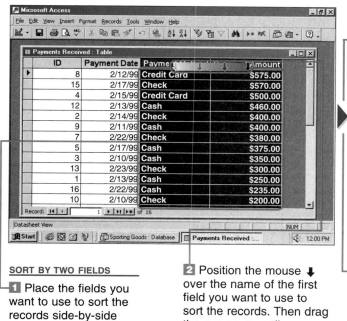

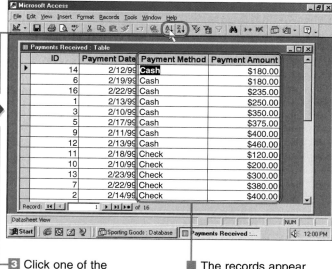

SORT BY TWO FIELDS

1 Place the fields you want to use to sort the records side-by-side and in the order you want to perform the sort. To rearrange fields, see page 45.

2 Position the mouse ↓ over the name of the first field you want to use to sort the records. Then drag the mouse ↓ until you highlight the second field.

3 Click one of the following buttons.

⭷ Sort A to Z, 1 to 9

⭷ Sort Z to A, 9 to 1

■ The records appear in the new order. In this example, the records are sorted by payment method. All records with the same payment method are also sorted by payment amount.

FIND DATA

You can search for data of interest in your database.

You can search for data in tables, queries and forms.

FIND DATA

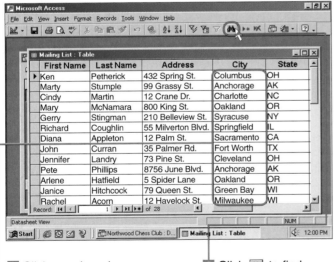

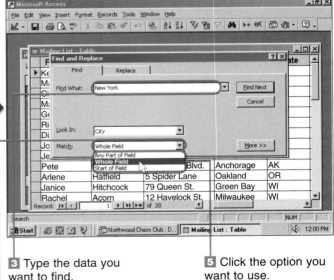

1 Click anywhere in the field containing the data you want to find.

2 Click 🔍 to find the data.

■ The Find and Replace dialog box appears.

3 Type the data you want to find.

4 To specify how you want to search for the data, click this area.

5 Click the option you want to use.

Note: For information on the available options, see the top of page 183.

? **How can I search for data in a field?**

Any Part of Field

Find data anywhere in the field. For example, **smith** finds **Smith**, **Smithson** and **Macsmith**.

Whole Field

Find data that is exactly the same. For example, **smith** finds **Smith**, but not **Smithson** or **Macsmith**.

Start of Field

Find data only at the beginning of the field. For example, **smith** finds **Smith** and **Smithson**, but not **Macsmith**.

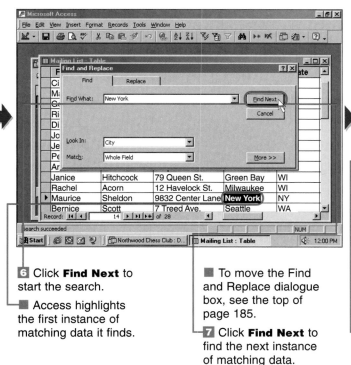

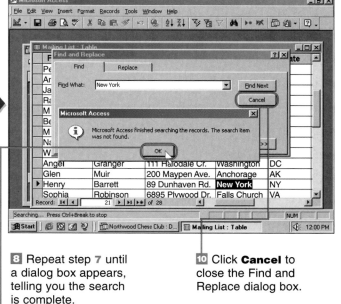

6 Click **Find Next** to start the search.

■ Access highlights the first instance of matching data it finds.

■ To move the Find and Replace dialogue box, see the top of page 185.

7 Click **Find Next** to find the next instance of matching data.

8 Repeat step **7** until a dialog box appears, telling you the search is complete.

9 Click **OK** to close the dialog box.

10 Click **Cancel** to close the Find and Replace dialog box.

REPLACE DATA

You can find and replace
data in a table, form or
query. The Replace feature
is useful when you want to
make the same change to
many records.

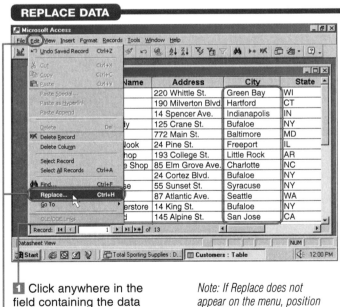

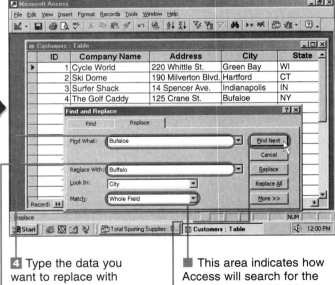

1 Click anywhere in the
field containing the data
you want to replace with
new data.

2 Click **Edit**.

3 Click **Replace**.

*Note: If Replace does not
appear on the menu, position
the mouse* ⬡ *over the bottom
of the menu to display all the
menu commands.*

■ The Find and Replace
dialog box appears.

4 Type the data you
want to replace with
new data.

5 Press the **Tab** key
and then type the
new data.

■ This area indicates how
Access will search for the
data. You can click this
area to change how Access
searches for the data. For
more information, see the
top of page 183.

6 Click **Find Next** to start
the search.

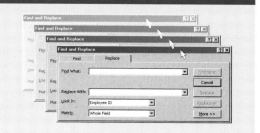

How do I move the Find and Replace dialog box?

To move the Find and Replace dialog box so you can clearly view the data in your table, position the mouse ⃕ over the title bar and then drag the dialog box to a new location.

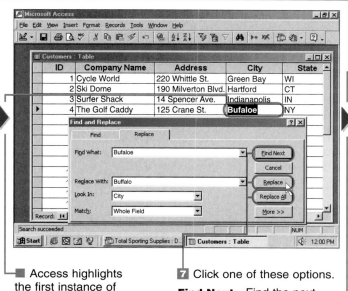

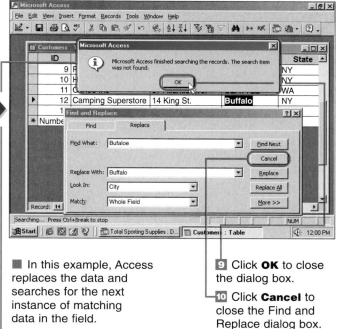

■ Access highlights the first instance of matching data in the field.

7 Click one of these options.

Find Next - Find the next instance of matching data in the field.

Replace - Replace the data.

Replace All - Replace the data and all other instances of matching data in the field.

■ In this example, Access replaces the data and searches for the next instance of matching data in the field.

8 Repeat step **7** until a dialog box appears, telling you the search is complete.

*Note: To end the search at any time, click **Cancel**.*

9 Click **OK** to close the dialog box.

10 Click **Cancel** to close the Find and Replace dialog box.

FILTER BY SELECTION

You can filter data in a table, form or query to display only records that contain data of interest. This can help you review and analyze information in your database.

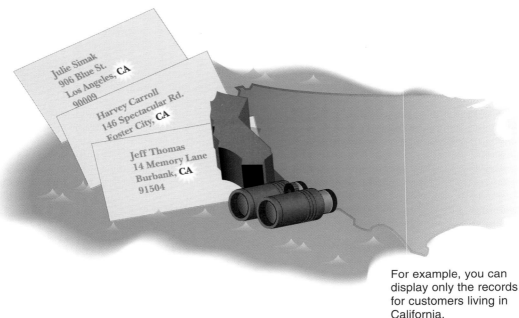

For example, you can display only the records for customers living in California.

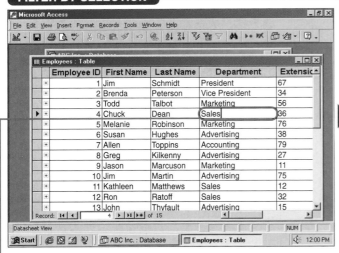

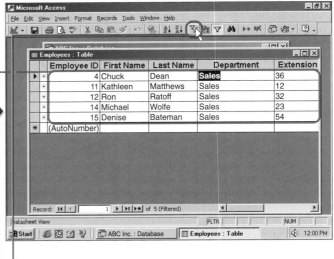

1 Click the data you want to use to filter the records.

Note: You can select data to change the way Access filters the records. For more information, see the top of page 187.

2 Click 🦋 to filter the records.

■ Access displays the records containing the data. All other records are hidden.

■ In this example, Access displays employees in the Sales department.

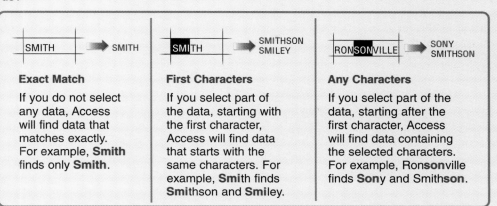

How can I change the way Access filters records?

You can select data to change the way Access filters records. To select data, see page 55.

Exact Match

If you do not select any data, Access will find data that matches exactly. For example, **Smith** finds only **Smith**.

First Characters

If you select part of the data, starting with the first character, Access will find data that starts with the same characters. For example, **Smith** finds **Smith**son and **Smi**ley.

Any Characters

If you select part of the data, starting after the first character, Access will find data containing the selected characters. For example, Ron**son**ville finds **Son**y and Smith**son**.

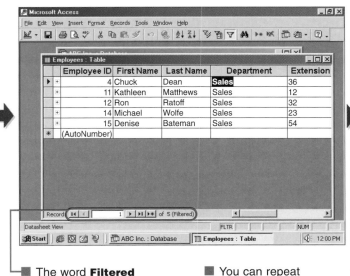

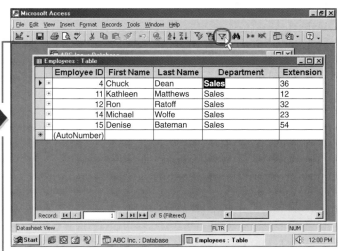

■ The word **Filtered** appears in this area to indicate that you are viewing filtered records.

■ You can repeat steps **1** and **2** to further filter the records.

3 When you finish reviewing the filtered records, click 🔽 to once again display all the records.

FILTER BY EXCLUSION

You can filter data in a table, form or query to hide records that contain specific data. This can help you review and analyze information of interest in your database.

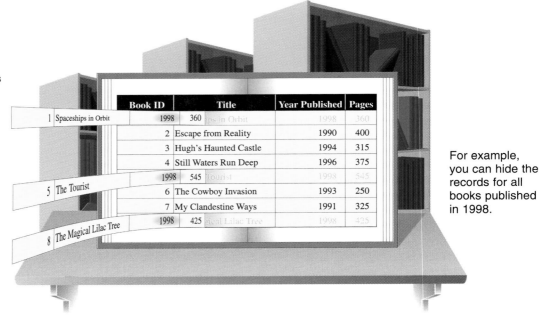

For example, you can hide the records for all books published in 1998.

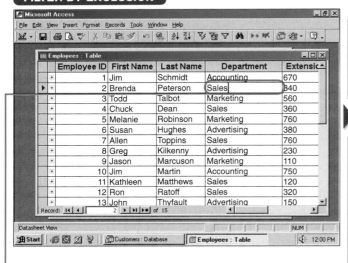

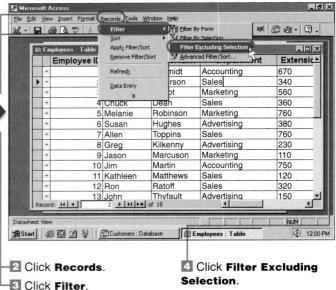

1 Click the data you want to use to filter the records. Access will hide all records that contain exactly the same data.

Note: You can select data to change the way Access filters the records. For more information, see the top of page 189.

2 Click **Records**.

3 Click **Filter**.

4 Click **Filter Excluding Selection**.

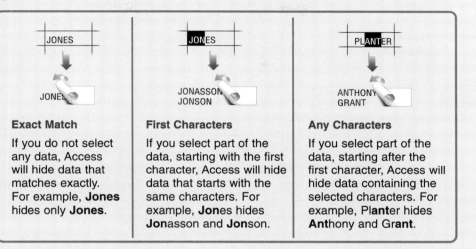

How can I change the way Access filters records?

You can select data to change the way Access filters records. To select data, see page 55.

Exact Match

If you do not select any data, Access will hide data that matches exactly. For example, **Jones** hides only **Jones**.

First Characters

If you select part of the data, starting with the first character, Access will hide data that starts with the same characters. For example, **Jon**es hides **Jon**asson and **Jon**son.

Any Characters

If you select part of the data, starting after the first character, Access will hide data containing the selected characters. For example, **Pl**ant**er** hides **Ant**hony and Gr**ant**.

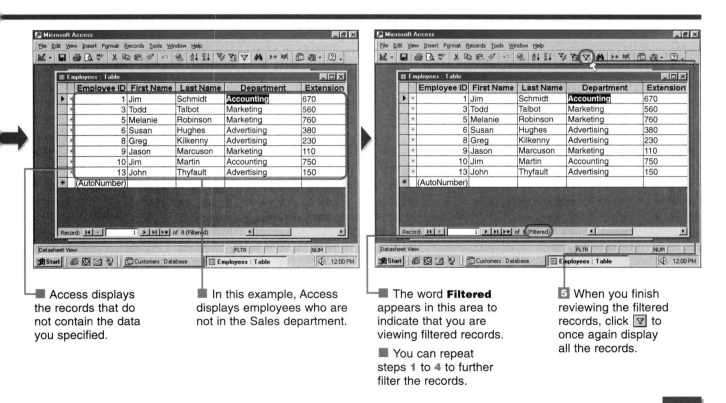

■ Access displays the records that do not contain the data you specified.

■ In this example, Access displays employees who are not in the Sales department.

─┐ The word **Filtered** appears in this area to indicate that you are viewing filtered records.

■ You can repeat steps **1** to **4** to further filter the records.

5 When you finish reviewing the filtered records, click ▼ to once again display all the records.

FILTER BY FORM

You can use the
Filter by Form
feature to find and
display records of
interest in a table,
form or query.

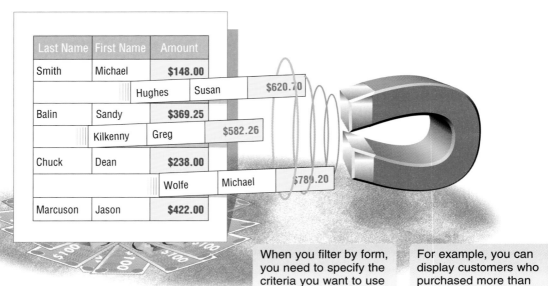

When you filter by form,
you need to specify the
criteria you want to use
to filter the records.

For example, you can
display customers who
purchased more than
$500.00 of your product.

FILTER BY FORM USING ONE CRITERIA

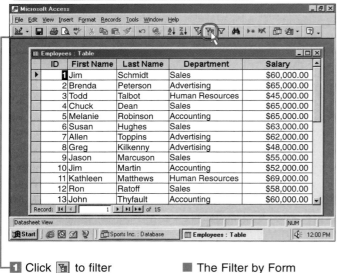

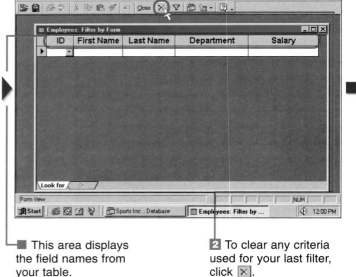

1 Click 🔽 to filter
by form.

■ The Filter by Form
window appears.

■ This area displays
the field names from
your table.

2 To clear any criteria
used for your last filter,
click ✕.

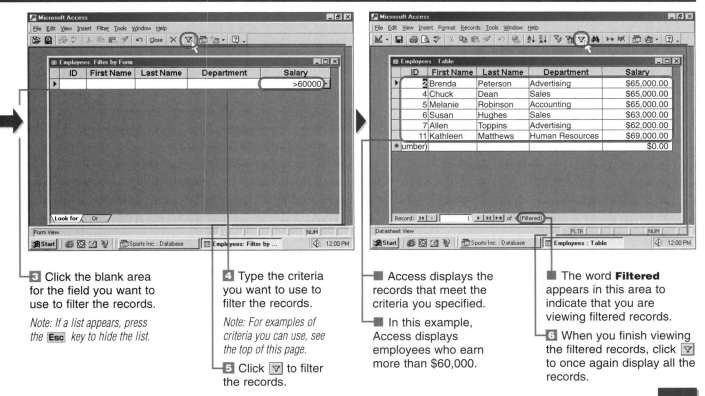

? **What criteria can I use to filter records?**

Here are some examples of criteria you can use to filter records. For more examples, see page 216.

Criteria	Description
<100	Less than 100
>100	Greater than 100
=Texas	Matches Texas
Between 100 and 200	Between 100 and 200
Like Mar*	Starts with "Mar"
Like *mar*	Contains "mar"

■3 Click the blank area for the field you want to use to filter the records.

Note: If a list appears, press the Esc *key to hide the list.*

■4 Type the criteria you want to use to filter the records.

Note: For examples of criteria you can use, see the top of this page.

■5 Click ▽ to filter the records.

■ Access displays the records that meet the criteria you specified.

■ In this example, Access displays employees who earn more than $60,000.

■ The word **Filtered** appears in this area to indicate that you are viewing filtered records.

■6 When you finish viewing the filtered records, click ▽ to once again display all the records.

FILTER BY FORM

You can use multiple criteria to filter your records. Access will find and display records that meet the criteria you specify.

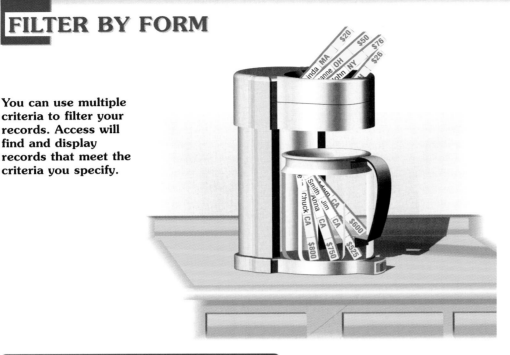

Criteria are conditions that identify which records you want to display. For examples of criteria, see page 191.

For example, you can display customers living in California who purchased more than $500.00 of your product.

FILTER BY FORM USING MULTIPLE CRITERIA

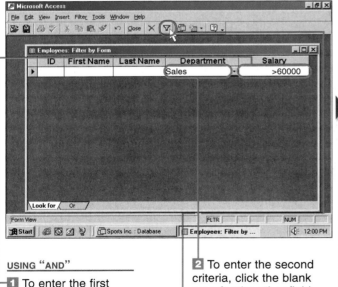

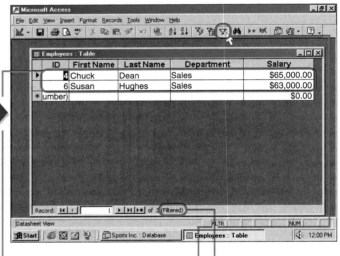

USING "AND"

1 To enter the first criteria you want to use to filter the records, perform steps 1 to 4 starting on page 190.

2 To enter the second criteria, click the blank area for the other field you want to use to filter the records. Then type the second criteria.

3 Click 🔽 to filter the records.

■ Access displays the records that meet both of the criteria you specified.

■ In this example, Access displays employees in the Sales department who earn more than $60,000.

■ The word **Filtered** appears in this area to indicate that you are viewing filtered records.

4 When you finish viewing the filtered records, click 🔽 to once again display all the records.

How can I use multiple criteria to filter records?

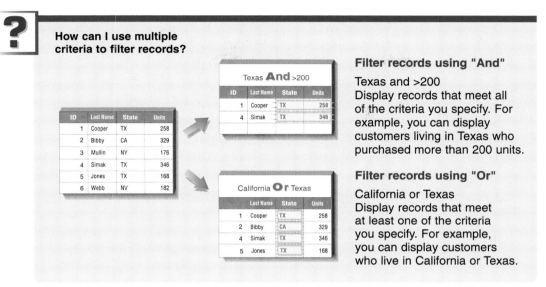

Filter records using "And"

Texas and >200
Display records that meet all of the criteria you specify. For example, you can display customers living in Texas who purchased more than 200 units.

Filter records using "Or"

California or Texas
Display records that meet at least one of the criteria you specify. For example, you can display customers who live in California or Texas.

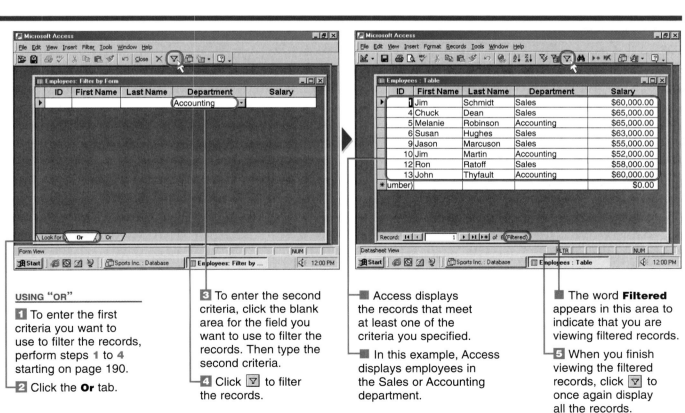

USING "OR"

1 To enter the first criteria you want to use to filter the records, perform steps 1 to 4 starting on page 190.

2 Click the **Or** tab.

3 To enter the second criteria, click the blank area for the field you want to use to filter the records. Then type the second criteria.

4 Click ▼ to filter the records.

■ Access displays the records that meet at least one of the criteria you specified.

■ In this example, Access displays employees in the Sales or Accounting department.

■ The word **Filtered** appears in this area to indicate that you are viewing filtered records.

5 When you finish viewing the filtered records, click ▼ to once again display all the records.

Which clients live in Florida?

Last Name	First Name	State
Davis	Sarah	Florida
Jones	Frank	Florida
Lee	Steven	Florida
Smith	Fred	Florida

Query

CHAPTER 9

Create Queries

Are you ready to create queries? This chapter teaches you how to create a query to find information of interest in your database.

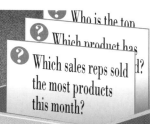

Who is the top
Which product has
Which sales reps sold d?
the most products
this month?

Queries

CREATE A QUERY IN THE DESIGN VIEW

You can create a query to find information of interest in your database.

Which wines were made before 1965?

When you create a query, you ask Access to find information that meets certain criteria or conditions.

When creating a query that uses more than one table, the tables should be related. For information on relationships, see page 128.

CREATE A QUERY IN THE DESIGN VIEW

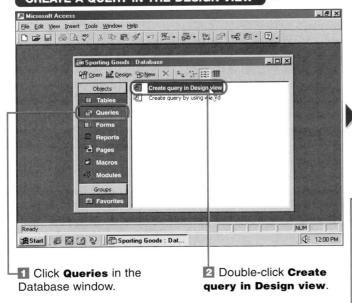

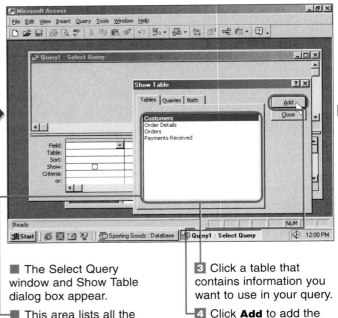

1 Click **Queries** in the Database window.

2 Double-click **Create query in Design view**.

■ The Select Query window and Show Table dialog box appear.

■ This area lists all the tables in your database.

3 Click a table that contains information you want to use in your query.

4 Click **Add** to add the table to your query.

How do I add another table to my query?

You can click 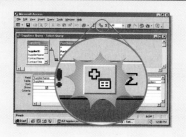 at any time to redisplay the Show Table dialog box and add another table to your query. To add another table to your query, perform steps **3** and **4** on page 196.

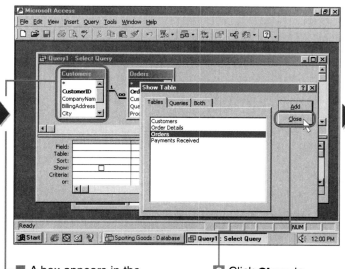

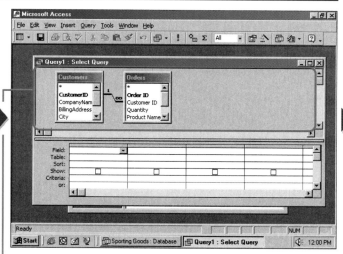

■ A box appears in the Select Query window, displaying the fields for the table you selected.

5 Repeat steps **3** and **4** for each table you want to use in your query.

6 Click **Close** to hide the Show Table dialog box.

■ Each box in this area displays the fields for one table.

Note: If the tables are related, Access displays a line joining the related fields. For information on relationships, see page 128.

■ If you accidentally added a table to the query, click the table and then press the `Delete` key. This removes the table from the query, but not from the database.

CONTINUED

CREATE A QUERY IN THE DESIGN VIEW

You can select which
fields you want to
include in your query.

Query Results

First Name	Last Name	Phone Number

For example, you may
want to include only the
name and phone number
of each customer.

CREATE A QUERY IN THE DESIGN VIEW (CONTINUED)

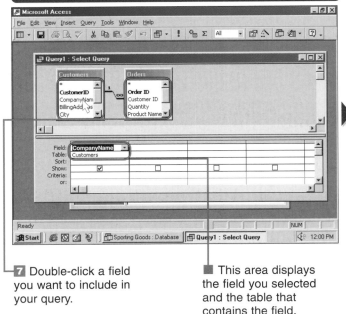

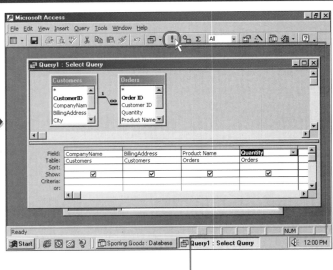

7 Double-click a field
you want to include in
your query.

■ This area displays
the field you selected
and the table that
contains the field.

8 Repeat step **7** for
each field you want to
include in your query.

*Note: To quickly select all
the fields in a table see
page 212.*

RUN THE QUERY

1 Click ! to run
the query.

Does a query store data?

No. When you save a query, Access only saves the design of the query. Each time you run a query, Access gathers the most current data from your database to determine the results of the query. For example, you can run the same query each month to display the top sales representatives for the month.

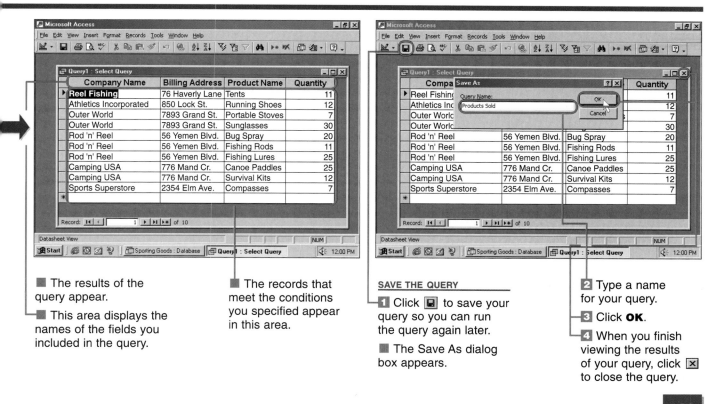

■ The results of the query appear.

■ This area displays the names of the fields you included in the query.

■ The records that meet the conditions you specified appear in this area.

SAVE THE QUERY

1 Click 🖬 to save your query so you can run the query again later.

■ The Save As dialog box appears.

2 Type a name for your query.

3 Click **OK**.

4 When you finish viewing the results of your query, click ⊠ to close the query.

CREATE A QUERY USING THE SIMPLE QUERY WIZARD

You can use the Simple
Query Wizard to create a
query. A query allows you
to find information of
interest in your database.

The Simple Query Wizard
will ask you a series of
questions and then set
up a query based on your
answers.

CREATE A QUERY USING THE SIMPLE QUERY WIZARD

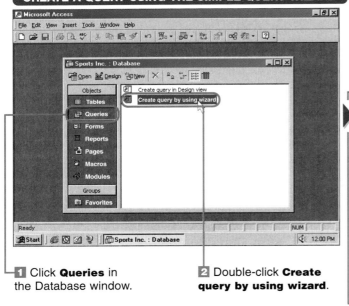

■1 Click **Queries** in
the Database window.

■2 Double-click **Create
query by using wizard**.

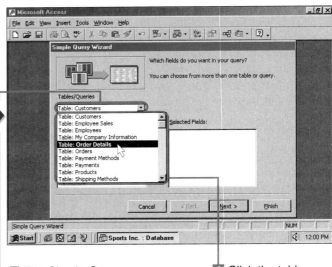

■ The Simple Query
Wizard appears.

■3 Click ⏷ in this
area to select the
table containing the
fields you want to
include in your query.

■4 Click the table
containing the fields.

?

Which tables in my database can I use to create a query?

You can use any table in your database to create a query. To create a query using data from more than one table, relationships must exist between the tables. For information on relationships, see page 128.

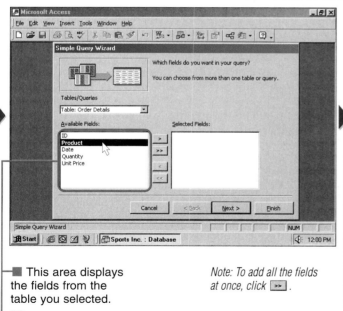

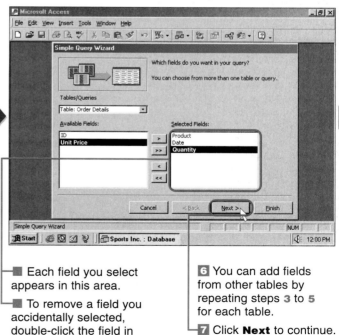

■ This area displays the fields from the table you selected.

5 Double-click each field you want to include in your query.

Note: To add all the fields at once, click ⏩ *.*

■ Each field you select appears in this area.

■ To remove a field you accidentally selected, double-click the field in this area.

Note: To remove all the fields at once, click ⏪ *.*

6 You can add fields from other tables by repeating steps 3 to 5 for each table.

7 Click **Next** to continue.

CONTINUED

CREATE A QUERY USING THE SIMPLE QUERY WIZARD

If your query contains information that Access can summarize, you can choose to show all the records or just the summary in the results of your query.

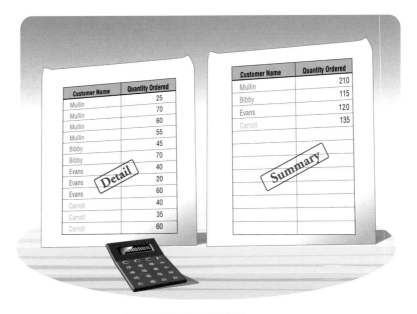

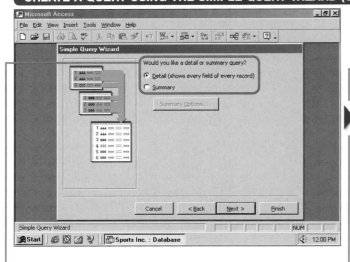

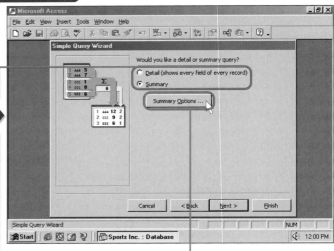

■ If your query contains information that Access can summarize, you can choose how you want to display the information in the results of your query.

Note: If this screen does not appear, skip to step 16 on page 205 to continue creating your query.

■8 Click the way you want to display the information in the results of your query (○ changes to ⊙). If you select **Detail**, skip to step 15 on page 204.

9 Click **Summary Options** to select how you want to summarize the information.

■ The Summary Options dialog box appears.

What calculations can I perform to summarize data in my query?

Sum
Add the values.

Avg
Calculate the average value.

Min
Find the smallest value.

Max
Find the largest value.

Count records
Count the number of records.

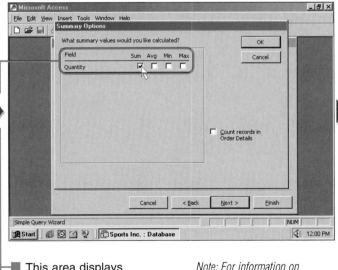

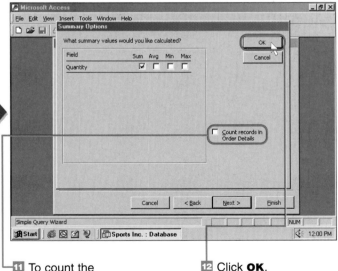

■ This area displays the fields you can summarize.

10 Click the box (☐) for each calculation you want to perform (☐ changes to ☑).

Note: For information on the calculations you can perform, see the top of this page.

11 To count the number of records in each group that Access summarizes, click this option (☐ changes to ☑).

12 Click **OK**.

CONTINUED

CREATE A QUERY USING THE SIMPLE QUERY WIZARD

If a field in your query contains dates, you can specify the way you want to group the dates.

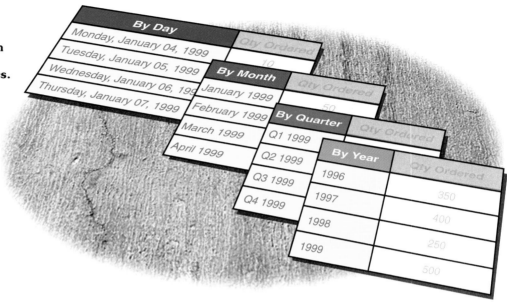

CREATE A QUERY USING THE SIMPLE QUERY WIZARD (CONTINUED)

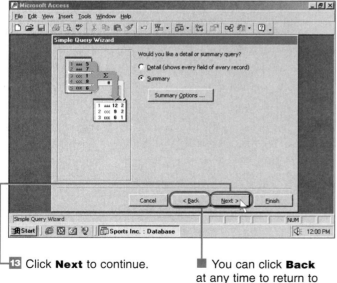

■13 Click **Next** to continue.

■ You can click **Back** at any time to return to a previous step and change your answers.

■ This screen appears if a field in your query contains dates.

■14 Click the way you want to group the dates in your query (○ changes to ⊙).

■15 Click **Next** to continue.

Why didn't my query summarize data the way I expected?

When creating a query, make sure you only include the fields you need. For example, to determine the total number of units sold by each employee, you should only include the Employee and Units Sold fields.

Employee	Units Sold
Abbott	8,800
Carey	7,400
Davis	3,900
Jones	3,700
Lance	7,700
McMillan	8,800

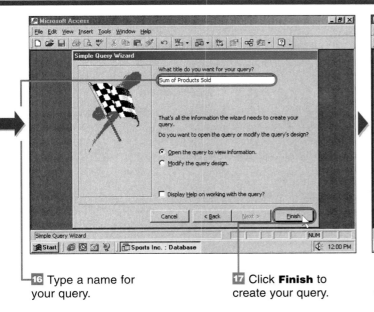

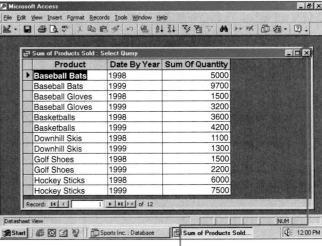

16 Type a name for your query.

17 Click **Finish** to create your query.

■ The results of your query appear.

■ When you finish viewing the results of your query, click ☒ to close the query.

Note: You can use the Design view to make changes to your query. To display your query in the Design view, see page 206.

CHANGE VIEW OF QUERY

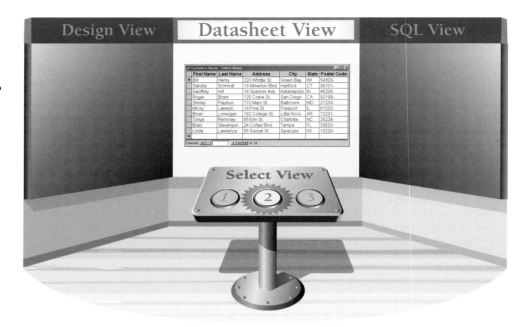

Design View | Datasheet View | SQL View

There are three ways you can view a query. Each view allows you to perform different tasks.

Select View
① ② ③

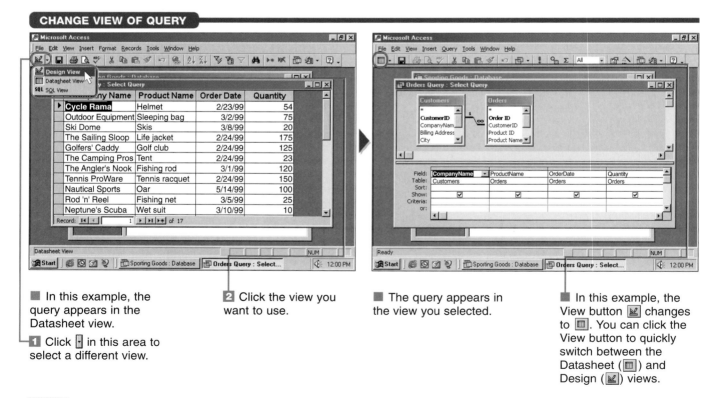

■ In this example, the query appears in the Datasheet view.

1 Click ● in this area to select a different view.

2 Click the view you want to use.

■ The query appears in the view you selected.

■ In this example, the View button 🔲 changes to 🔲. You can click the View button to quickly switch between the Datasheet (🔲) and Design (🔲) views.

206

THE QUERY VIEWS

Design View

The Design view allows you to plan your query. You can use this view to tell Access what data you want to find, where Access can find the data and how you want to display the results.

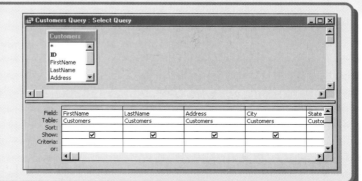

Datasheet View

The Datasheet view displays the results of your query. The field names appear across the top of the window. Each row shows the information for one record that meets the criteria or conditions you specified.

SQL View

SQL (Structured Query Language) is a computer language. When you create a query, Access creates the SQL statements that describe your query. The SQL view displays the SQL statements for your query. You do not need to use this view to effectively use Access.

```
SELECT Customers.FirstName, Customers.LastName, Customers.Address, Customers.City, Customers.State,
Customers.PostalCode
FROM Customers;
```

OPEN A QUERY

You can open a query to display the results of the query on your screen. This lets you review and make changes to the query.

Each time you open a query, Access will use the most current data from your database to determine the results of the query.

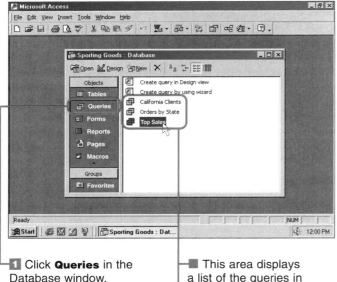

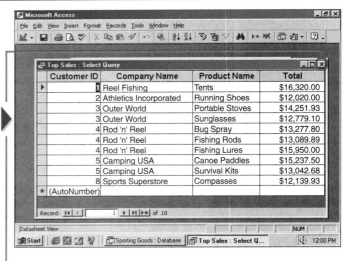

1 Click **Queries** in the Database window.

■ This area displays a list of the queries in your database.

2 Double-click the query you want to open.

■ The query opens. You can now review the results of the query.

■ When you finish working with the query, click ☒ to close the query.

■ A dialog box will appear if you did not save changes you made to the design of the query. Click **Yes** to save the changes.

You can change the
order of fields in a
query. Rearranging
fields in a query will
affect the order that
the fields appear in
the query results.

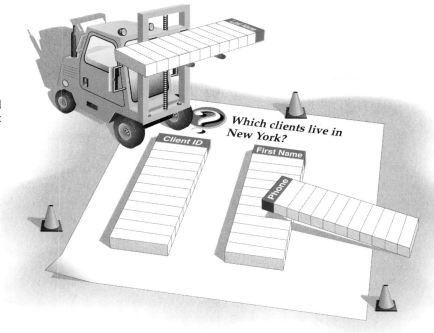

Which clients live in
New York?

Client ID

First Name

Phone

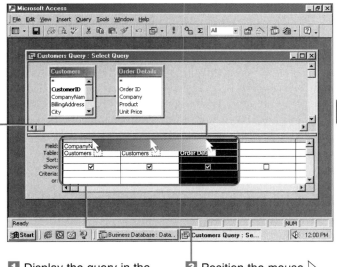

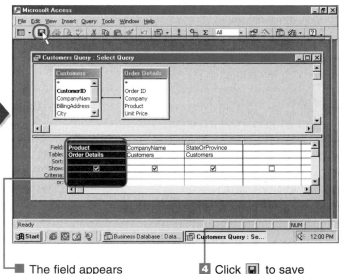

1 Display the query in the
Design view. To change the
view, see page 206.

2 Position the mouse ⊾
directly above the field you
want to move (⊾ changes
to ↓) and then click to
select the field.

3 Position the mouse ⊾
directly above the selected
field and then drag the
field to a new location.

*Note: A thick line shows where
the field will appear.*

■ The field appears
in the new location.

4 Click 🔲 to save
your change.

DELETE A FIELD

You can delete a field
you no longer need
from your query.

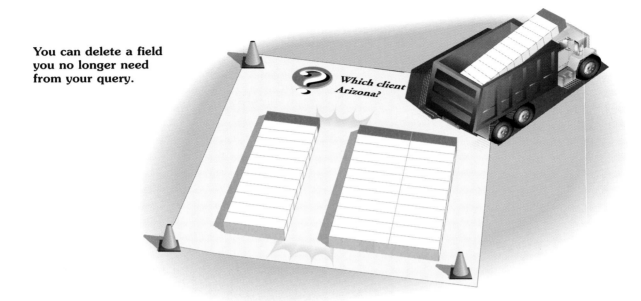

Which client
Arizona?

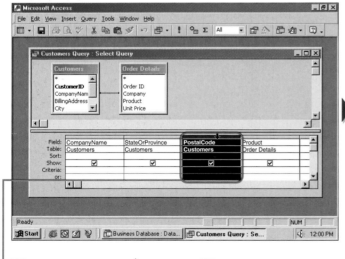

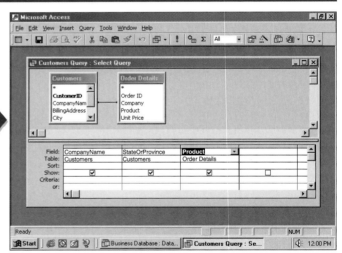

1 Position the mouse ⬡
directly above the field you
want to delete (⬡ changes
to ↓) and then click to
select the field.

2 Press the **Delete** key.

■ The field disappears
from your query.

You can hide a field used in a query. Hiding a field is useful when you need a field to find information in your database, but do not want the field to appear in the results of your query.

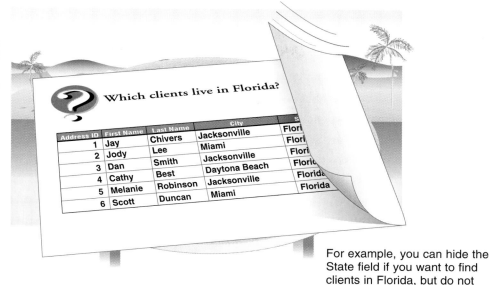

Which clients live in Florida?

Address ID	First Name	Last Name	City	S...
1	Jay	Chivers	Jacksonville	Flori...
2	Jody	Lee	Miami	Flori...
3	Dan	Smith	Jacksonville	Flori...
4	Cathy	Best	Daytona Beach	Flori...
5	Melanie	Robinson	Jacksonville	Florida...
6	Scott	Duncan	Miami	Florida...

For example, you can hide the State field if you want to find clients in Florida, but do not want the State field to appear in the query results.

HIDE A FIELD

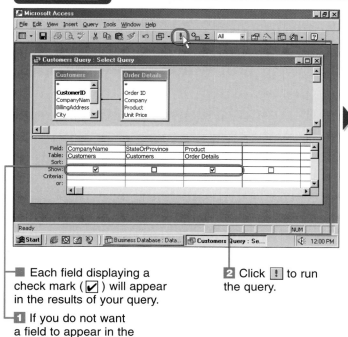

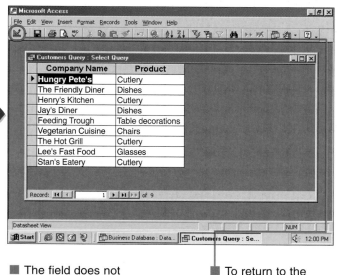

■ Each field displaying a check mark (☑) will appear in the results of your query.

1 If you do not want a field to appear in the results of your query, click the **Show** box for the field (☑ changes to ☐).

2 Click ! to run the query.

■ The field does not appear in the results of the query.

■ To return to the Design view, click ☒.

SELECT ALL FIELDS

When creating a query, you can select all the fields in a table at once. This allows you to quickly add all the fields in the table to your query.

Recipe ID	Recipe Name	Meal	Vegetarian
1	Chicken Stir-fry	Dinner	No
2	Omelet	Breakfast	Yes
3	Veggie Pizza	Lunch	Yes
4	Lasagna	Dinner	No
5	Pancakes	Breakfast	Yes
6	Pork Chops	Dinner	No
7	Garden Salad	Lunch	Yes

USING THE TABLE HEADING

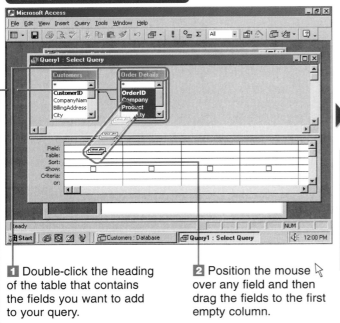

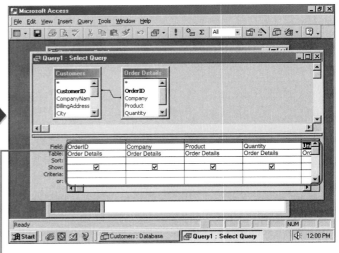

1 Double-click the heading of the table that contains the fields you want to add to your query.

■ All the fields in the table are selected.

2 Position the mouse over any field and then drag the fields to the first empty column.

■ Each field from the table appears in its own column.

212

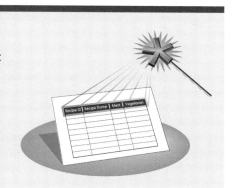

Why would I use the asterisk (∗) to select all the fields in a table?

You should use the asterisk to select all the fields in a table if you plan to later add fields to the table. When you add a field to the table, Access will automatically include the new field in the query. If you do not use the asterisk and you add a field to the table, you must manually add the new field to the query.

USING THE ASTERISK

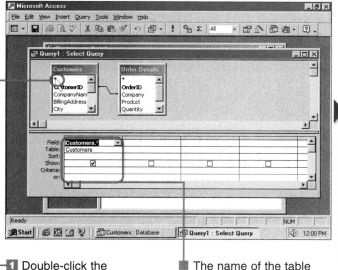

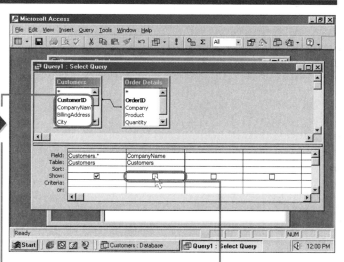

1 Double-click the asterisk (∗) in the table that contains the fields you want to add to your query.

◼ The name of the table followed by an asterisk (∗) appears in a column. All the fields in the table will appear in the results of your query.

2 To set criteria or other options for a specific field in the table, double-click the field to place the field in a separate column.

Note: To set criteria, see page 215.

3 Click the **Show** box for the field (☑ changes to ☐) to ensure the field will not appear twice in the results of your query.

SORT QUERY RESULTS

You can sort the results of a query to better organize the results. This can help you quickly find information of interest.

Sort "scores" in ascending order

There are two ways you can sort the results of a query.

Ascending

Sorts A to Z, 1 to 9

Descending

Sorts Z to A, 9 to 1

SORT QUERY RESULTS

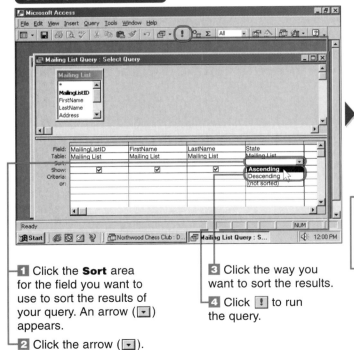

1 Click the **Sort** area for the field you want to use to sort the results of your query. An arrow (▾) appears.

2 Click the arrow (▾).

3 Click the way you want to sort the results.

4 Click ! to run the query.

■ The records appear in the order you specified. In this example, the records are sorted alphabetically by state.

■ To return to the Design view, click ⬚.

■ To no longer use a field to sort the query results, repeat steps **1** to **3**, except select **(not sorted)** in step **3**.

You can use criteria to find specific records in your database. Criteria are conditions that identify which records you want to find.

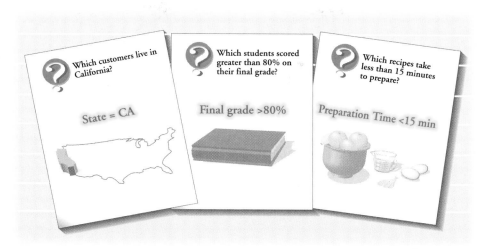

Which customers live in California?

State = CA

Which students scored greater than 80% on their final grade?

Final grade >80%

Which recipes take less than 15 minutes to prepare?

Preparation Time <15 min

For example, you can use criteria to find customers who live in California.

USING CRITERIA

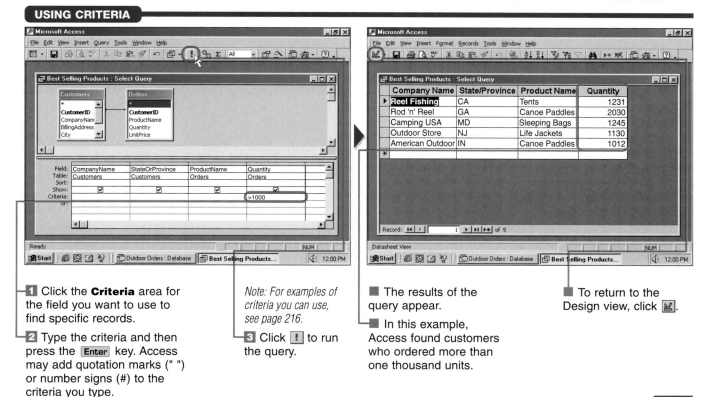

1 Click the **Criteria** area for the field you want to use to find specific records.

2 Type the criteria and then press the **Enter** key. Access may add quotation marks (" ") or number signs (#) to the criteria you type.

Note: For examples of criteria you can use, see page 216.

3 Click ! to run the query.

■ The results of the query appear.

■ In this example, Access found customers who ordered more than one thousand units.

■ To return to the Design view, click ⊠.

EXAMPLES OF CRITERIA

Here are examples of criteria that you can use to find records in your database. Criteria are conditions that identify the records you want to find.

Exact matches

=100   Finds the number 100.

=California   Finds the word California.

=1/5/99   Finds the date 5-Jan-99.

Note: You can leave out the equal sign (=) when searching for an exact match.

Less than

<100
Finds numbers less than 100.

<N
Finds text starting with the letters A to M.

<1/5/99
Finds dates before 5-Jan-99.

Less than or equal to

<=100   Finds numbers less than or equal to 100.

<=N   Finds the letter N and text starting with the letters A to M.

<=1/5/99   Finds dates on and before 5-Jan-99.

Greater than

>100
Finds numbers greater than 100.

>N
Finds text starting with the letters N to Z.

>1/5/99
Finds dates after 5-Jan-99.

Greater than or equal to

>=100   Finds numbers greater than or equal to 100.

>=N   Finds the letter N and text starting with the letters N to Z.

>=1/5/99   Finds dates on and after 5-Jan-99.

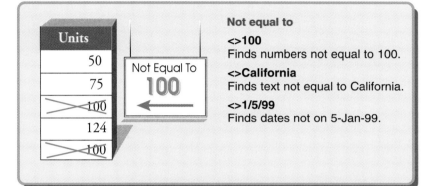

Not equal to

<>100
Finds numbers not equal to 100.

<>California
Finds text not equal to California.

<>1/5/99
Finds dates not on 5-Jan-99.

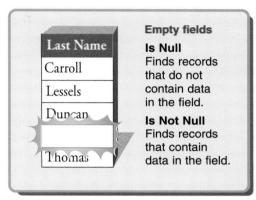

Empty fields

Is Null
Finds records that do not contain data in the field.

Is Not Null
Finds records that contain data in the field.

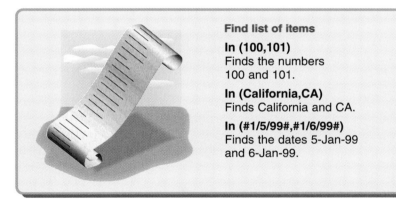

Find list of items

In (100,101)
Finds the numbers 100 and 101.

In (California,CA)
Finds California and CA.

In (#1/5/99#,#1/6/99#)
Finds the dates 5-Jan-99 and 6-Jan-99.

Between...And...

Between 100 And 200
Finds numbers from 100 to 200.

Between A And D
Finds the letter D and text starting with the letters A to C.

Between 1/5/99 And 1/15/99
Finds dates on and between 5-Jan-99 and 15-Jan-99.

Wildcards

The asterisk (*) wildcard represents one or more characters. The question mark (?) wildcard represents a single character.

Like Br*   Finds text starting with **Br**, such as **Br**enda and **Br**own.

Like *ar*   Finds text containing **ar**, such as **Ar**nold and M**ar**c.

Like Wend?   Finds 5-letter words starting with **Wend**, such as **Wend**i and **Wend**y.

RENAME A QUERY

You can change the name of a query to better describe the information the query displays.

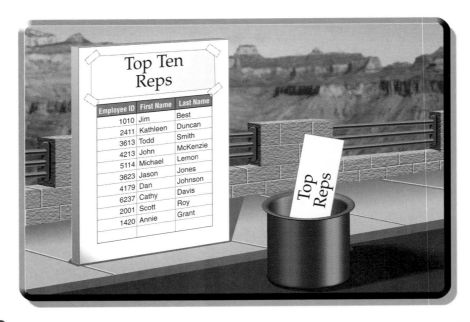

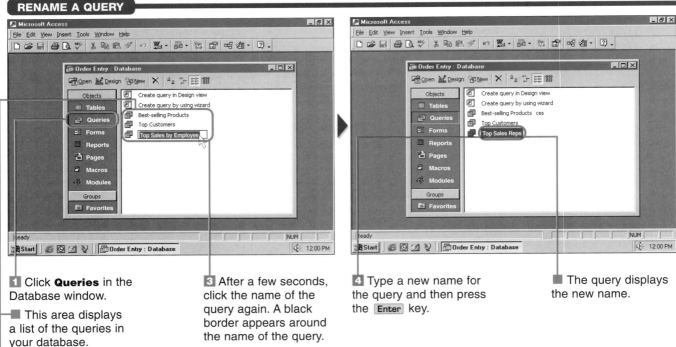

1 Click **Queries** in the Database window.

■ This area displays a list of the queries in your database.

2 Click the name of the query you want to rename.

3 After a few seconds, click the name of the query again. A black border appears around the name of the query.

Note: If you accidentally double-click the name of the query, the query will open.

4 Type a new name for the query and then press the **Enter** key.

■ The query displays the new name.

If you no longer
need a query, you
can permanently
delete the query
from your database.

Top Ten
Reps

Employee ID	First Name	Last Name
1010	Jim	Best
2411	Kathleen	Duncan
3613	Todd	Smith
4213	John	McKenzie

DELETE A QUERY

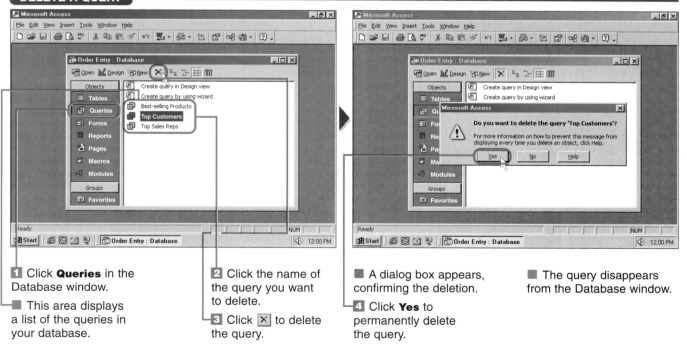

■1 Click **Queries** in the
Database window.

■ This area displays
a list of the queries in
your database.

■2 Click the name of
the query you want
to delete.

■3 Click X to delete
the query.

■ A dialog box appears,
confirming the deletion.

■4 Click **Yes** to
permanently delete
the query.

■ The query disappears
from the Database window.

DISPLAY TOP OR BOTTOM VALUES

You can have Access display only the top or bottom values in the results of your query.

TOP 5 ORDERS

Company	Product	Total Ordered
Sports R Us	Skis	898
Golf & Skis Inc.	Ski Pants	742
Ski Ski Ski!	Racing Helmet	616
#1 Skis Inc.	Ski Goggles	425
Downhill Plus	Ski Boots	306

For example, you can display the top five orders or the ten lowest-selling products.

DISPLAY TOP OR BOTTOM VALUES

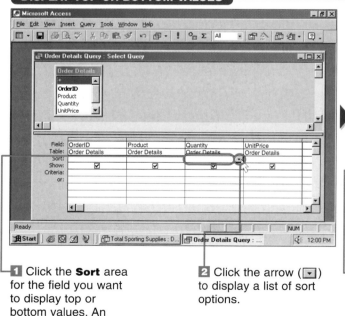

1 Click the **Sort** area for the field you want to display top or bottom values. An arrow ( ) appears.

2 Click the arrow ( ) to display a list of sort options.

3 Click the way you want to sort the records.

Ascending
Display bottom values

Descending
Display top values

4 Click in this area to specify the number or percentage of records you want to display in the results of your query.

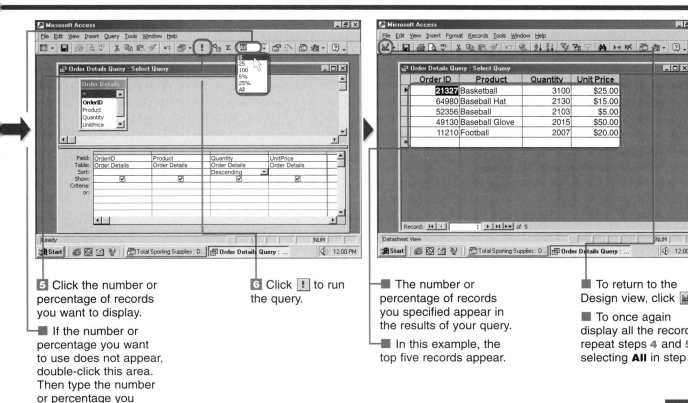

Why didn't the results of my query appear the way I expected?

If you have sorted other fields in your query, Access may not display top or bottom values properly. To remove a sort from a field, perform steps **1** to **3** on page 222, except select **(not sorted)** in step **3**.

? Find Top 5 Products Sold

Product	Units Sold
Superior Race Top	4,068
Extreme Socks	3,749
Baldwin Shorts	2,562
Stay Cool Hat	2,378
Dual Purpose Shades	1,584

5 Click the number or percentage of records you want to display.

■ If the number or percentage you want to use does not appear, double-click this area. Then type the number or percentage you want to use.

6 Click **!** to run the query.

■ The number or percentage of records you specified appear in the results of your query.

■ In this example, the top five records appear.

■ To return to the Design view, click 📈.

■ To once again display all the records, repeat steps **4** and **5**, selecting **All** in step **5**.

USING MULTIPLE CRITERIA

You can use multiple criteria to find records in your database. Using the "Or" condition allows you to find records that meet at least one of the criteria you specify.

Criteria are conditions that identify which records you want to find. For examples of criteria, see page 216.

USING "OR" WITH ONE FIELD

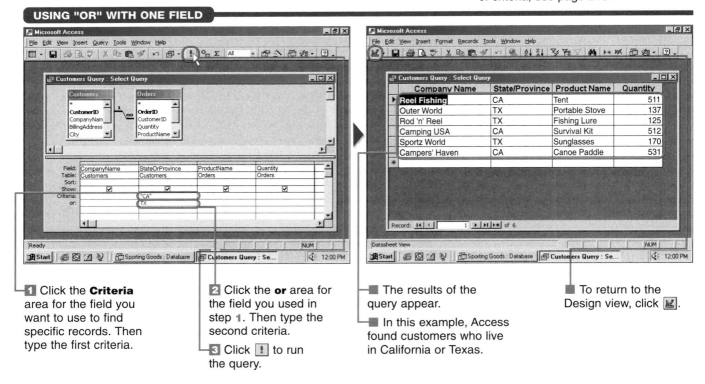

■1 Click the **Criteria** area for the field you want to use to find specific records. Then type the first criteria.

■2 Click the **or** area for the field you used in step 1. Then type the second criteria.

■3 Click [!] to run the query.

■ The results of the query appear.

■ In this example, Access found customers who live in California or Texas.

■ To return to the Design view, click [M].

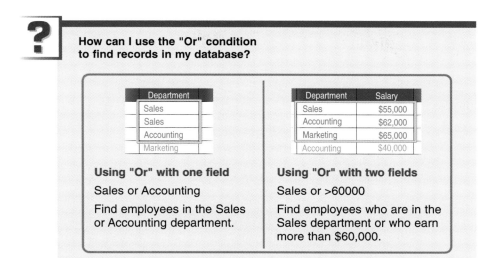

How can I use the "Or" condition to find records in my database?

Department
Sales
Sales
Accounting
Marketing

Department	Salary
Sales	$55,000
Accounting	$62,000
Marketing	$65,000
Accounting	$40,000

Using "Or" with one field

Sales or Accounting

Find employees in the Sales or Accounting department.

Using "Or" with two fields

Sales or >60000

Find employees who are in the Sales department or who earn more than $60,000.

USING "OR" WITH TWO FIELDS

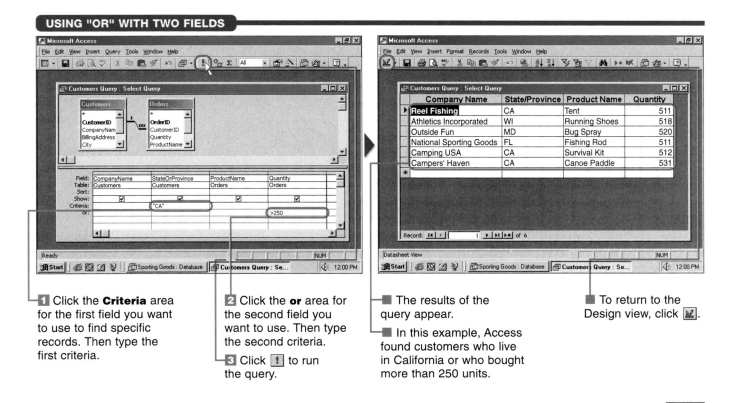

■1 Click the **Criteria** area for the first field you want to use to find specific records. Then type the first criteria.

■2 Click the **or** area for the second field you want to use. Then type the second criteria.

■3 Click ![run] to run the query.

■ The results of the query appear.

■ In this example, Access found customers who live in California or who bought more than 250 units.

■ To return to the Design view, click ![design].

USING MULTIPLE CRITERIA

You can use multiple criteria to find records in your database. Using the "And" condition allows you to find records that meet all of the criteria you specify.

Recipe ID	Recipe Name	Calories/Serving	Vegetarian
1	Chicken Stir-fry	180	No
2	Omelet	200	Yes
3	Veggie		
4	Lasa		
5	Panc		

Find: Vegetarian
And
Under 225 Calories

Recipe ID	Recipe Name	Calories/Serving	Vegetarian
2	Omelet	200	Yes
3	Veggie Pizza	215	Yes
5	Pancakes	180	Yes

Criteria are conditions that identify which records you want to find. For examples of criteria, see page 216.

USING "AND" WITH ONE FIELD

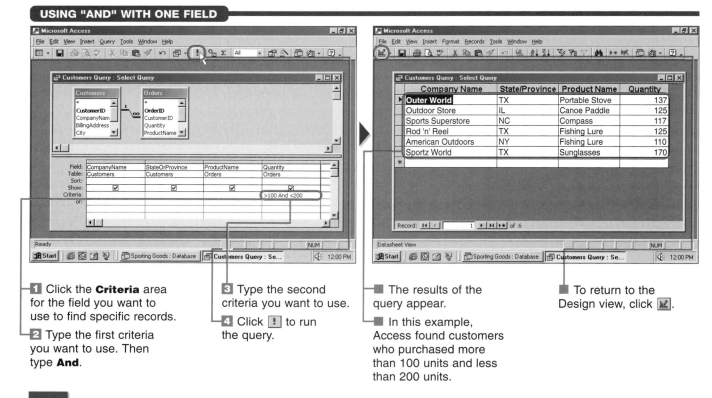

■1 Click the **Criteria** area for the field you want to use to find specific records.

■2 Type the first criteria you want to use. Then type **And**.

■3 Type the second criteria you want to use.

■4 Click ! to run the query.

■ The results of the query appear.

■ In this example, Access found customers who purchased more than 100 units and less than 200 units.

■ To return to the Design view, click 🔲.

226

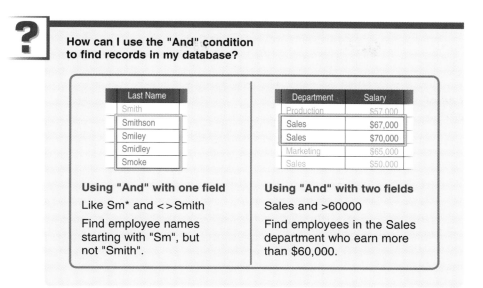

How can I use the "And" condition to find records in my database?

Last Name
Smith
Smithson
Smiley
Smidley
Smoke

Department	Salary
Production	$57,000
Sales	$67,000
Sales	$70,000
Marketing	$65,000
Sales	$50,000

Using "And" with one field

Like Sm* and <>Smith

Find employee names starting with "Sm", but not "Smith".

Using "And" with two fields

Sales and >60000

Find employees in the Sales department who earn more than $60,000.

USING "AND" WITH TWO FIELDS

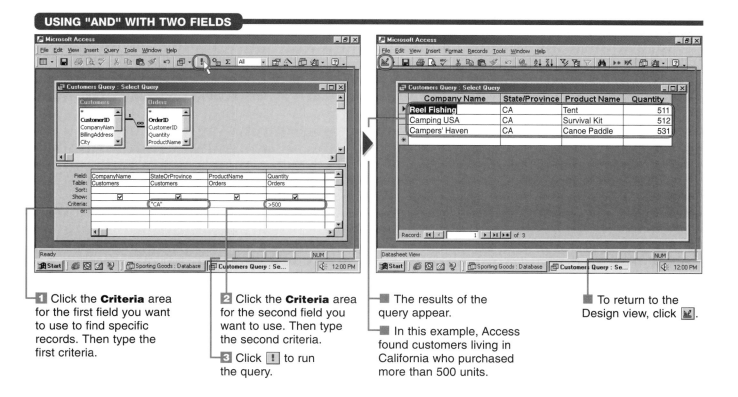

1 Click the **Criteria** area for the first field you want to use to find specific records. Then type the first criteria.

2 Click the **Criteria** area for the second field you want to use. Then type the second criteria.

3 Click ! to run the query.

■ The results of the query appear.

■ In this example, Access found customers living in California who purchased more than 500 units.

■ To return to the Design view, click ■.

PERFORM CALCULATIONS

You can perform calculations on each record in your database. You can then review and analyze the results.

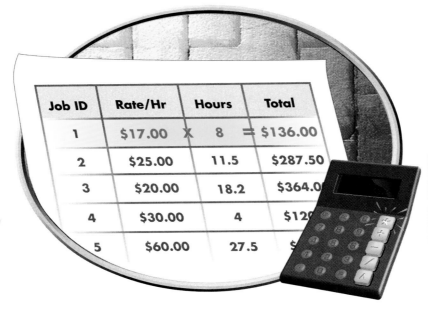

Job ID	Rate/Hr	Hours	Total
1	$17.00 X	8 =	$136.00
2	$25.00	11.5	$287.50
3	$20.00	18.2	$364.0
4	$30.00	4	$12
5	$60.00	27.5	$

You can use these operators to perform calculations.

+ Add
- Subtract
* Multiply
/ Divide
^ Raise to a power

PERFORM CALCULATIONS

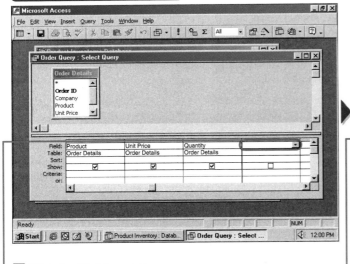

1 Click the **Field** area in the first empty column.

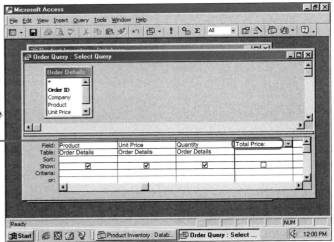

2 Type a name for the field that will display the results of the calculations, followed by a colon (:). Then press the **Spacebar** to leave a blank space.

How do I enter an expression to perform a calculation?

[Orders]![Quantity]*[Orders]![Price]

To enter a field in an expression, type the name of the table containing the field in square brackets (**[Orders]**) followed by an exclamation mark (**!**). Then type the field name in square brackets (**[Quantity]**). Make sure you type the table and field names exactly.

Orders		
Quantity	Price	Total
100	$42	$4,200
50	$50	$2,500
70	$75	$5,250
30	$36	$1,080
90	$45	$4,050

[Quantity]*[Price]

If a field exists in only one table, you do not need to enter the table name.

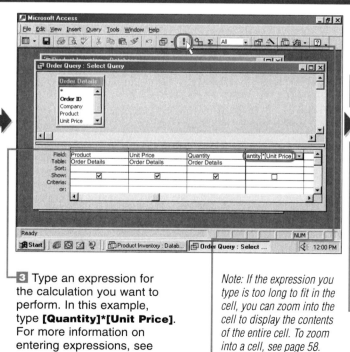

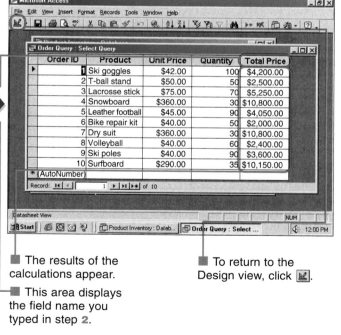

3 Type an expression for the calculation you want to perform. In this example, type **[Quantity]*[Unit Price]**. For more information on entering expressions, see the top of this page.

Note: If the expression you type is too long to fit in the cell, you can zoom into the cell to display the contents of the entire cell. To zoom into a cell, see page 58.

4 Click **!** to run the query.

■ The results of the calculations appear.

■ This area displays the field name you typed in step **2**.

■ To return to the Design view, click ▨.

CHANGE FORMAT OF CALCULATED DATA

After performing calculations in your query, you can change the way calculated data appears in the results of the query.

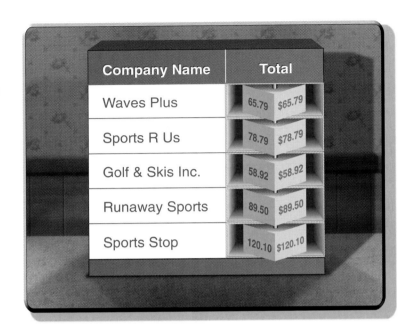

Company Name	Total
Waves Plus	65.79 $65.79
Sports R Us	78.79 $78.79
Golf & Skis Inc.	58.92 $58.92
Runaway Sports	89.50 $89.50
Sports Stop	120.10 $120.10

To perform calculations in your query, see page 228.

CHANGE FORMAT OF CALCULATED DATA

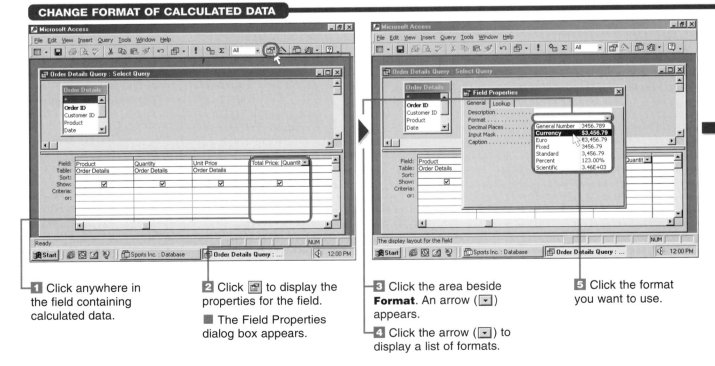

1 Click anywhere in the field containing calculated data.

2 Click 🖼 to display the properties for the field.

■ The Field Properties dialog box appears.

3 Click the area beside **Format**. An arrow (▼) appears.

4 Click the arrow (▼) to display a list of formats.

5 Click the format you want to use.

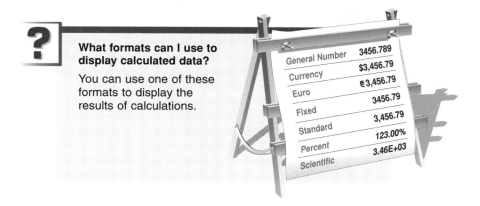

What formats can I use to display calculated data?

You can use one of these formats to display the results of calculations.

General Number	3456.789
Currency	$3,456.79
Euro	€3,456.79
Fixed	3456.79
Standard	3,456.79
Percent	123.00%
Scientific	3.46E+03

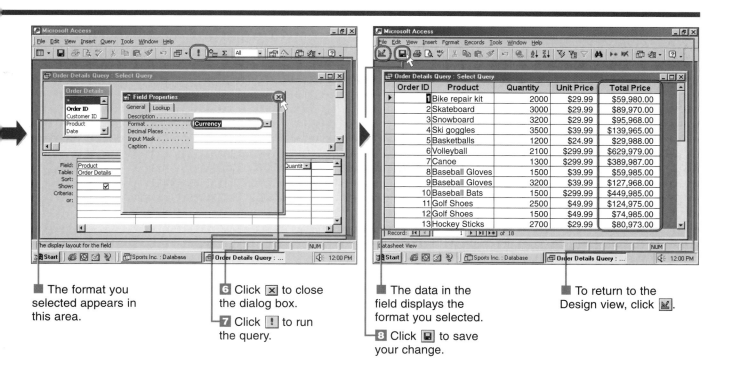

■ The format you selected appears in this area.

6 Click ☒ to close the dialog box.

7 Click ! to run the query.

■ The data in the field displays the format you selected.

8 Click 🔲 to save your change.

■ To return to the Design view, click ☑.

USING PARAMETERS

You can use a
parameter to specify
the information you
want to find each time
you run a query.

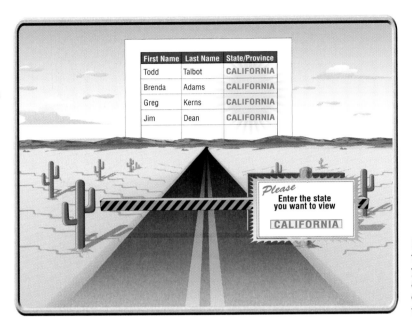

For example, each
time you run a query,
you can have Access
ask you for the name
of the state you want
to find.

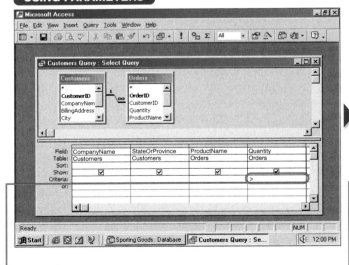

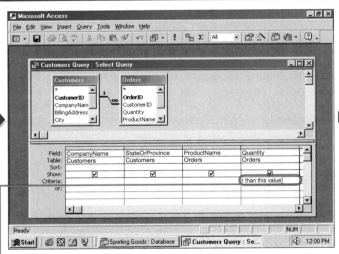

■1 Click the **Criteria**
area for the field you
want to use a parameter.

■2 Type an operator
for the parameter.

*Note: For examples of
operators you can use,
see the top of page 233.*

■3 Type the message you
want Access to display
when you run the query.
Enclose the message in
square brackets [ ].

*Note: If the message you type
is too long to fit in the cell,
you can zoom into the cell to
display the contents of the
entire cell. To zoom into a
cell, see page 58.*

When entering a parameter, what operators can I use?

Operator	Result
=	Find data equal to the value you enter.
>	Find data greater than the value you enter.
>=	Find data greater than or equal to the value you enter.
<	Find data less than the value you enter.
<=	Find data less than or equal to the value you enter.
<>	Find data not equal to the value you enter.

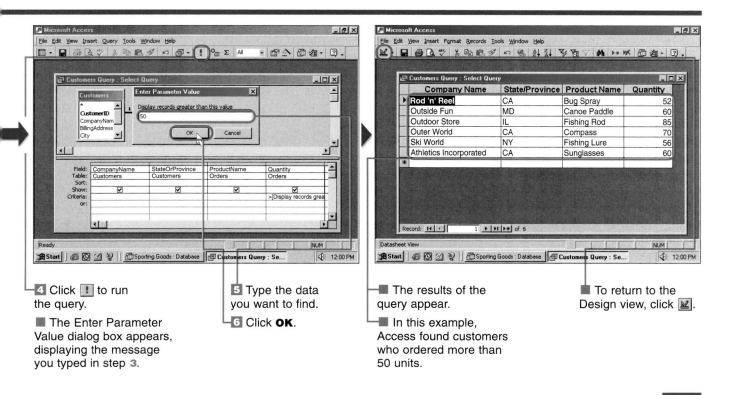

- Click ! to run the query.

■ The Enter Parameter Value dialog box appears, displaying the message you typed in step 3.

5 Type the data you want to find.

6 Click **OK**.

■ The results of the query appear.

■ In this example, Access found customers who ordered more than 50 units.

■ To return to the Design view, click ▣.

SUMMARIZE DATA

You can summarize the data in a field to help you analyze the data.

COMPANY	QTY ORDERED
Wild Adventures	40
Sports Inc.	60
Racquets Plus	70
Ski World	30
Bike Time Inc.	25
The Ski Club	60
Mountain Top	90
Biking Time	30

= 405

For example, you can summarize data in the Quantity Ordered field to determine the total amount of products ordered.

SUMMARIZE DATA FOR ONE FIELD

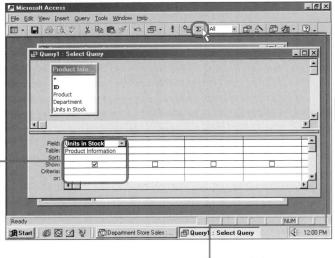

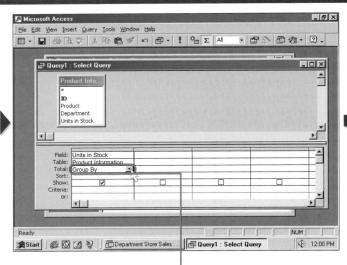

■1 Create a query that includes only the field you want to summarize. To create a query in the Design view, see page 196.

■2 Click Σ to display the Total row.

■ The Total row appears.

Note: You can repeat step 2 at any time to remove the Total row.

■3 Click the **Total** area for the field. An arrow (▾) appears.

■4 Click the arrow (▾) to display a list of calculations you can perform.

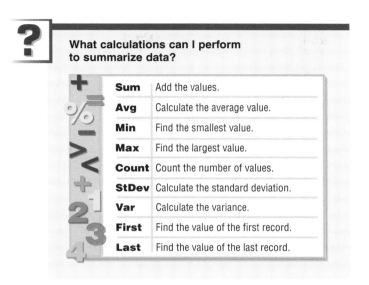

What calculations can I perform to summarize data?

Sum	Add the values.
Avg	Calculate the average value.
Min	Find the smallest value.
Max	Find the largest value.
Count	Count the number of values.
StDev	Calculate the standard deviation.
Var	Calculate the variance.
First	Find the value of the first record.
Last	Find the value of the last record.

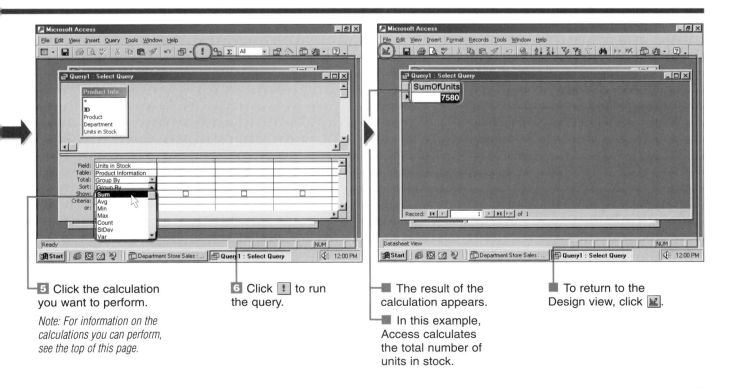

▬5 Click the calculation you want to perform.

Note: For information on the calculations you can perform, see the top of this page.

▬6 Click ! to run the query.

■ The result of the calculation appears.

■ In this example, Access calculates the total number of units in stock.

■ To return to the Design view, click 🖾.

SUMMARIZE DATA

You can group records
in your database and
summarize the data
for each group.

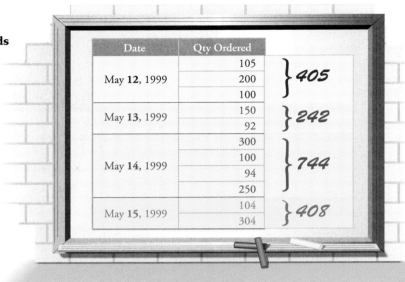

Date	Qty Ordered	
May 12, 1999	105	
	200	} 405
	100	
May 13, 1999	150	} 242
	92	
May 14, 1999	300	
	100	} 744
	94	
	250	
May 15, 1999	104	} 408
	304	

For example, you can
group records by date
and determine the total
number of orders for
each day.

SUMMARIZE DATA FOR GROUPED RECORDS

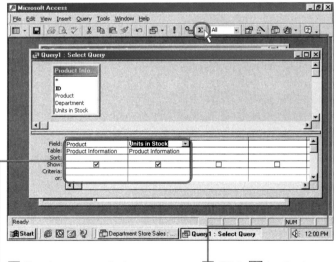

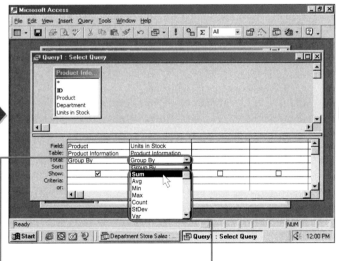

1 Create a query that
includes only the field
you want to use to group
your records and the field
you want to summarize.
To create a query in the
Design view, see page 196.

2 Click Σ to display
the Total row.

■ The Total row
appears.

*Note: You can repeat step 2
at any time to remove the
Total row.*

3 Click the **Total** area
for the field you want to
summarize. An arrow (▼)
appears.

4 Click the arrow (▼) to
display a list of calculations
you can perform.

5 Click the calculation
you want to perform.

*Note: For information on the
calculations you can perform,
see the top of page 235.*

?

Can I use more than one field to group records?

You can group records using more than one field. For example, to determine the total amount of each product purchased by each company, use the Company and Product fields to group records and the Quantity Ordered field to summarize data.

COMPANY	PRODUCT	QUANTITY ORDERED
Fitness Minds	A	40
Fitness Minds	B	60
Racquets Plus	A	80
Racquets Plus	B	30
Ski World	A	25
Ski World	B	60
SportStop	A	90
SportStop	B	100

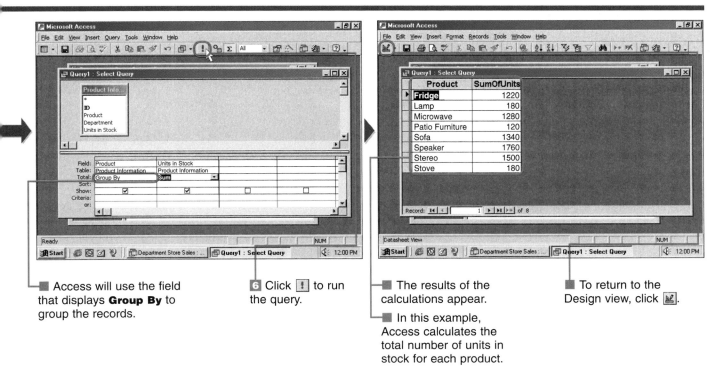

■ Access will use the field that displays **Group By** to group the records.

6 Click ! to run the query.

■ The results of the calculations appear.

■ In this example, Access calculates the total number of units in stock for each product.

■ To return to the Design view, click ⬚.

FIND UNMATCHED RECORDS

You can find records in one table that do not have matching records in another table.

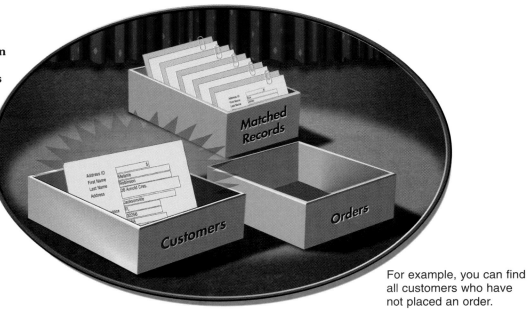

For example, you can find all customers who have not placed an order.

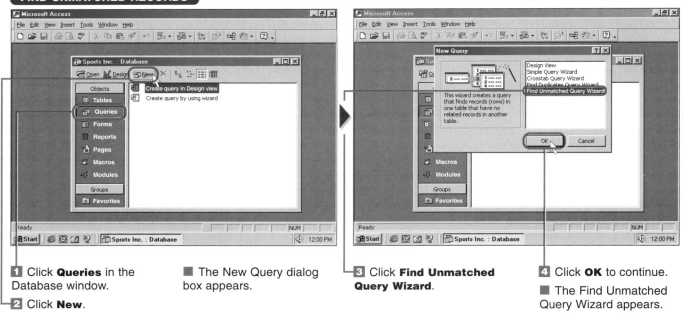

1 Click **Queries** in the Database window.

2 Click **New**.

■ The New Query dialog box appears.

3 Click **Find Unmatched Query Wizard**.

4 Click **OK** to continue.

■ The Find Unmatched Query Wizard appears.

238

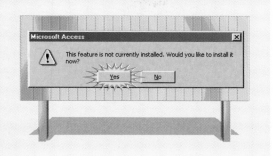

Why does this error message appear?

This error message appears if the Find Unmatched Query Wizard is not installed on your computer. Insert the CD-ROM disc you used to install Access into your CD-ROM drive and then click **Yes** to install the wizard.

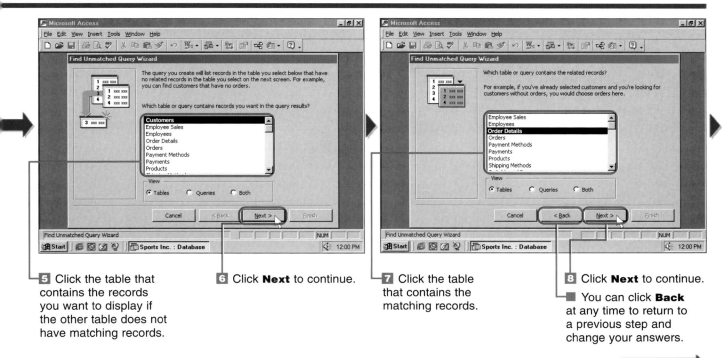

5 Click the table that contains the records you want to display if the other table does not have matching records.

6 Click **Next** to continue.

7 Click the table that contains the matching records.

8 Click **Next** to continue.

■ You can click **Back** at any time to return to a previous step and change your answers.

CONTINUED

FIND UNMATCHED RECORDS

When using the
Find Unmatched
Query Wizard, you
need to select the
field that appears
in both tables.

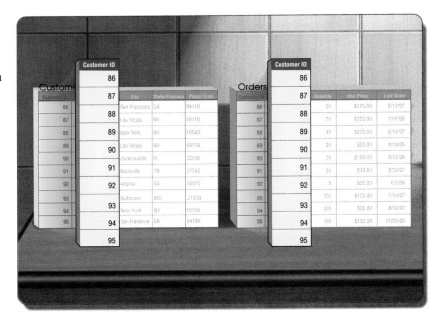

For example, the
Customer ID field
may appear in a
table containing
customer information
and in a table
containing orders.

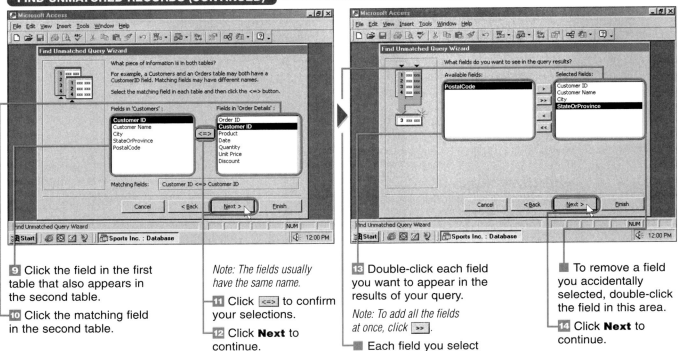

9 Click the field in the first
table that also appears in
the second table.

10 Click the matching field
in the second table.

*Note: The fields usually
have the same name.*

11 Click [<=>] to confirm
your selections.

12 Click **Next** to
continue.

13 Double-click each field
you want to appear in the
results of your query.

*Note: To add all the fields
at once, click [>>].*

■ Each field you select
appears in this area.

■ To remove a field
you accidentally
selected, double-click
the field in this area.

14 Click **Next** to
continue.

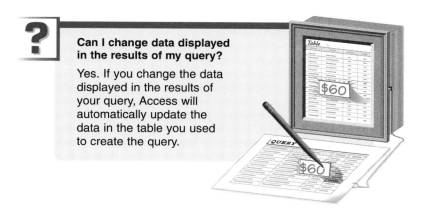

Can I change data displayed in the results of my query?

Yes. If you change the data displayed in the results of your query, Access will automatically update the data in the table you used to create the query.

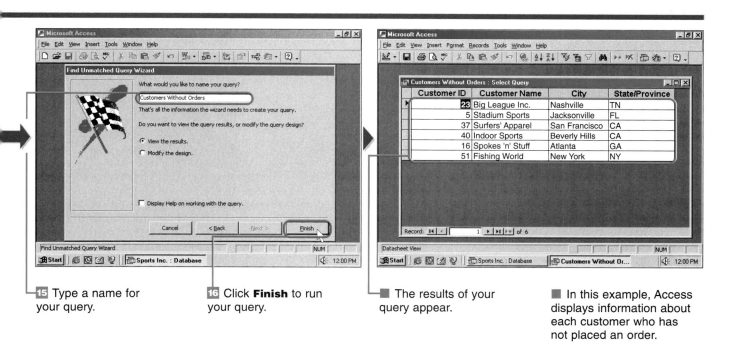

🔲15 Type a name for your query.

🔲16 Click **Finish** to run your query.

■ The results of your query appear.

■ In this example, Access displays information about each customer who has not placed an order.

First Quarter Sales

Product   *Baseball Bat*

Month	Quantity Sold	Unit Price
		$29.99
January	3200	
		$29.99
February	3000	
		$29.99
March	2000	

Summary for 'Product' = Baseball Bat (3 detail records)

Sum   8200

Product   *Baseball Glove*

Month	Quantity Sold	Unit Price
		$39.99
January	3200	

CHAPTER 11

Create Reports

Would you like to present your data in a professional-looking report? This chapter teaches you how to create and work with reports.

CREATE A REPORT USING THE REPORT WIZARD

You can use the Report Wizard to create a professionally designed report that summarizes data in your database.

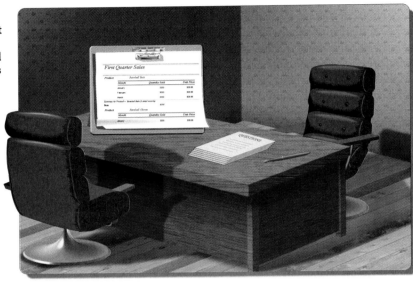

The Report Wizard asks you a series of questions and then creates a report based on your answers.

CREATE A REPORT USING THE REPORT WIZARD

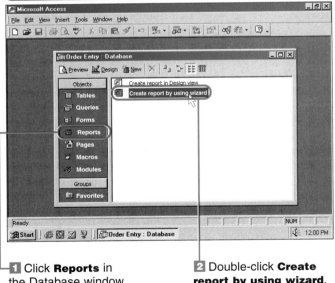

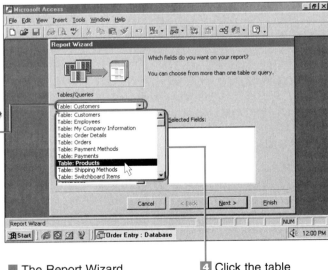

1 Click **Reports** in the Database window.

2 Double-click **Create report by using wizard**.

■ The Report Wizard appears.

3 Click ▼ in this area to select the table containing the fields you want to include in your report.

4 Click the table containing the fields.

Which tables in my database can I use to create a report?

You can use any table in your database to create a report. To create a report using data from more than one table, relationships must exist between the tables. For information on relationships, see page 128.

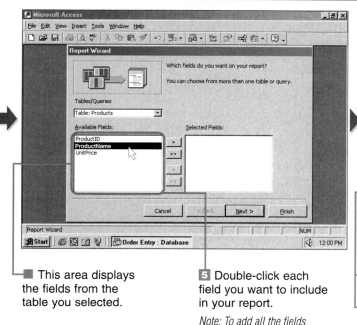

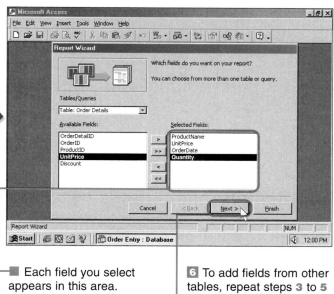

■ This area displays the fields from the table you selected.

5 Double-click each field you want to include in your report.

Note: To add all the fields at once, click ➤➤.

■ Each field you select appears in this area.

■ To remove a field you accidentally selected, double-click the field in this area.

Note: To remove all the fields at once, click ◀◀.

6 To add fields from other tables, repeat steps **3** to **5** for each table.

7 Click **Next** to continue.

CONTINUED ▶

CREATE A REPORT USING THE REPORT WIZARD

You can choose how you want to group data in your report. Grouping data helps you organize and summarize the data in your report.

For example, you can group all the customers from the same state together in your report.

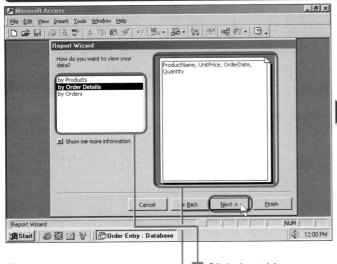

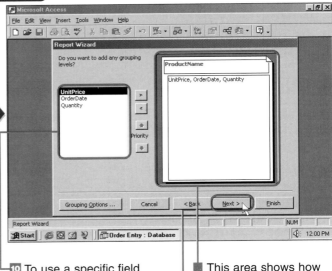

■ If you selected fields from more than one table, you can choose the table you want to use to group data in your report.

Note: If this screen does not appear, skip to step 10.

8 Click the table you want to use to group data in your report.

■ This area shows how Access will group data in your report.

9 Click **Next** to continue.

10 To use a specific field to group data in your report, double-click the field you want to use.

■ This area shows how Access will group data in your report.

11 Click **Next** to continue.

Why would I sort the records in my report?

Why would I sort the records in my report?

You can sort the records in your report to better organize the data. For example, you can alphabetically sort records by the Last Name field to make it easier to find customers of interest. If the same last name appears more than once in the field, you can sort by a second field, such as First Name.

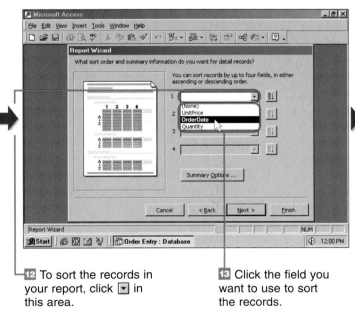

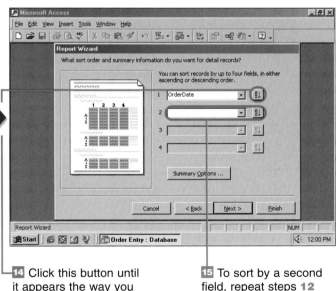

12 To sort the records in your report, click ▼ in this area.

Note: For information on sorting, see the top of this page.

13 Click the field you want to use to sort the records.

14 Click this button until it appears the way you want to sort the records.

Sort A to Z, 1 to 9

Sort Z to A, 9 to 1

15 To sort by a second field, repeat steps **12** to **14** in this area.

CONTINUED

CREATE A REPORT USING THE REPORT WIZARD

You can perform
calculations in your
report to summarize
your data.

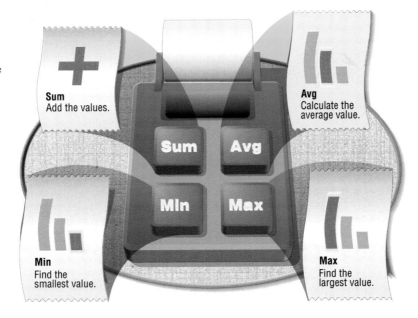

Sum
Add the values.

Avg
Calculate the
average value.

Min
Find the
smallest value.

Max
Find the
largest value.

CREATE A REPORT USING THE REPORT WIZARD (CONTINUED)

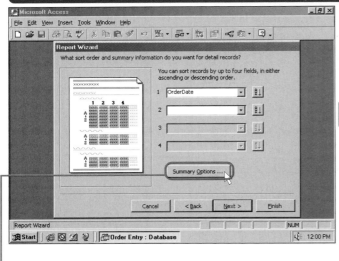

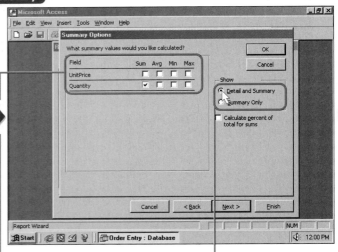

■16 To perform calculations
in your report, click
Summary Options.

*Note: Summary Options may
not be available for some
reports. If Summary Options is
not available, skip to step 21 to
continue creating your report.*

■ The Summary Options
dialog box appears.

■ This area displays the
fields you can perform
calculations on.

■17 Click the box (☐) for
each calculation you want
to perform (☐ changes
to ☑).

■18 Click an option to
specify if you want to
display all the records
and the summary
or just the summary
(○ changes to ◉).
For more information,
see the top of page 249.

248

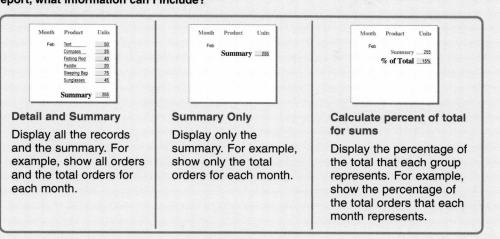

When performing calculations in my report, what information can I include?

Detail and Summary

Display all the records and the summary. For example, show all orders and the total orders for each month.

Summary Only

Display only the summary. For example, show only the total orders for each month.

Calculate percent of total for sums

Display the percentage of the total that each group represents. For example, show the percentage of the total orders that each month represents.

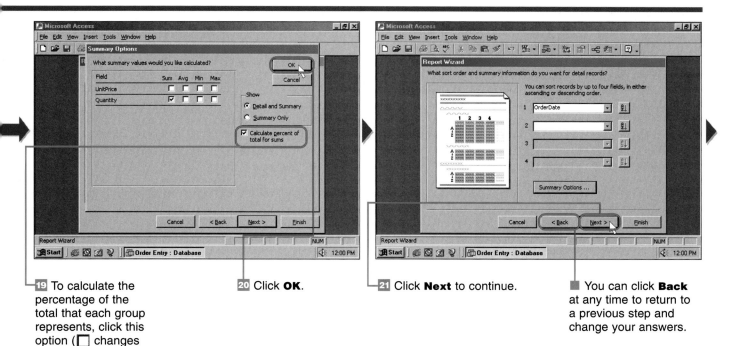

-19 To calculate the percentage of the total that each group represents, click this option (☐ changes to ☑).

-20 Click **OK**.

-21 Click **Next** to continue.

■ You can click **Back** at any time to return to a previous step and change your answers.

CONTINUED

CREATE A REPORT USING THE REPORT WIZARD

You can choose from several layouts for your report. The layout determines the arrangement of information in your report.

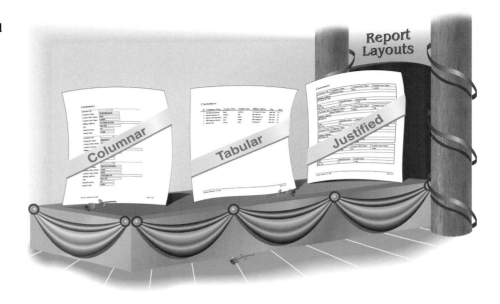

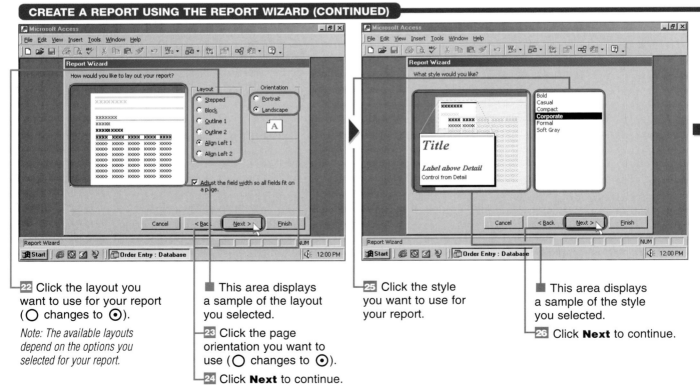

■22 Click the layout you want to use for your report (○ changes to ◉).

Note: The available layouts depend on the options you selected for your report.

■ This area displays a sample of the layout you selected.

■23 Click the page orientation you want to use (○ changes to ◉).

■24 Click **Next** to continue.

■25 Click the style you want to use for your report.

■ This area displays a sample of the style you selected.

■26 Click **Next** to continue.

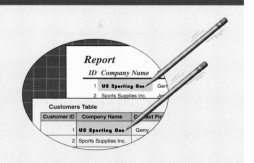

Do I need to create a new report each time I change the data in my database?

No. Each time you open a report, Access gathers the most current data from your database to create the report. This ensures that the report always displays the most up-to-date information.

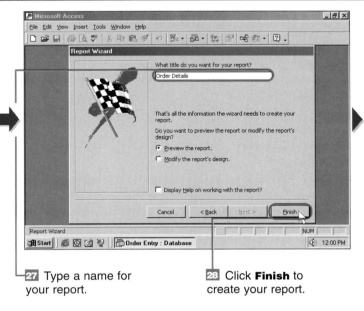

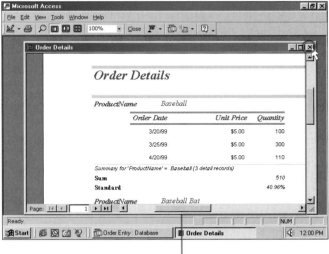

■ A window appears, displaying your report.

Note: To move through the pages in a report, see page 256.

-27 Type a name for your report.

-28 Click **Finish** to create your report.

-29 When you finish viewing your report, click ☒ to close the report.

CREATE A REPORT USING AN AUTOREPORT

You can use the AutoReport Wizard to quickly create a report that displays the information from a table in your database.

Columnar AutoReport

Displays records in a column.

Tabular AutoReport

Displays records in rows.

CREATE A REPORT USING AN AUTOREPORT

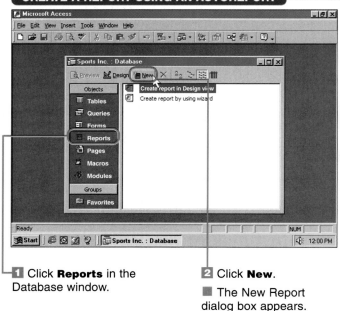

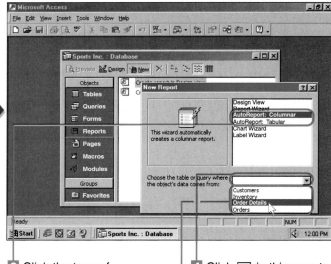

1 Click **Reports** in the Database window.

2 Click **New**.

■ The New Report dialog box appears.

3 Click the type of AutoReport you want to create.

4 Click ▼ in this area to select the table containing the data you want to include in your report.

5 Click the table containing the data.

252

Can I change the data displayed
in a report?

If you want to make changes to
the data displayed in a report, you
must change the data in the table
you used to create the report.
Changes you make to data in the
table will automatically appear
in the report the next time you
open the report.

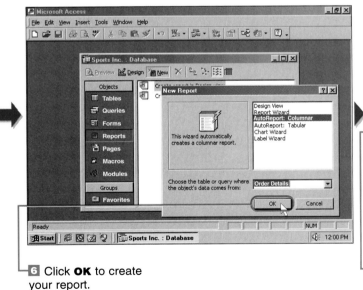

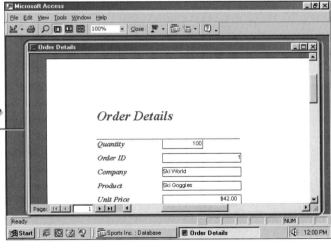

6 Click **OK** to create
your report.

■ A window appears,
displaying your report.

*Note: To move through
the pages of a report,
see page 256.*

CONTINUED

CREATE A REPORT USING AN AUTOREPORT

After you create a report using the AutoReport Wizard, you need to save the report to store it for future use.

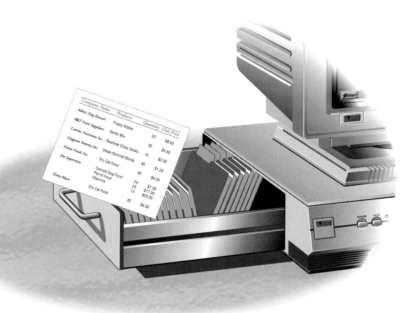

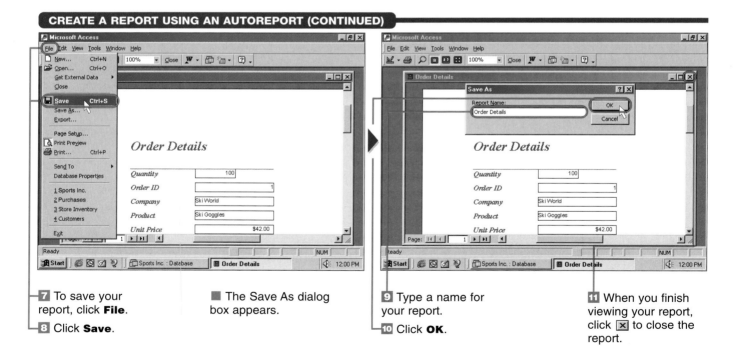

7 To save your report, click **File**.

8 Click **Save**.

■ The Save As dialog box appears.

9 Type a name for your report.

10 Click **OK**.

11 When you finish viewing your report, click ⊠ to close the report.

You can open a
report to display
the contents of
the report on
your screen.

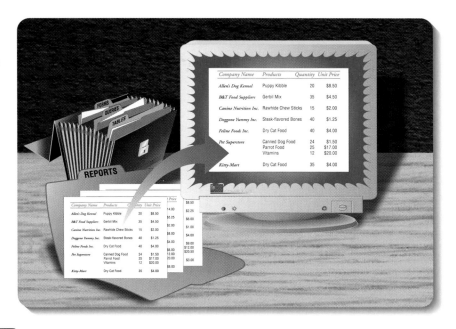

Each time you open
a report, Access
gathers the most
current data from
your database to
create the report.

OPEN A REPORT

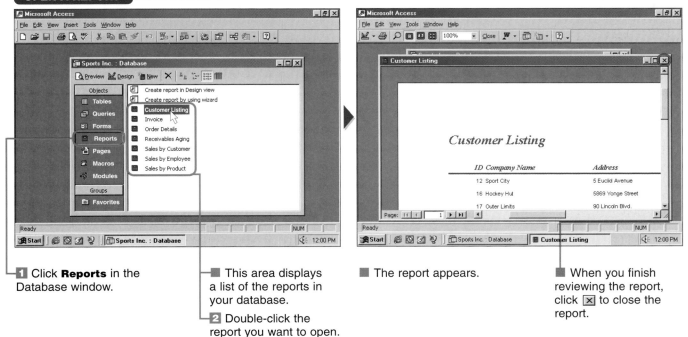

■1 Click **Reports** in the
Database window.

■ This area displays
a list of the reports in
your database.

■2 Double-click the
report you want to open.

■ The report appears.

■ When you finish
reviewing the report,
click ⊠ to close the
report.

MOVE THROUGH PAGES

If your report contains
more than one page,
you can move through
the pages to review
the information.

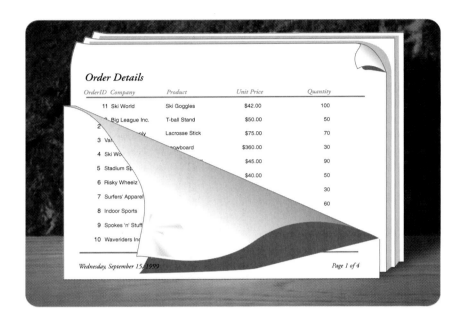

■ This area shows the
number of the page
displayed on your screen.

1 If your report contains
more than one page, click
one of these buttons to
display another page.

*Note: If a button is dimmed, the
button is currently not available.*

◄◄	First page
◄	Previous page
►	Next page
►►	Last page

You can display an entire page of a report on your screen to view the overall appearance of the page. You can also magnify an area of a page to view the area in more detail.

ZOOM IN OR OUT

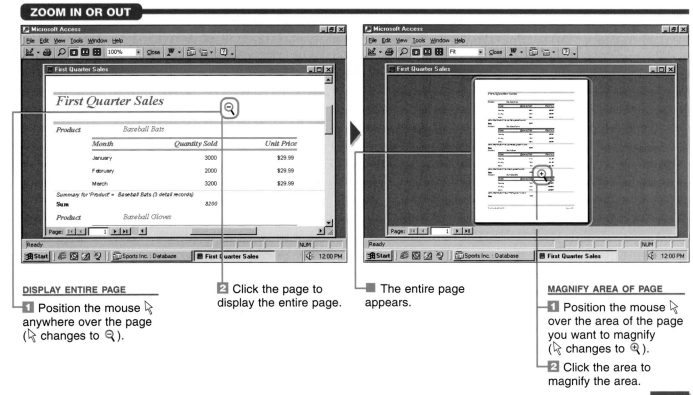

DISPLAY ENTIRE PAGE

1 Position the mouse ℛ anywhere over the page (ℛ changes to 🔍).

2 Click the page to display the entire page.

■ The entire page appears.

MAGNIFY AREA OF PAGE

1 Position the mouse ℛ over the area of the page you want to magnify (ℛ changes to 🔍).

2 Click the area to magnify the area.

CHANGE VIEW OF REPORT

There are three
ways you can
view a report.
Each view allows
you to perform
different tasks.

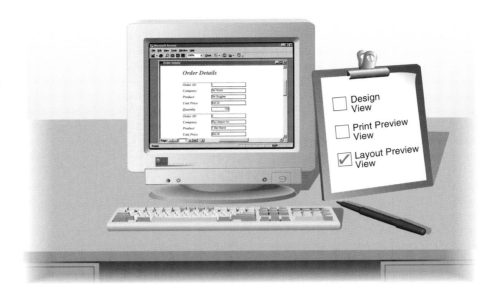

- [ ] Design View
- [ ] Print Preview View
- [x] Layout Preview View

CHANGE VIEW OF REPORT

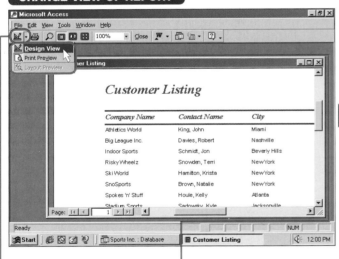

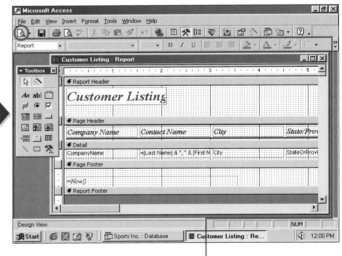

■ In this example, the report appears in the Print Preview view.

1 Click ┊ in this area to select a different view.

Note: If the view you want does not appear on the menu, position the mouse � over the bottom of the menu to display all the views.

2 Click the view you want to use.

Note: The available views depend on the view you are currently using.

■ The report appears in the view you selected.

■ In this example, the View button 🖼 changes to 🔍. You can click the View button to quickly switch between the Print Preview (🔍) and Design (🖼) views.

258

Design View

The Design view allows you to change the layout and design of a report. This view displays small, evenly spaced dots to help you line up the items in a report. Information in this view appears in several sections, such as the Report Header and Page Footer sections.

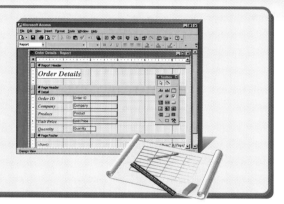

Print Preview View

The Print Preview view allows you to see how a report will look when printed. You can use this view to move through the pages in a report and examine how each page will print.

Layout Preview View

The Layout Preview view allows you to quickly view the layout and style of a report. This view is similar to the Print Preview view, but may not display all the data in the report.

ADD A PICTURE

You can add a picture to enhance the appearance of your report. For example, you can add your company logo or a picture of your products.

You can use a drawing program to create your own pictures or use a scanner to scan pictures into your computer. You can also buy pictures at computer stores or obtain pictures on the Internet.

ADD A PICTURE

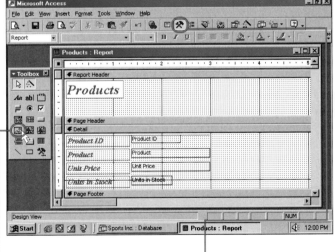

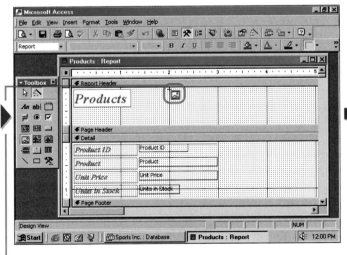

1 Display the report you want to change in the Design view. To change the view, see page 258.

2 Click  to add a picture to your report.

■ If 📷 is not available, click 🔨 to display the Toolbox toolbar.

3 Click where you want the top left corner of the picture to appear in your report.

■ The Insert Picture dialog box appears.

What section of a report can I add a picture to?

You can add a picture to any section of a report. For example, if you want the picture to appear at the top of the report, add the picture to the Report Header section.

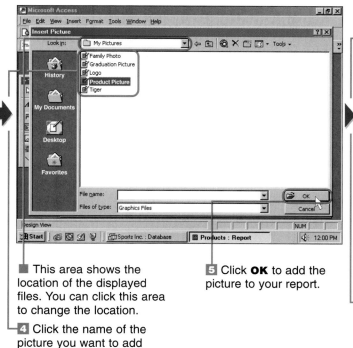

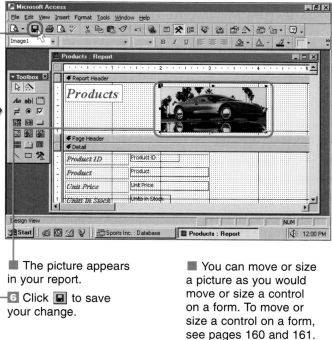

■ This area shows the location of the displayed files. You can click this area to change the location.

4 Click the name of the picture you want to add to your report.

5 Click **OK** to add the picture to your report.

■ The picture appears in your report.

6 Click 🖫 to save your change.

■ You can move or size a picture as you would move or size a control on a form. To move or size a control on a form, see pages 160 and 161.

RENAME A REPORT

You can change the
name of a report to
better describe the
information the
report displays.

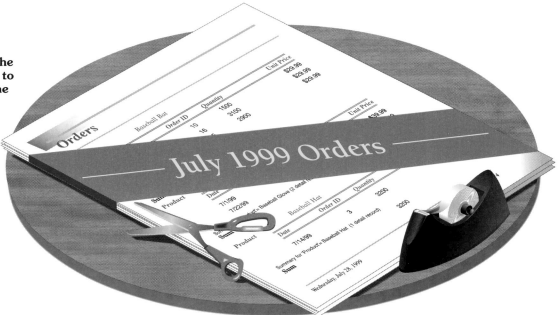

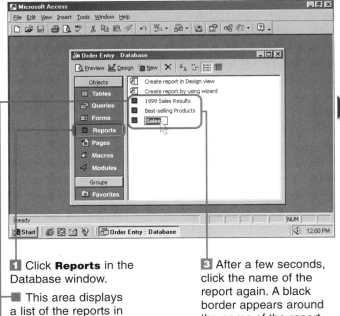

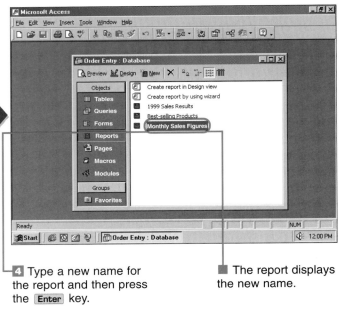

1 Click **Reports** in the
Database window.

■ This area displays
a list of the reports in
your database.

2 Click the name of the
report you want to rename.

3 After a few seconds,
click the name of the
report again. A black
border appears around
the name of the report.

*Note: If you accidentally
double-click the name of the
report, the report will open.*

4 Type a new name for
the report and then press
the **Enter** key.

■ The report displays
the new name.

262

If you no longer
need a report, you
can permanently
delete the report
from your database.

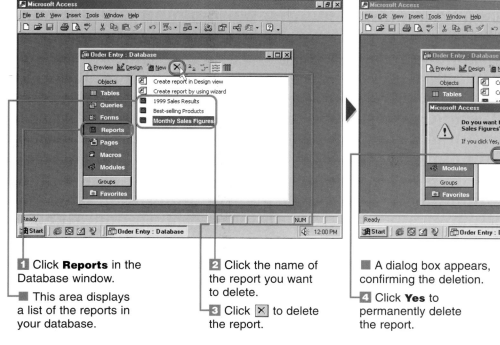

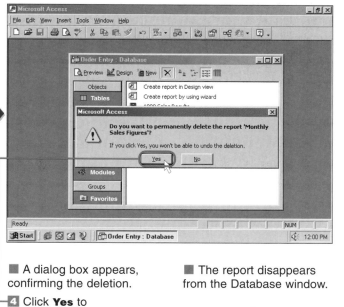

1 Click **Reports** in the
Database window.

■ This area displays
a list of the reports in
your database.

2 Click the name of
the report you want
to delete.

3 Click ☒ to delete
the report.

■ A dialog box appears,
confirming the deletion.

4 Click **Yes** to
permanently delete
the report.

■ The report disappears
from the Database window.

CHAPTER 12

Print Information

Are you wondering how to produce a paper copy of information in your database? In this chapter you will learn how to print information and create mailing labels.

PREVIEW BEFORE PRINTING

You can use the Print Preview feature to see how a table, query, form or report will look when printed. This lets you confirm that the printed pages will appear the way you want.

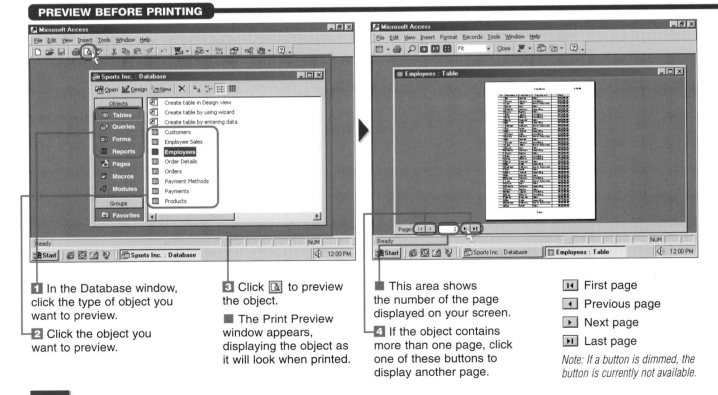

1 In the Database window, click the type of object you want to preview.

2 Click the object you want to preview.

3 Click 🔍 to preview the object.

■ The Print Preview window appears, displaying the object as it will look when printed.

■ This area shows the number of the page displayed on your screen.

4 If the object contains more than one page, click one of these buttons to display another page.

◀◀	First page
◀	Previous page
▶	Next page
▶▶	Last page

Note: If a button is dimmed, the button is currently not available.

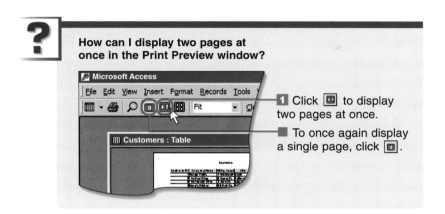

How can I display two pages at once in the Print Preview window?

1 Click 🔲 to display two pages at once.

■ To once again display a single page, click 🔲.

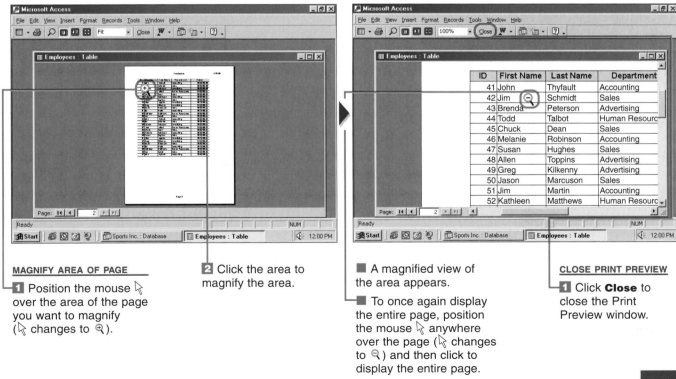

MAGNIFY AREA OF PAGE

1 Position the mouse ⬚ over the area of the page you want to magnify (⬚ changes to ⊕).

2 Click the area to magnify the area.

■ A magnified view of the area appears.

■ To once again display the entire page, position the mouse ⬚ anywhere over the page (⬚ changes to ⊖) and then click to display the entire page.

CLOSE PRINT PREVIEW

1 Click **Close** to close the Print Preview window.

CHANGE PAGE SETUP

You can change the way
information appears on
a printed page.

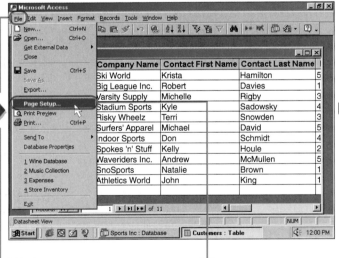

CHANGE PAGE SETUP

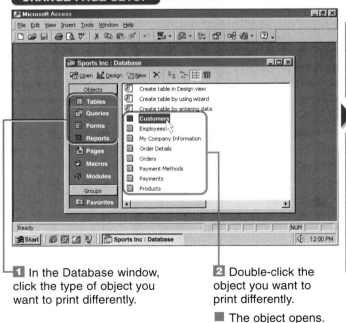

1 In the Database window,
click the type of object you
want to print differently.

2 Double-click the
object you want to
print differently.

■ The object opens.

3 Click **File**.

4 Click **Page Setup**.

■ The Page Setup
dialog box appears.

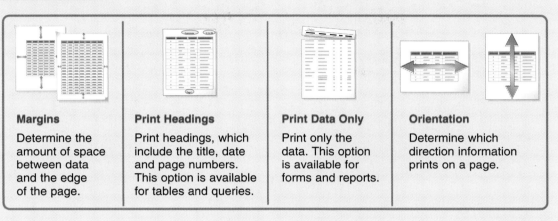

What page setup options does Access offer?

Margins

Determine the amount of space between data and the edge of the page.

Print Headings

Print headings, which include the title, date and page numbers. This option is available for tables and queries.

Print Data Only

Print only the data. This option is available for forms and reports.

Orientation

Determine which direction information prints on a page.

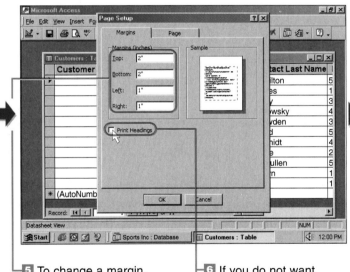

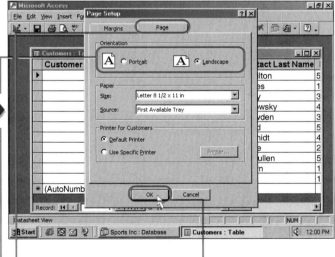

5 To change a margin, double-click the box beside the margin. Then type a new margin.

6 If you do not want to print the title, date or page numbers, click **Print Headings** (☑ changes to ☐).

■ If this area displays the Print Data Only option and you only want to print the data, click the option (☐ changes to ☑).

7 To change the page orientation, click the **Page** tab.

8 Click the page orientation you want to use (○ changes to ◉).

9 Click **OK** to confirm your changes.

Note: You can use the Print Preview feature to preview the changes you made. To use the Print Preview feature, see page 266.

PRINT INFORMATION

You can produce a paper
copy of a table, query,
form or report.

When you print a table
or query, Access prints
the title, date and page
number on each page.

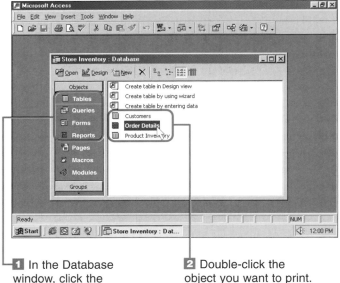

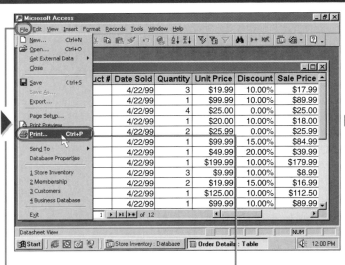

1 In the Database
window, click the
type of object you
want to print.

2 Double-click the
object you want to print.

■ The object opens.

■ If more than one record
appears on your screen and
you only want to print a few
records, select the records
you want to print. To select
records, see page 54.

3 Click **File**.

4 Click **Print**.

■ The Print dialog
box appears.

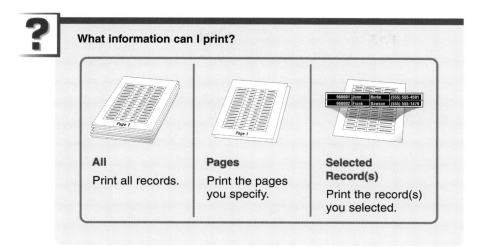

What information can I print?

All
Print all records.

Pages
Print the pages you specify.

Selected Record(s)
Print the record(s) you selected.

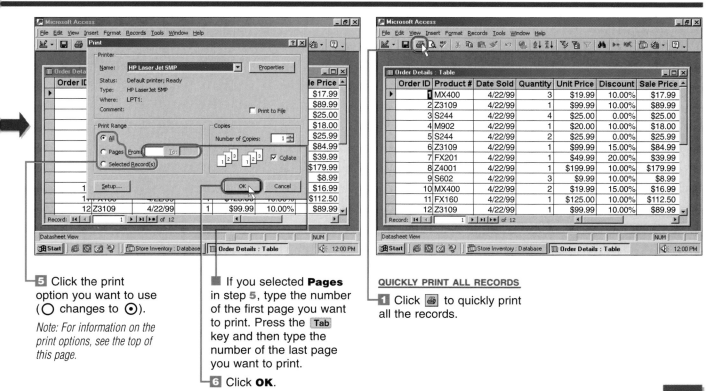

5 Click the print option you want to use (○ changes to ⦿).

Note: For information on the print options, see the top of this page.

■ If you selected **Pages** in step **5**, type the number of the first page you want to print. Press the Tab key and then type the number of the last page you want to print.

6 Click **OK**.

QUICKLY PRINT ALL RECORDS

1 Click 🖨 to quickly print all the records.

CREATE MAILING LABELS

You can create a mailing label for every person in a table. You can use mailing labels for addressing envelopes and packages and creating name tags.

The Label Wizard asks you a series of questions and then creates mailing labels based on your answers.

CREATE MAILING LABELS

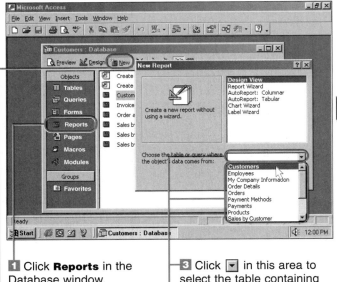

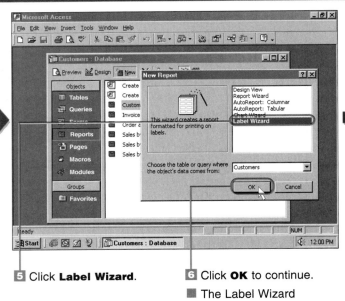

1 Click **Reports** in the Database window.

2 Click **New**.

■ The New Report dialog box appears.

3 Click ▼ in this area to select the table containing the names and addresses you want to appear on the labels.

4 Click the table you want to use.

5 Click **Label Wizard**.

6 Click **OK** to continue.

■ The Label Wizard appears.

What types of labels can I use?

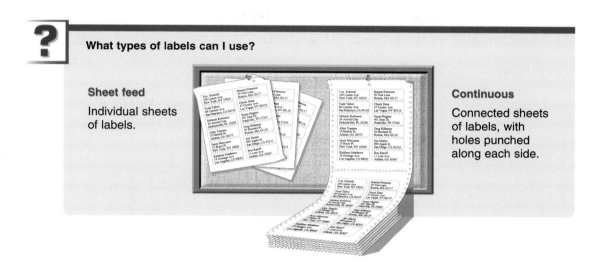

Sheet feed

Individual sheets
of labels.

Continuous

Connected sheets
of labels, with
holes punched
along each side.

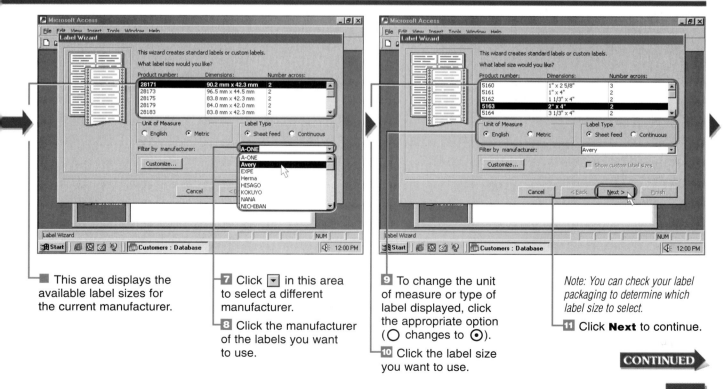

■ This area displays the
available label sizes for
the current manufacturer.

7 Click ▼ in this area
to select a different
manufacturer.

8 Click the manufacturer
of the labels you want
to use.

9 To change the unit
of measure or type of
label displayed, click
the appropriate option
(○ changes to ⊙).

10 Click the label size
you want to use.

*Note: You can check your label
packaging to determine which
label size to select.*

11 Click **Next** to continue.

CONTINUED ▶

CREATE MAILING LABELS

You can change how text will appear on your mailing labels.

The changes you make to the appearance of text will affect all the text on every mailing label. You cannot change the appearance of text for part of a label.

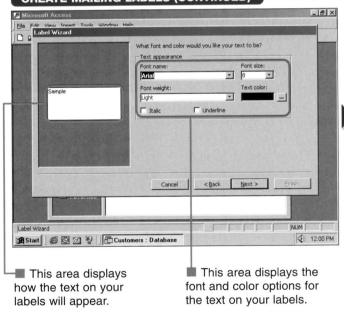

■ This area displays how the text on your labels will appear.

■ This area displays the font and color options for the text on your labels.

12 To change the appearance of the text on your labels, click ▼ for the font option you want to change. A list appears.

13 Click the option you want to use.

14 Click **Next** to continue.

■ You can click **Back** at any time to return to a previous step and change your answers.

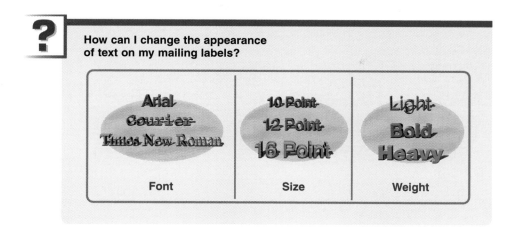

How can I change the appearance
of text on my mailing labels?

Font	Size	Weight
Arial	10 Point	Light
Courier	12 Point	Bold
Times New Roman	16 Point	Heavy

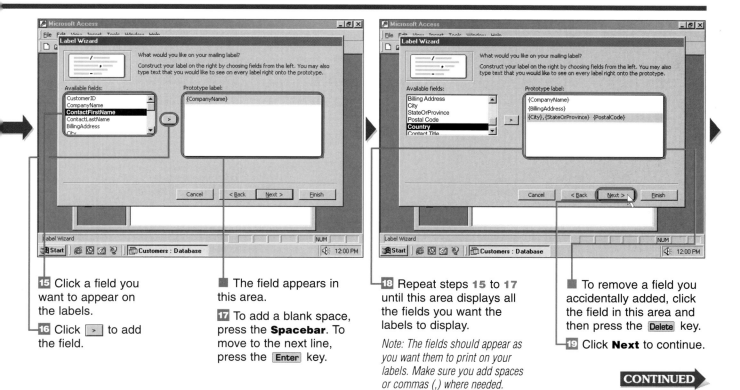

15 Click a field you want to appear on the labels.

16 Click ▸ to add the field.

■ The field appears in this area.

17 To add a blank space, press the **Spacebar**. To move to the next line, press the **Enter** key.

18 Repeat steps **15** to **17** until this area displays all the fields you want the labels to display.

Note: The fields should appear as you want them to print on your labels. Make sure you add spaces or commas (,) where needed.

■ To remove a field you accidentally added, click the field in this area and then press the **Delete** key.

19 Click **Next** to continue.

CONTINUED ▸

CREATE MAILING LABELS

You can sort your
mailing labels to
specify how you
want to organize
the labels.

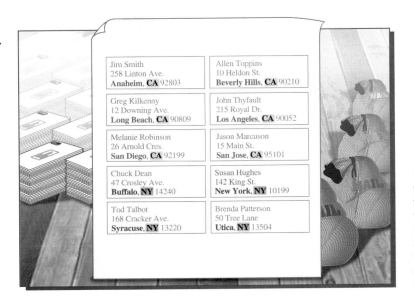

For example, you can sort
your mailing labels by state
to place all the labels for
the same state together.
If the same state appears
on several labels, you can
sort by a second field, such
as city, to further organize
the labels.

CREATE MAILING LABELS (CONTINUED)

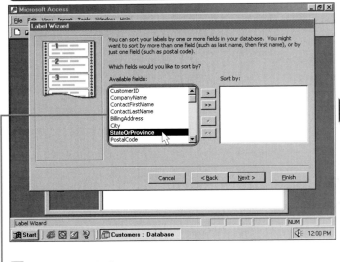

20 To sort the labels,
double-click the field
you want to use to
sort the labels.

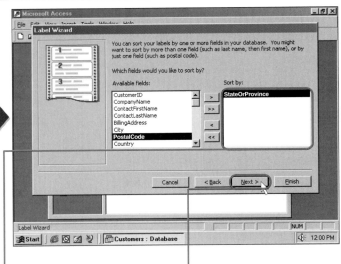

■ The field you selected
appears in this area.

■ To remove a field you
accidentally selected,
double-click the field
in this area.

■ To sort by a second
field, repeat step **20** for
the field.

21 Click **Next** to continue.

How do I edit mailing labels I created?

To edit mailing labels, you must change the data in the table you used to create the labels. For example, to change the address of a customer, you must change the data in the table that stores the customer's address. Changes you make to the data in the table will automatically appear in the labels.

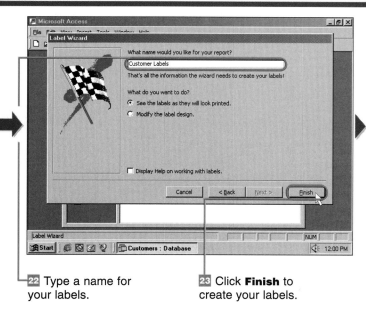

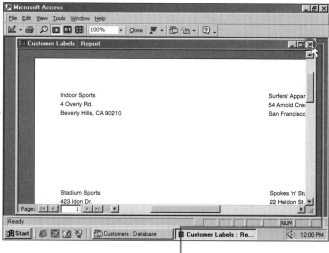

22 Type a name for your labels.

23 Click **Finish** to create your labels.

■ A window appears, displaying a label for each person in your table.

Note: To print the labels, see page 270.

24 When you finish viewing the labels, click ☒ to close the window.

■ Access stores your labels as a report. For information on working with reports, see pages 255 to 257.

CHAPTER 13

Access and the Internet

Would you like to use Access to share information with other people on the Internet? Learn how in this chapter.

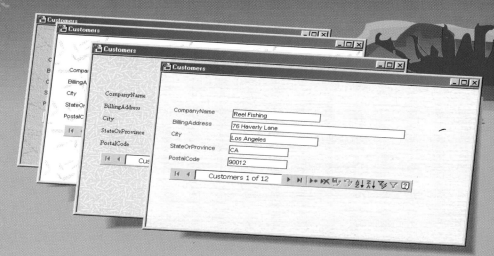

CREATE A DATA ACCESS PAGE

You can use the Page
Wizard to create a data
access page. A data
access page is a Web
page that allows you
to view and edit data
in your database from
the Internet or your
company's intranet.

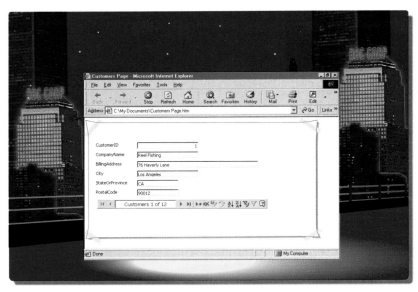

An intranet is
a small version
of the Internet
within a company.

To create a data
access page, you
must have Internet
Explorer 5 or
a later version
installed on your
computer.

CREATE A DATA ACCESS PAGE

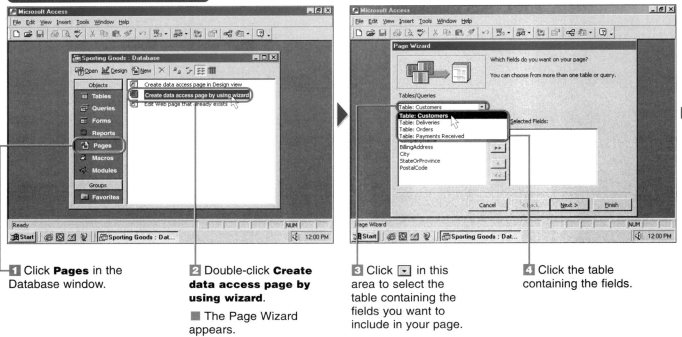

1 Click **Pages** in the
Database window.

2 Double-click **Create
data access page by
using wizard**.

■ The Page Wizard
appears.

3 Click ▾ in this
area to select the
table containing the
fields you want to
include in your page.

4 Click the table
containing the fields.

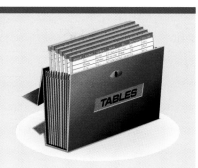

Which tables in my database can I use to create a data access page?

You can use any table in your database to create a data access page. To create a data access page using data from more than one table, relationships must exist between the tables. For information on relationships, see page 128.

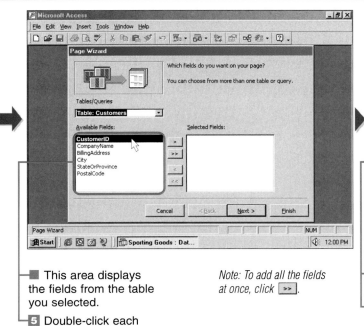

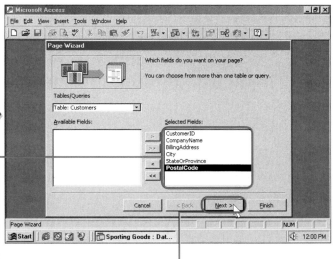

■ This area displays the fields from the table you selected.

5 Double-click each field you want to include in your page.

Note: To add all the fields at once, click ⟩⟩ *.*

■ Each field you select appears in this area.

6 To remove a field you accidentally selected, double-click the field in this area.

Note: To remove all the fields at once, click ⟨⟨ *.*

7 To add fields from other tables, repeat steps **3** to **6** for each table.

8 Click **Next** to continue.

CONTINUED

CREATE A DATA ACCESS PAGE

You can group data in
your data access page.
Grouping data helps
you organize the
data in your page.

For example, you can
group all the customers
from the same state
together in your page.

CREATE A DATA ACCESS PAGE (CONTINUED)

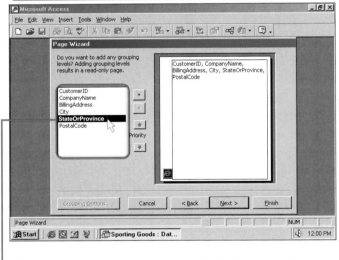

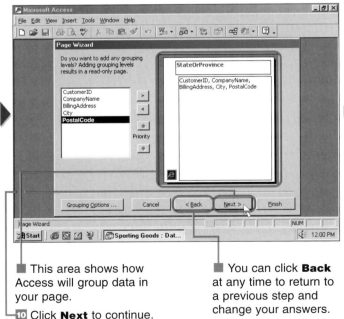

■ 9 If you want to group data
in your page, double-click
the field you want to use
to group the data.

*Note: If you group data, you
will not be able to edit data
in the page.*

■ This area shows how
Access will group data in
your page.

■ 10 Click **Next** to continue.

■ You can click **Back**
at any time to return to
a previous step and
change your answers.

Why would I sort the records in my page?

You can sort the records in your page to better organize the data. For example, you can sort records alphabetically by the Last Name field to make it easier to find customers of interest. If the same last name appears more than once in the field, you can sort by a second field, such as First Name, to further organize the data.

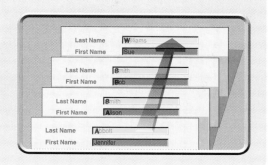

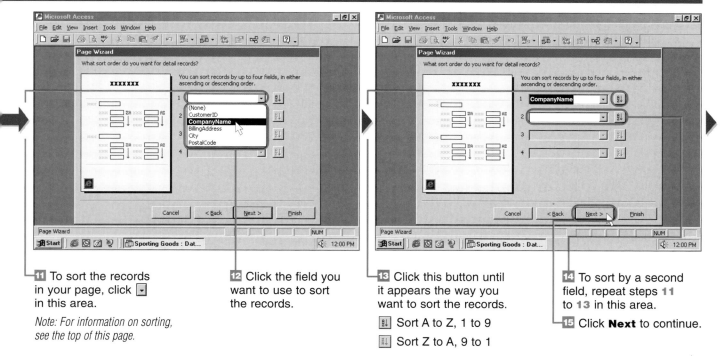

11 To sort the records in your page, click ⏷ in this area.

Note: For information on sorting, see the top of this page.

12 Click the field you want to use to sort the records.

13 Click this button until it appears the way you want to sort the records.

⏶↓ Sort A to Z, 1 to 9

⏷↓ Sort Z to A, 9 to 1

14 To sort by a second field, repeat steps **11** to **13** in this area.

15 Click **Next** to continue.

CONTINUED ▶

CREATE A DATA ACCESS PAGE

When creating a data
access page, you
can give the page
a descriptive title.

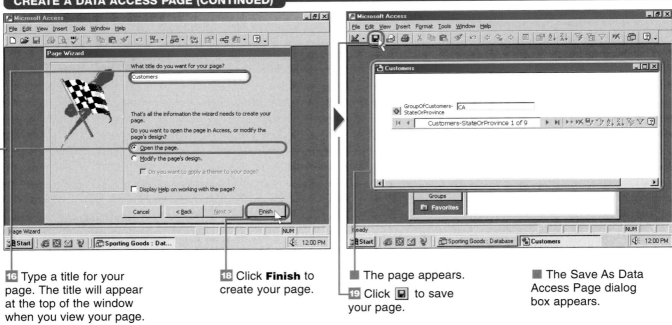

16 Type a title for your
page. The title will appear
at the top of the window
when you view your page.

17 Click this option to
open the page when you
finish creating the page
(○ changes to ⊙).

18 Click **Finish** to
create your page.

■ The page appears.

19 Click 🔲 to save
your page.

■ The Save As Data
Access Page dialog
box appears.

284

? **How do I open a data access page I created?**

Access stores your data access page in the location you specified in the Save As Data Access Page dialog box. You can open the page as you would open any file on your computer.

Access displays the name of the data access page in the Database window. To open a data access page using the Database window, see page 286.

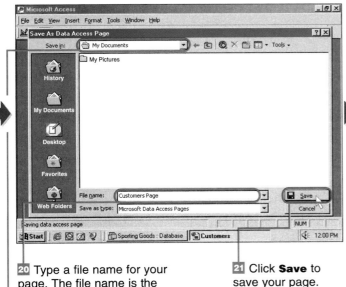

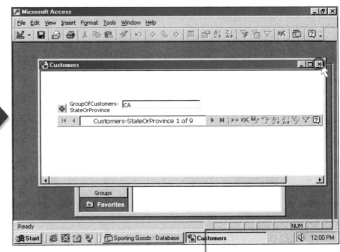

20 Type a file name for your page. The file name is the name you use to store the page on your computer.

■ This area shows the location where Access will store your page. You can click this area to change the location.

21 Click **Save** to save your page.

■ Access saves the page on your computer.

Note: To move through records in a data access page, see page 288.

22 When you finish reviewing the page, click ☒ to close the page.

Note: To make the page available for other people to view, see the top of page 293.

OPEN A DATA ACCESS PAGE

You can open a data access page to display its contents on your screen. This lets you review and make changes to the page.

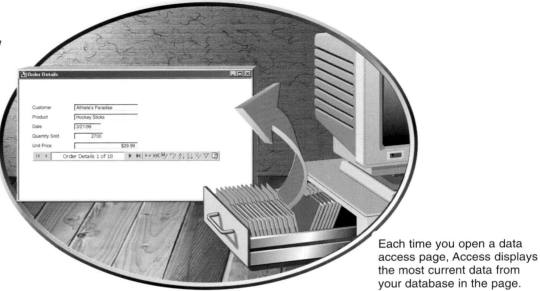

Each time you open a data access page, Access displays the most current data from your database in the page.

OPEN A DATA ACCESS PAGE

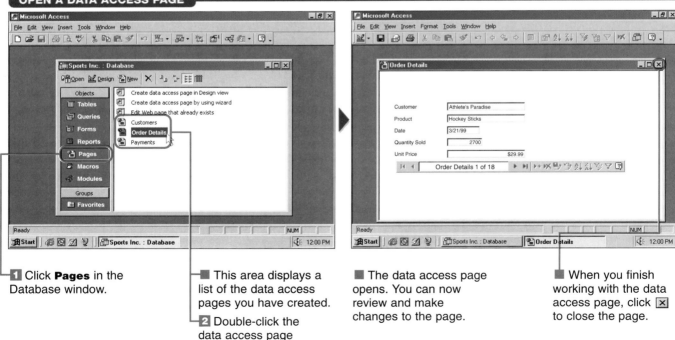

■ Click **Pages** in the Database window.

■ This area displays a list of the data access pages you have created.

2 Double-click the data access page you want to open.

■ The data access page opens. You can now review and make changes to the page.

■ When you finish working with the data access page, click ⊠ to close the page.

CHANGE VIEW OF DATA ACCESS PAGE

There are two ways you can view a data access page. Each view allows you to perform different tasks.

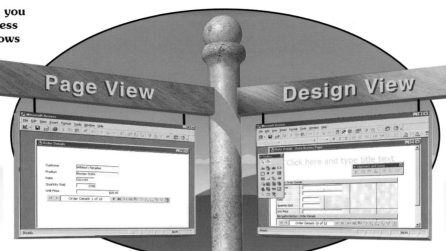

Page View

Design View

Page view

Allows you to view and edit the information displayed in a data access page.

Design view

Allows you to change the design of a data access page.

CHANGE VIEW OF DATA ACCESS PAGE

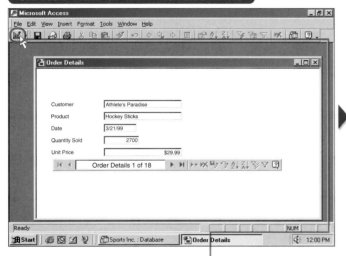

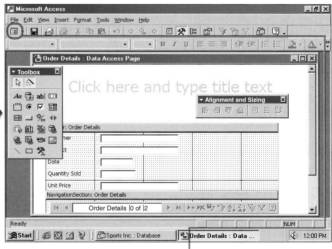

■ In this example, the data access page appears in the Page view.

1 Click ![icon] to display the data access page in the Design view.

■ The data access page appears in the Design view.

■ The View button ![icon] changes to ![icon]. You can click the View button to quickly switch between the Page (![icon]) and Design (![icon]) views.

MOVE THROUGH RECORDS IN A DATA ACCESS PAGE

You can move through the records in a data access page to review and edit information.

MOVE THROUGH RECORDS IN A DATA ACCESS PAGE

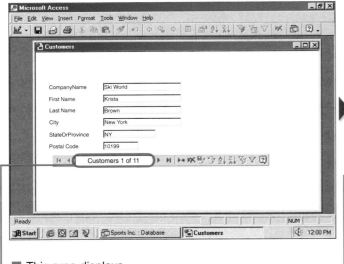

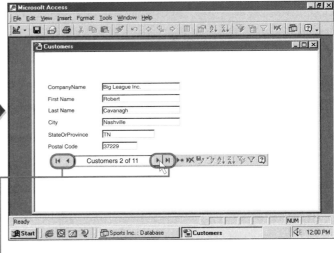

■ This area displays the number of the current record and the total number of records.

1 To move to another record, click one of these buttons.

|◄| First record

|◄| Previous record

|►| Next record

|►| Last record

Can I edit the data in my data access page?

Yes. When you change the data in a data access page, Access will also change the data in the table you used to create the page.

If you chose to group data when you created your data access page, you cannot edit the data in the page.

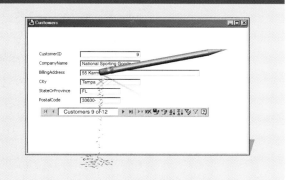

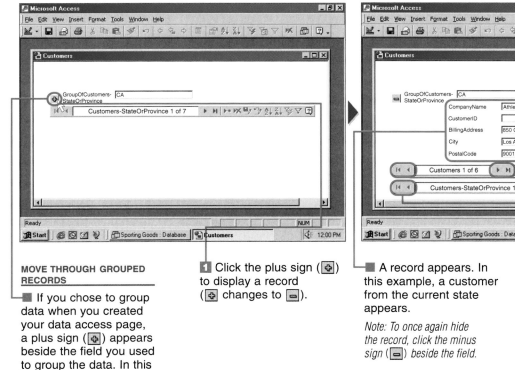

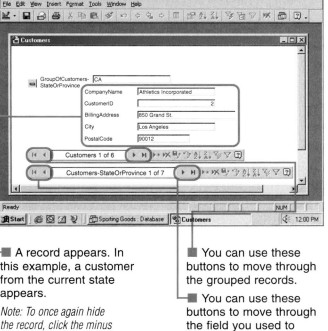

MOVE THROUGH GROUPED RECORDS

■ If you chose to group data when you created your data access page, a plus sign (⊞) appears beside the field you used to group the data. In this example, records are grouped by state.

1 Click the plus sign (⊞) to display a record (⊞ changes to ⊟).

■ A record appears. In this example, a customer from the current state appears.

Note: To once again hide the record, click the minus sign (⊟) beside the field.

■ You can use these buttons to move through the grouped records.

■ You can use these buttons to move through the field you used to group the records.

APPLY A THEME TO A DATA ACCESS PAGE

Access offers many ready-to-use designs, called themes, that you can use to enhance the appearance of your data access page.

APPLY A THEME TO A DATA ACCESS PAGE

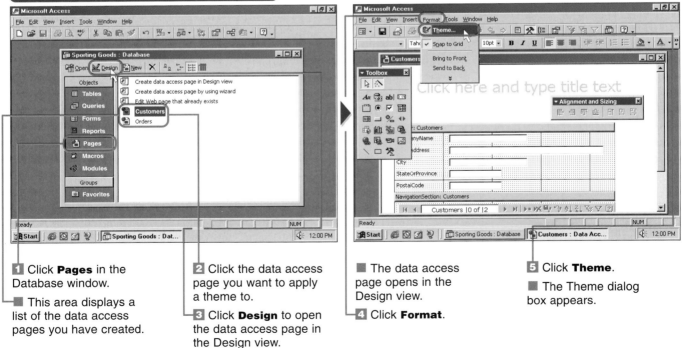

1 Click **Pages** in the Database window.

■ This area displays a list of the data access pages you have created.

2 Click the data access page you want to apply a theme to.

3 Click **Design** to open the data access page in the Design view.

■ The data access page opens in the Design view.

4 Click **Format**.

5 Click **Theme**.

■ The Theme dialog box appears.

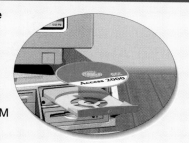

Why didn't a sample of the theme I selected appear?

If a sample of the theme you selected does not appear, the theme is not installed on your computer. To install the theme, insert the CD-ROM disc you used to install Access into your CD-ROM drive. Then click **Install**.

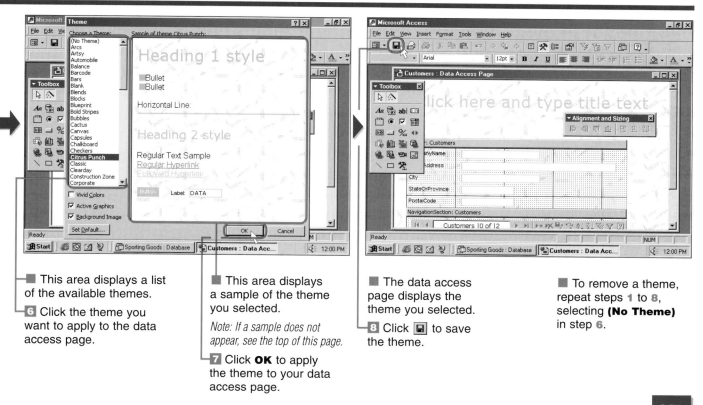

■ This area displays a list of the available themes.

◾6 Click the theme you want to apply to the data access page.

■ This area displays a sample of the theme you selected.

Note: If a sample does not appear, see the top of this page.

◾7 Click **OK** to apply the theme to your data access page.

■ The data access page displays the theme you selected.

◾8 Click 🖫 to save the theme.

■ To remove a theme, repeat steps 1 to 8, selecting **(No Theme)** in step 6.

SAVE A DATABASE OBJECT AS A WEB PAGE

You can save a table, query, form or report as a Web page. This lets you place the database object on the Internet or your company's intranet.

An intranet is a small version of the Internet within a company.

The Web page you create will not update to display changes you make to data in your database. If you want your Web page to always display the most current data, see page 280 to create a data access page.

SAVE A DATABASE OBJECT AS A WEB PAGE

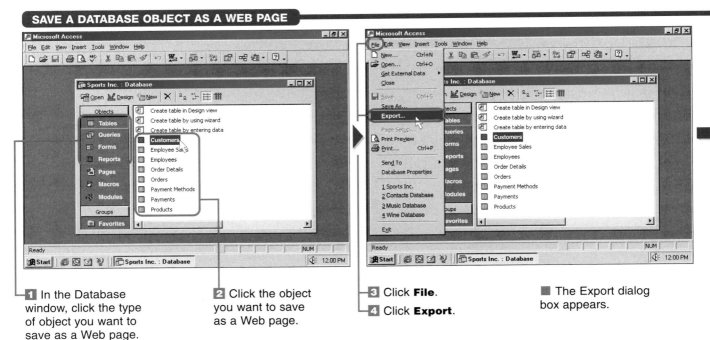

1 In the Database window, click the type of object you want to save as a Web page.

2 Click the object you want to save as a Web page.

3 Click **File**.

4 Click **Export**.

■ The Export dialog box appears.

How do I make my Web page available for other people to view?

To make a Web page available on the Internet or your company's intranet, you need to transfer the page to a Web server. A Web server is a computer that stores Web pages. Once you publish a Web page on a Web server, the page will be available for other people to view. For more information on publishing a Web page, contact your network administrator or Internet service provider.

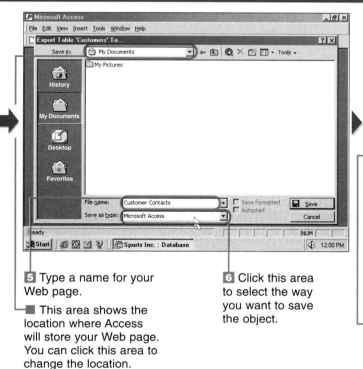

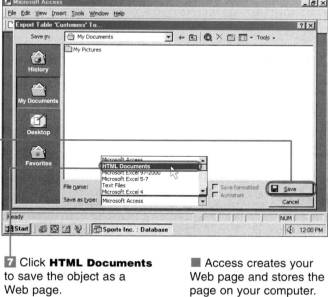

5 Type a name for your Web page.

■ This area shows the location where Access will store your Web page. You can click this area to change the location.

6 Click this area to select the way you want to save the object.

7 Click **HTML Documents** to save the object as a Web page.

8 Click **Save**.

*Note: If the HTML Output Options dialog box appears, click **OK** to continue.*

■ Access creates your Web page and stores the page on your computer. You can open the Web page as you would open any file on your computer. You cannot open the Web page from within Access.

INDEX

INDEX

as database objects, 7, 27
delete, 155
fields
    add, 164
    formats, change, 170-171
labels, add, 165
magnify pages, in Print Preview, 267
margins, change, 268-269
open, 148
pages, setup, change, 268-269
pictures, add, 176-177
preview, 266-267
print, 270-271
records
    add, 152
    delete, 153
    move through, 149
    sort, 180-181
rename, 154
save as Web pages, 292-293
size, change, 163
text
    bold, 167
    fonts, change, 168
    italicize, 167
    size, 169
    underline, 167
views, change, 158-159
freeze fields, in tables, 72-72

G

greater than (>), criteria, 216
greater than or equal to (>=), criteria, 216
gridlines
    color, change, in tables, 68-69
    remove, in tables, 68-69
group
    data
        in data access pages, 282
        in reports, 246
    dates in queries, 204

H

headings
    print, 268-269
    tables, select fields in queries using, 212
help, 30-31
hide
    fields
        in queries, 211
        in tables, 70-71

Office Assistant, 31
    toolbars, 23
History folder, 19
Hyperlink data types, 85
hyperlinks
    add to records, in tables, 120-123
    select, in tables, 123

I

index, create for fields in tables, 100-101
input masks, create in tables, 102-105, 106-107
Internet, and Access, 280-293
intranets, 120, 280
italicize
    data, in tables, 66-67
    text
        in forms, 167
        on mailing labels, 274

K

keyboards, move through data in tables using, 53
keys. *See* primary keys

L

labels
    add to forms, 165
    mailing
        create, 272-277
        edit, 277
        font options, change, 274
        sort, 276
    text, change, 166
Layout Preview view, 259
    display reports in, 258
less than (<), criteria, 216
less than or equal to (<=), criteria, 216
lookup columns, create, 108-111
Lookup Wizard data types, 85

M

magnify pages
    in Print Preview, 267
    of reports, 257
mailing labels
    create, 272-277
    edit, 277
    font options, change, 274
    sort, 276
margins, change, 268-269

INDEX

INDEX

summarize, data
    in queries, 202-203, 234-235, 236-237
    in reports, 248-249
switch between windows, 28
switchboards, 16
symbols left of records in tables, 57

T

Table Wizard, use, 38-41
tables
    add to queries, 197
    background color, change, 68-69
    cell effects, add, 68-69
    close, 42
    consider when planning databases, 8
    create
        in Datasheet view, 34-37
        using Table Wizard, 38-41
    data
        bold, 66-67
        color, change, 66-67
        copy, 62-63
        filter
            by exclusion, 188-189
            by form, 190-191, 192-193
            by selection, 186-187
        find, 182-183
        fonts, change, 66-67
        italicize, 66-67
        move, 62-63
            through, 52-53
        replace, 184-185
        select, 54-55
        size, 66-67
    as database objects, 6, 27
    delete, 49
    fields
        add
            in Datasheet view, 46
            in Design view, 78-79
        captions, add, 92-93
        decimal places, change number of, 90-91
        default values, set, 94-95
        delete
            in Datasheet view, 47
            in Design view, 80
        descriptions, add, 83
        display hidden, 71
        formats, select, 86-87

freeze, 72-73
hide, 70-71
index, create, 100-101
input masks, create, 102-105, 106-107
lookup columns, create, 108-111
properties, display, 82
rearrange
    in Datasheet view, 45
    in Design view, 81
rename, 44
require data entry for, 96-97
select all, in queries, 212
size, change, 88-89
unfreeze, 73
validation rules, add, 98-99
Yes/No, create, 112-115
gridlines
    color, change, 68-69
    remove, 68-69
hyperlinks
    add to records, 120-123
    select, 123
magnify pages in Print Preview, 267
mailing labels, create using, 272-277
open, 42
pages, setup, change, 268-269
parts of, 35
pictures, add to records, 116-119
preview, 266-267
primary key, set, 126-127
print, 270-271
records
    add, 64
    delete, 65
    select all, 55
    sort, 180-181
referential integrity, enforce, 132-133
relationships
    consider when planning databases, 9
    create, 128-131
rename, 48
save, 35
    as Web pages, 292-293
spelling, check, 60-61
subdatasheets, display, 59
symbols next to records, 57
views, 76-77
Yes/No fields, 85, 112-115
zoom into, 58

OVER 6 MILLION

OTHER 3-D Visual SERIES

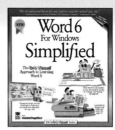

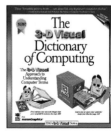

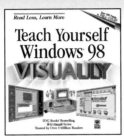

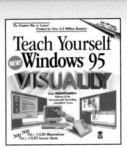
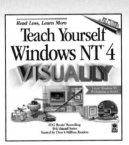

ORDER FORM

TRADE & INDIVIDUAL ORDERS

Phone: **(800) 762-2974**
or **(317) 596-5200**
(8 a.m. – 6 p.m., CST, weekdays)
FAX : **(800) 550-2747**
or **(317) 596-5692**

EDUCATIONAL ORDERS & DISCOUNTS

Phone: **(800) 434-2086**
(8:30 a.m.–5:00 p.m., CST, weekdays)
FAX : **(317) 596-5499**

CORPORATE ORDERS FOR 3-D VISUAL™ SERIES

Phone: **(800) 469-6616**
(8 a.m.–5 p.m., EST, weekdays)
FAX : **(905) 890-9434**

Qty	ISBN	Title	Price	Total

Shipping & Handling Charges

	Description	First book	Each add'l. book	Total
Domestic	Normal	$4.50	$1.50	$
	Two Day Air	$8.50	$2.50	$
	Overnight	$18.00	$3.00	$
International	Surface	$8.00	$8.00	$
	Airmail	$16.00	$16.00	$
	DHL Air	$17.00	$17.00	$

Subtotal _____

*CA residents add
applicable sales tax* _____

*IN, MA and MD
residents add
5% sales tax* _____

*IL residents add
6.25% sales tax* _____

*RI residents add
7% sales tax* _____

*TX residents add
8.25% sales tax* _____

Shipping _____

Total _____

Ship to:

Name _____

Address _____

Company _____

City/State/Zip _____

Daytime Phone _____

Payment: □ Check to IDG Books (US Funds Only)

□ Visa □ Mastercard □ American Express

Card # _____ Exp. _____ Signature _____